Psalms for All Seasons

Psalms for All Seasons

Rediscovering the Riches of Their Original Design

O. PALMER ROBERTSON

THE BANNER OF TRUTH TRUST

THE BANNER OF TRUTH TRUST

Head Office
3 Murrayfield Road
Edinburgh, EH12 6EL
UK

North America Office
610 Alexander Spring Road
Carlisle, PA 17015
USA

banneroftruth.org

First published as *Psalms in Congregational Celebration*
by Evangelical Press, Darlington, 1995
First Banner of Truth edition 2025

*

ISBN
Print: 978 1 80040 538 7
Epub: 978 1 80040 539 4

*

Typeset in 11/13 pt Adobe Garamond Pro at
The Banner of Truth Trust, Edinburgh

Printed in the USA by
Versa Press, Inc.,
East Peoria, IL

Contents

Introduction

The Psalms always have played a vital role in the worship of God's people. This fact should not be surprising, since they were inspired of God for this very purpose. The whole expanse of human reaching out to God in praise, in petition, in confession, in lamentation finds its quintessential expression in these imperishable monuments to God's presence in the souls of men.

But, sadly, with all the attention on 'new forms' of worship in the modern church, little reclaiming of the riches of the Psalms in their fulness has yet been realized. On a limited scale the Psalms are sung in the cadences of the old psalters. In a previous generation, public worship almost always included a 'responsive reading' from the book of Psalms. More recently, countless choruses have centred on a repetition in song of one verse, or even one phrase, of one psalm. But the full-orbed testimony of the Psalter, as it touches every possible experience of weal and woe in the life of God's people, has not found a voice in the current worship of the church.

Yet perhaps nothing could be more needed. How else can it be communicated adequately to God's people that only the person with 'clean hands and a pure heart' can enter the house of the Lord? (Psa. 24:4). What better way could be devised to enforce the folly of the fool who says there is no God, than to have that neglected truth reiterated by the multiple voices of the holy ones assembled for adoration and worship in his presence? (Psa. 14:1). How could comfort for Christians suffering under the oppression of the proud be communicated more effectively than by a community of believers joining in united testimony to the sudden devastation that God brings on his enemies? (Psa. 73:2, 3, 18, 19).

So the present work represents an effort to capture for congregations the vitality of the varied message of the Psalms. In introducing this work, something needs to be said about the form being employed, the translation of the various psalms and the rationale behind the selection of these particular psalms.

Form

Generally it is recognized that parallelism of structure functions as the major element characterizing Hebrew poetry. But very seldom is this central feature represented in English translations of the Psalms. In the present treatment, an effort has been made to retain this parallelism as fully as possible so that today's reader may profit from the insight into emphasis and meaning provided by the inspired writers through the literary vehicle of parallelism. As a consequence it is hoped that the original intent of the inspired author will be more immediately apparent to the modern reader.

The reader also will note the distinction being made among various speakers in this translation. Sometimes the assembled congregation responds to the speech of an individual. At other times more than one individual take their turns in addressing the congregation. Again, at some points one portion of the congregation responds antiphonally to another grouping of the assembly.

In many cases, the psalm itself clearly indicates these changes of speakers. The single individual of Psalm 118, the 'I' of this psalm, offers his threefold testimony to God's deliverance (verses 5-7, 10-14, 17-19). Then a community of believers responds with their praise to God for his saving work (verses 8, 9, 15, 16, 23-25). By apportioning the various sections of this psalm between an individual speaker and the assembled congregation, the message of this portion of God's word may be communicated more immediately to the worshippers.

It can be anticipated that this form of public reading will appear awkward and foreign at first. But the rationale for the variation in speakers will quickly become apparent, and the increased benefit in understanding should encourage a congregation to 'give it a try.' It may be observed that the distinctions among speakers as represented in these current translations were instantly apparent to the original readers of the biblical text, and this advantage should not be lightly forfeited by the current community of believers.

Translation

Various theories of Bible translation are represented in the numerous modern versions available today. Paraphrased versions take great liberties in transferring thought-patterns from biblical languages into proposed modern equivalents. More literal translations carry over the original text word-for-word into modern dialect. The current translation stays very close to the verbal representations of the original text. But 'dynamic equivalents' have been offered regularly when it was essential for the transferral of the true meaning of the text into modern English.

Selection

The choice of psalms treated in this present work could have been dictated by the arrangement of the Psalter itself, so that the first twenty-five psalms would have determined the selection. But a reader familiar with the Psalter knows that these opening psalms concentrate heavily on David's response to his enemies. In order to achieve a greater variety in subject matter, style and structure, a selection has been made across the breadth of the Psalter. Themes covered in these twenty-five representative psalms include:

specifically Messianic psalms (Psa. 2; 80; 110)
praise psalms (Psa. 113; 146)
psalms involving confession of sin (Psa. 32)
didactic psalms (Psa. 1; 15; 126)
psalms of trust (Psa. 11; 91)
thanksgiving psalms (Psa. 118)
psalms of historical recollection (Psa. 106)

The table of contents offers a brief description of the topics of the various psalms being treated. This listing of topics may help the worship leader to identify a psalm that suits the theme of a particular worship service. It is hoped that congregations and individuals will be able to make immediate use of all these various types of psalms, since they represent the breadth of experience of the people of God in every age. By the employment of this variety of inspired, poetic expressions in the worship services of God's people, the breadth, length, depth and height of the life of the redeemed may be experienced more fully.

In sum, it is hoped that the celebration of the truth in these psalms may enrich the life of faith for God's people. By rehearsing in their worship services the expressions of Messianic hope, the inspired praises of their Creator and Redeemer, the solemn acknowledgements of wrongdoing and the remembrances of God's faithfulness in the past, the faith of the redeemed should be strengthened to meet the challenge of today's world.

A pdf of the psalms selected for this volume is available to download and reproduce for congregational use by scanning this QR code:

Psalm 1

The Way of the Righteous

Reader: 1 How blessed is the person
1st Congr.: who will not walk
2nd Congr.: in the counsel of the wicked;
1st Congr.: and will not stand
2nd Congr.: in the way of sinners;
1st Congr.: and will not sit
2nd Congr.: in the seat of the scoffers.

Reader: 2 For with the law of the Covenant Lord
All: is his delight,
Reader: and in his law he meditates
All: day and night.

Reader: 3 So he shall be like a tree
planted by watering streams
that bears its fruit
in its time.
1st Congr.: Its leaf
shall never wither.
2nd Congr.: So everything he does
always prospers.

Reader: 4 Never will it be so
All: for the wicked!

Reader: For they will be like a hollow shell
All: that the wind blows about.

Reader: 5 For evil people never will stand
All: at the time of judgment,
Reader: nor sinners
All: with the righteous when they assemble.

Reader: 6 For the Covenant LORD loves
All: the lifestyle of the righteous,
All: but the lifestyle of the wicked
Reader: will lead to ruin.

The Way of the Righteous—*Magnifying God's Law*

Introduction

Psalms 1 and 2 stand as twin pillars forming an entry to the literary temple of the Psalter, inviting men to come and worship the Lord. The first psalm magnifies the law; the second psalm magnifies the Messiah. The first psalm begins by declaring the blessedness of the man who honours God's law; the second psalm ends by declaring the blessedness of the man who honours God's Messiah.

Now you are invited to enter the temple of the Psalter and consider a contrast between two kinds of people in the world. One person lives in the presence of God, and the other ignores the reality of God. One person has a happy life of fruitfulness, while the other acts out nothing more than a miserable sham. One finally enters the fulness of fellowship with God and his people, while the other is cast forever into the misery of eternal loneliness.

Consider three aspects of this vivid contrast of lifestyles in Psalm 1: a contrast in the way of life; a contrast in the fruit of life; and a contrast in the end of life.

1. A contrast in the way of life

The first word of the psalmist pronounces God's blessing on one particular way of life. This benediction echoes the ancient blessings declared over the covenant people of God in the book of Deuteronomy:

> Blessed shall you be in the city, and blessed shall you be in the field …
>
> Blessed shall you be in when you come in, and blessed shall you be when you go out …

> The LORD will command the blessing on you in your barns and in all that you undertake …
>
> The LORD will open to you his good treasury, the heavens, to give the rain to your land in its season and to bless all the work of your hands. And you shall lend to many nations, but you shall not borrow. And the Lord will make you the head, and not the tail …
>
> (Deut. 28:3, 6, 8, 12, 13).

This benediction that opens the book of Psalms also anticipates the beatitudes of Jesus in the Sermon on the Mount:

> Blessed are the poor in spirit,
> for theirs is the kingdom of heaven.
> Blessed are those who mourn,
> for they shall be comforted.
> Blessed are the meek,
> for they shall inherit the earth.
> Blessed are those who hunger and thirst for righteousness,
> for they shall be satisfied.
> Blessed are the merciful,
> for they shall receive mercy.
> Blessed are the pure in heart,
> for they shall see God.
> Blessed are the peacemakers,
> for they shall be called sons of God.
> Blessed are those who are persecuted for righteousness' sake,
> for theirs is the kingdom of heaven
>
> (Matt. 5:3-10).

What man is there who would not want to experience all these blessings? Who would not hope that his life would go well for him in all these ways?

If you walk in the way commended by the psalmist, you can be a happy, blessed person despite all the sin and misery in the world. God's word assures it, if you will believe it.

The opening word of Psalm 1 might better be translated, 'How *happy*' is this man. Not only is he blessed without; he is contented within. Some people have many blessings but no happiness. But the man whom God blesses has both inner joy and outer benediction from the Lord.

The negative aspect

The prescription for this happy life begins with a negative note. Given the fallen, sinful condition of the world, how could it be otherwise? This man who receives God's blessings

> will *not* walk
>   in the counsel of the wicked;
> will *not* stand
>   in the way of sinners;
> will *not* sit
>   in the seat of scoffers.

This point must be learned early in life if anyone wishes to avoid great grief. The person who would walk according to the law of the Lord must learn how to say 'No!' and to say it without apology. Happiness in life often depends on a person's ability to refuse to go the way of the crowd. The broad way of this world leads to destruction. Steadfastly resisting the proposals of the unrighteous is the only way to stay on the narrow path that leads to life.

The psalmist promises blessing to those who resist the downward sequence that first 'walks,' then 'stands' and finally 'sits' with sinners. Each step of the way leads a person deeper and deeper into the trap of those who disrespect the Lord and his law. First a person listens to the seemingly wise counsel of sinners. He may insist on retaining his own freedom to decide whether or not he will follow the counsel of the wicked. But soon he is moving easily along the well-travelled road. Eventually he finds himself quite comfortable in the company of unbelieving scoffers and settles down to their lifestyle.

But happy is the person who will not walk in the counsel of the ungodly. Though he may fall into sin, he never delights in it. He continually says 'No' to worldly wisdom and steadfastly refuses any honour that might come from association with the wicked.

The positive aspect

The positive description of the way of life blessed by God is explained in verse 2:

> With the law of the Covenant LORD
>   is his delight,
> And in his law he meditates
>   day and night.

Negative purity is not enough. The man who would be blessed must take his delight in knowing and doing the will of God as well as avoiding temptation to sin. Every night and every day he must meditate on the law of God so he can understand fully its implications for his life.

According to the law-code of Deuteronomy, the King of Israel was required to have his own personal copy of God's law for his daily contemplation (Deut. 17:18, 19). But the remainder of the people were expected to commit the law to memory so they also could meditate constantly on its application to their lives.

The people who lived in the days of the psalmist were just as busy as we. They had to chop their wood and spin their yarn as a part of providing for every day's needs. But they found time to inject Scripture into their lives by memorization and meditation. As the people were going through their day, they were 'mumbling' the words of Scripture to themselves, for that is the actual meaning of the word 'to meditate.' Perhaps in some ways they were better off than we, not having all the versions, commentaries and printed Bibles that have become our intellectual crutches, our excuses for not actually knowing the Scriptures.

Today we have the whole of the Old and New Testaments, while for many centuries God's people had only the first five books of Moses. We have printed Bibles in a variety of versions, and Scripture on recorded tapes that can be played as we drive about in our cars. Yet the people of old may have known their Bibles better than we. They understood that God's blessing came through constant application of his word to their lives. But do we?

Meditating on the law of the Lord is not a burden but a delight. The happy man finds his heart lifted up in joy because of the truth he finds in the word of God. Its guidance for his life leads him out of darkness into the joy of the Lord.

John Calvin says, 'God is favourable to none but those who devote themselves to the study of divine truth.'[1] Studying the law of God, particularly as it is embodied in the person of Jesus Christ, is the most important thing a person can do to assure happiness throughout life. Even the most active of people cannot afford to neglect the daily searching of the Scriptures. As Joshua was being prepared for a lifetime of leading God's people into battle, he was instructed to meditate on the word of God night and day (Josh. 1:8). His demanding responsibilities did not excuse him from the obligation to delve deeply into the meaning of God's Word for his day.

So the contrast between two ways of life is established. One way neglects, rejects, violates and mocks the word of God. The other way delights in God's law and meditates on it constantly.

Be sure you meditate on God's word daily, savouring its every truth. Never stop studying the word of God. Then you will experience true happiness.

2. A contrast in the fruit of life

Consider next the contrasting fruit produced by the lives of these two persons.

The fruit of the person who seeks after God

First, look at the fruit of the person who seeks after God:

> He shall be like a tree
>   planted by watering streams
> that bears its fruit
>   in its time.

[1] *Psalms*, I, p. 2.

Its leaf
  will never wither.
So everything he does
  always prospers

(verse 3).

The person who lives by the law of God may be likened to the tree of life planted by God in the garden of Eden (Gen. 2:9). The product of his life may be compared to the fruit produced by the tree described in the last chapter of the book of Revelation, which bore a different fruit every month of the year (Rev. 22:2). Positioned by watering streams that come down from heaven, the man who loves God's law remains green and fertile even in times of drought.

At times the wicked may seem to produce more fruit than the righteous. But the roots of people who live contrary to the law of the Lord are carnal and shallow, drawing their nourishment only from earthly things. The wicked look for instantaneous gratification. So when drought comes, they dry up and perish. All their fruit withers. In contrast, the person who honours the law of the Lord waits patiently for a fruit far more lasting. 'In its time' is his motto. His life will bear fruit 'in its time.'

All during this waiting period, the leaf of the godly never withers. In the most trying of times, the signs of life are always evident. If people would only look more closely, they could see the difference between the life-fruit of the righteous and the wicked. But people all too often are impatient, judging by the standard of immediate outward success rather than by the standard of eternal worth.

Everything the godly does eventually prospers. Even hard times bless the person who loves the law of the Lord. Every saint of the Lord can testify to the blessings that have come to him through sickness, sorrow, disappointment and setback. If a person genuinely accepts the promises of the word of God to be true, he can enjoy anticipating these blessings even before they materialize.

The fruit of the wicked

The fruit produced by the life of the wicked is set in sharpest contrast:

> Never will it be so
>   for the wicked!
> For they will be like a hollow shell
>   that the wind blows about
>
> (verse 4).

Never will there be an exception to this principle. Fruitfulness on the part of the wicked is only a delusion. It is a mirage. Instead of having a truly productive life, those who scoff at God and his truth will be like a hollow shell, like chaff that separates from the wheat. The threshing instrument puts pressure on both the husk and the kernel. But the purity and worth of the one are confirmed, while the other is proven to have no true value.

The winds of change sweep away the illusion of fruitfulness presented by the wicked. Political uncertainty blows him about. Financial ups and downs cast him first this way and then that. Personal whim continually unsettles him. In the end, his life proves to be useless and fruitless.

The righteous also will experience his ups and downs in life. He is not insulated from the winds of change. But in contrast with the wicked, his constant faith in the word of the Lord upholds him. He overcomes even in his trials.

So what is the prospect for fruit in your life? Can you look back and see the hand of the Lord prospering everything you do? Only as a person puts his continual trust in the Christ who justifies sinners and makes them love his law can he expect to experience this blessedness, this happiness described by the psalmist.

3. A contrast at the end of life

First the psalmist contrasts the *way* of the wicked and the righteous. Then the permanent *fruit* produced by the righteous is set over against the perishing fruit of the wicked. Now the psalmist contrasts the end of life for the wicked and the righteous.

The end of life for the wicked

Those who are absorbed in seeking the pleasures of this life naturally have an aversion towards thinking about life's end. If they consider the termination of their lives, their best hope is found in the expectation of annihilation.

But the Lord has set an order in the world that will not allow men to live undisturbed with the vain hope that their last earthly breath will end it all. Near-brushes with death frequently implant serious doubt in this futile hope. Conscience strikes terror in the heart as it raises the dread spectre of accountability. For God has many ways of making it plain that 'it is appointed for man to die once, and after that comes judgment' (Heb. 9:27).

More significantly, God raised Jesus Christ from the dead as a testimony to all men. His resurrection witnesses to the fact of accountability. After unjust maltreatment by wicked men he was vindicated by being lifted up in glory, which clearly indicates that God will see to it that the righteous will be rewarded and the wicked punished. According to the psalmist:

> Evil people never will stand
>   at the time of judgment,
> Nor sinners
>   with the righteous when they assemble
>
> (verse 5).

There will be a renewal of life after death, followed by a great judgment that will separate the wicked from the righteous. The sheep who have heard and hearkened to the voice of Jesus Christ will stand on God's right hand, and the goats who have resisted his voice will stand on the left. The final destinies of men will reinforce the contrast already begun in this life. While the godly and the wicked may mix together for the present, no intermingling will occur in the life to come.

What will be the end of those who seek their counsel among sinners, pattern their lives by the way of the wicked, and join in the mockery of God and his true standards of moral uprightness? In the end, they never will stand in the day when God calls men to account. Their lives, their actions, their motives will not survive the test of his holy scrutiny. They will be justly condemned on the Day of Judgment.

The day is coming, and it is near. Never will an evil person be able to fool the Lord on that day. Those who are too cowardly to take a stand for God in this life will not stand on judgment day. Those who do not centre their lives on Jesus Christ never will have joyful fellowship with him in eternity. Even at the various testing-points throughout this life, the wicked will not stand. God always will find the wicked at fault. So he will live perpetually under the condemnation of the Lord.

The end of life for the righteous

In sharpest contrast, the righteous will enjoy a glorious assembly on the Day of Judgment with God and all his people. It will be a great gathering. The electricity of human jubilation will fill the air. It will be like a holiday homecoming or a great church convention. Refreshing conversation with all the saints of old will enrich the soul.

Don't get anxious. If you have an aversion to crowds, you will not be overpowered in that final assembly. It will be just right for you. You will enjoy the pleasure of good friends without strain, just the way you have always wanted to.

But wicked, sinful scoffers whose lifestyles have not been affected by Jesus Christ will not be present. They cannot possibly share in the assembly of the righteous. Even in this life, their gatherings are hollow, empty pretences of accord. Their judgment at the end will confine them to absolute aloneness in the terrors of outer darkness for eternity.

The reason for the contrast

But why? What is the root reason for this great contrast in the destinies of men? Why will the righteous enjoy the blessings of eternity as part of a great assembly in the presence of God? Why will the wicked be excluded, confined to eternal aloneness?

Why? Because:

The Covenant LORD loves
    the lifestyle of the righteous,
    but the lifestyle of the wicked
will lead to ruin

(verse 6).

Why are the righteous so blessed? Because the Lord loves them. The text actually says the Lord 'knows' the way of the righteous. But the word conveys the idea of knowing thoroughly and approvingly, even to the point of loving. As a consequence, all they do is blessed by him. Their entire lifestyle meets his fullest approval and receives the blessing of his final reward.

But the lifestyle of the wicked leads only to misery. Their way of life disintegrates into nothingness.

Conclusion

So the book of Psalms begins with a lesson in contrasts. There can be no middle ground. Either you are among the righteous or you are among the wicked. Your place is determined by your faith in the word of God. Either you believe in God as he has been revealed in Jesus Christ, delighting in his law. Or you follow the counsel of the wicked, the sinful and the scoffers, living according to their faithless way.

The psalms are especially designed to reinforce the truth of God's law. As these poetic words are recited and sung regularly in worship, let their truth become ingrained in your soul as a determinative factor for the whole of your life.

Psalm 2
Submitting to the Son

1st Congr.: 1Why do the nations
    rage?
2nd Congr.: And the peoples
    plot vainly?

1st Congr.: 2Kings of the earth
    take their stand;
2nd Congr.: and potentates
    are set
All: against the Lord of the Covenant,
    and against his Messiah:

Chorus: 3'Let us break
    their bands
and fling from us
    their fetters.'

1st Congr.: 4He who sits in heaven
    laughs;
2nd Congr.: the Lord
    mocks them.

1st Congr.: 5Then he will address them
    in his wrath;

2nd Congr.: and in his fierceness
he will terrify them:

1st Reader: 6 'For I have installed my king
on Zion my holy mountain.'

2nd Reader: 7 'I will proclaim the decree
of the Covenant LORD.
He said to me:

1st Reader: "You are my Son;
this day
I have given birth to you.

8 "Ask of me
and I will give you
the nations
as your inheritance,
and as your possession
the ends of the earth.

9 "You will herd them
with a rod of iron;
as the bowl of a potter
you will smash them."'

3rd Reader: 10 And now, you kings
act wisely;

All: yield to correction,
you who judge the earth.

3rd Reader: 11 Serve the Covenant LORD
with fear;

All: and rejoice
with trembling.

3rd Reader: 12 Kiss the Son to avert his anger,
or you will perish in the way.
For his anger will consume in a moment.

All: Blessed are all who trust in him.

Submitting to the Son—
Magnifying God's Messiah

Introduction

As Psalm 1 opens with a pronouncement of blessing, Psalm 2 concludes by pronouncing a blessing. Psalm 1 declares the person blessed who delights in God's law; Psalm 2 pronounces its benediction on the person who trusts in God's Messiah.

These two blessings must go together. The law without the Messiah only condemns. Only by trusting Messiah's mediatorship with the Father can a person stand before the scrutiny of God's law without trembling from dread due to clear condemnation. Only by understanding Messiah's power to deliver from sin's control in his or her life can a person meditate with delight on the law.

So this psalm centres on the Messiah and the blessings he brings to his people. By constant faith in him, the rich blessing of righteousness and all that it brings can be claimed by all who are a part of his kingdom.

New Testament references to the psalm

This psalm has no designated author in the Psalter. But the New Testament indicates that King David, the anointed one of the Lord, the 'messiah' of his day, composed this poem (Acts 4:25). So the message about the 'Messiah' in these verses has application to the life-experience of David even as it anticipates the reign of God's greater Anointed One, the Lord Jesus Christ (Acts 4:25-27). In referring to this psalm, the apostle Peter builds on the parallelism between the experiences of David and Jesus. The apostle indicates this mutual relationship by referring to both David and Jesus by the term *pais*, a title that simultaneously designates each of these men as God's 'servant' who is also God's 'son.' Though Jesus is unique in his person as Son of God, his ministry was foreshadowed by the life of David, God's anointed servant.

Along with Psalm 110, Psalm 2 shares the honour of being the psalm quoted most often in the New Testament. Sample quotations of this psalm include:

> 'Why do the nations rage?' (verse 1). This phrase is applied by the New Testament to the ragings of religious leaders against Jesus and his disciples (Acts 4:25-27).
>
> 'You are my son, this day I have given birth to you' (verse 7). These words celebrating God's giving 'birth' to the Messianic King are interpreted by Paul as a figure of speech anticipating the resurrection of Jesus Christ (Acts 13:32, 33).
>
> 'You shall herd them with a rod of iron' (verse 9). The book of Revelation applies this description of the lordship of Messiah to the final reign of the glorified Christ over all the nations (Rev. 19:11-16).

This broad usage by the New Testament indicates that Psalm 2 has a variety of lessons to teach the new covenant believer. But the central message may be summarized as follows: the LORD of the Covenant establishes his Messiah's eternal reign despite the opposition of kings and nations.

Form and outline

A variety of parallel structures in the regular style of Hebrew poetry are skilfully employed to underscore various points throughout the psalm. In addition, Psalm 2 is divided into four stanzas basically the same in length, marked in the English text by three verses apiece.

An outline of the psalm may follow this natural stanza structure: haughty men plot vainly against Messiah (1-3); the Lord mocks their rebellious efforts (4-6); Messiah proclaims his God-appointed position (7-9); mighty men are charged to submit (10-12).

1. Haughty men plot vainly against Messiah (verses 1-3)

Why do they do it?

Why do the nations
  rage?

(verse 1).

What is the point? What do the nations expect to accomplish? *That* the nations rage against the control of the Lord and his Messiah there can be no question. Over and over again the peoples of this earth show their folly. They take a bold stand; they set themselves against the Lord and against his Messiah. *How* they rage is also basically clear. They deny that the Covenant LORD created this universe, insisting that somehow of itself, or by some other god, the world came into being. So they deny that they are stewards accountable to God. They also deny the consistent testimony of their consciences that it is wrong to break the law of their Creator God. They lie, loot and look with lust, and so they make the original mistake of man in claiming the prerogative for himself to determine what is good and what is evil, what is right and what is wrong.

But why? What can the peoples of the earth expect to gain from this rebellion against the rule of the one true God?

Their rebellion is all in vain. They are like a person who jumps out of an aeroplane, supposing that somehow he can escape the inevitability of hitting the ground.

All through the ages men have tried to escape the sovereignty of the one true God, and his ordering of the universe. But all their efforts have been in vain. Even those who follow the trail of various religious expressions rebel in vain against the Lord and his Messiah, Jesus Christ the Son of God.

This plotting to overthrow the rightful rule of the Lord and his Messiah is not confined to isolated cases here and there. Entire nations and peoples, kings and potentates take their stand together. A 'plot' emerges. They scheme together in order to accomplish their goal.

They conspire against him

A corporate spirit of rebellion often is more determined than the revolt of the individual. When governments aggressively assault neighbouring nations, exploit the poor to satisfy the tastes of the rich, operate an unsound fiscal policy, tolerate inefficiency and fail to provide swift punishment for wrong-doers, they are rebelling against the Lord and his Christ. When trade unions tolerate poor workmanship, imply that it is disloyal to the union to put in eight hours of real work for eight hours on the job, and promote violence and intimidation to attain their goals, they are rebelling against the Lord and his Christ. When management amasses wealth by paying inadequate wages, requires its workers to report unnecessarily on Sundays and leads companies into bankruptcy while retaining large sums for its executives, it is rebelling against the Lord and his Christ. When universities show favouritism towards atheistic teaching, deny the basic values of honest enquiry, and provide a safe harbour for depraved morals, they are rebelling against the Lord and his Christ.

Unitedly and as individuals, the nations, peoples, kings and potentates of the earth agree on a single goal:

> Let us break
>   their bands,
> and fling from us
>   their fetters
>
> (verse 3).

They have twisted the very structural order of things, and have declared evil to be good, and freedom to be bondage. But despite the slanderous reports of unbelievers, Christianity is no more a bondage to men than are wings a bondage to birds. For Christ invites men to enjoy the 'glorious liberty of the children of God' (Rom. 8:21 KJV).

It is all in vain

Sometimes the Christian feels intimidated by the conglomerations set against him. How can he make a way for himself and his family when the structures of government, labour, management and the educational systems of the day oppose the values that mean the most to him?

The confrontation of Christians with the 'powers that be' is not something new that has first arisen in our modern culture. In Acts 4 Peter interprets the opposition the apostles faced as a manifestation of the principles described in Psalm 2. He quotes this psalm and then explains: 'for truly in this city there were gathered together against your holy servant Jesus, whom you anointed, both Herod and Pontius Pilate, along with the Gentiles and the peoples of Israel' (Acts 4:27). Political and religious authorities, Gentile and Jewish in origin, agreed on one point despite the rivalry that normally separated them. Jesus must be destroyed, and his followers must be suppressed. But what did they accomplish?

It was all in vain. They were able to do only what God's power and will had determined beforehand should happen (Acts 4:28). Though they represented all the forces that human resources could muster, they could not suppress the plan of God. As a matter of fact, in their ragings they assisted in the realization of exactly what God had planned all along.

Can you learn this lesson? Can you put your heart to rest? Are you willing to accept delays in the realization of your Christ-honouring goals, trusting that the same principles are at work today that have worked through all the centuries? In vain men attempt to thwart the purposes of God and his people. By their best efforts they only bring about what his power and will have decided beforehand should happen.

So ends the first scene of this psalm. On earth the nations plot against the Lord and his Messiah. But all their schemings are in vain.

The second and third scenes of this psalm are set in heaven. They depict the response of God and his Messiah to the revolt on earth.

2. The Lord mocks their rebellious efforts (verses 4-6)

How should you respond to the plotting of wicked men against God and his righteous purposes? You should respond by trusting in the Lord's control and by praying that God will intervene to maintain his own glory.

Now how does God himself respond to these provocations?

He laughs at their efforts

He who sits in heaven
  laughs;
the Lord
  mocks them

(verse 4).

From a human perspective, the Lord's failure to respond instantly to the rebellion of men appears to confirm the suggestion that he will not get directly involved in earthly matters. He will let the problems of the world work themselves out. But the Lord's delays only establish his patience towards sinners, and ultimately manifest his complete control of the situation at hand. God is not threatened by the rebellious contortions of men. He is quite capable of bringing them up short whenever he wishes. In the meantime, he continues to be in control, laughing at their efforts to overthrow his sovereignty.

He speaks of his Son

But then …! Then he suddenly speaks to them in his wrath. By just a slight display of the power at his disposal, he shows how quickly he can turn their spirit of bold revolt into trembling cowardice. All God must do is speak, just as he once did at Sinai. His voice is enough to cause the cedars to tremble and the desert to shake (Psa. 29:5, 8). His speaking is enough to subdue men.

What does he say when he finally responds to the rebellious? He speaks all about Jesus. In reaction to the rebellions of men, he reveals an important fact about his Son Jesus Christ.

I have installed my king
  on Zion my holy mountain

(verse 6).

The Lord does not speak in vague, abstract terms. He does not seek some common denominator of religious truth to which all men might agree. God speaks pointedly about his Son, and about the fact that he has already been established as King on his holy mountain. From his exalted vantage-point, God's anointed King surveys the revolts of men. Seated at God's right hand, he has been given all authority in heaven and on earth.

Why is it that whole nations often turn to search out the Christian faith in a time of national calamity? Why is it that men are often opened to the gospel by the trouble that comes to them? People in prisons and hospitals may listen eagerly to words about the Saviour just at the time when rebellion against God might be expected. Why are they open to God rather than closed in resentment against him?

Why? Because *then* God speaks to them. Having humbled them as a way of softening their hearts, he then speaks the good news of the gospel.

You can be an instrument of God by relaying his message to the hardened unbeliever. You can never know by a person's outward appearance whether he or she has been prepared for the gospel or not. Sometimes your word will be like the gentle touch on a piece of ripe fruit barely clinging to the branch of a tree. It falls into your hand at the slightest nudge.

Why does it happen that way? Because if you are speaking all about Jesus, the voice of God comes through your words. By your testimony the Lord may subdue his strongest enemies under your feet. In this way he mocks their rebellious efforts, showing that they are to no avail.

3. Messiah proclaims his God-appointed position (verses 7-9)

So how does Jesus Christ himself view all these developments? Kings and nations rebel against the righteous ways of God. The Father in turn designates the Son as his emissary to earth. So how does the Son of God respond to the rebellious counsels of men? How does he react to crises among the nations of the world today? He reacts in two ways.

The divine sonship of Christ

First, he asserts the uniqueness of his divine sonship. He is God's appointed King to rule in this world on the Lord's behalf:

> I will proclaim the decree
> of the Covenant LORD.
> He said to me:
> 'You are my Son;
> this day
> I have given birth to you'
>
> (verse 7).

After a long winter, writers often speak of the 'birth' of spring. At that time the world is transformed from the deadness of winter into the special glory of springtime. In a similar way, this reference to the 'birth' of the Son of God speaks figuratively of his resurrection. By that event Jesus was transformed from a condition of humiliation to one of glory and power. Paul the apostle makes this point quite plainly when declaring the good news at Antioch: 'We bring you the good news that what God promised to the fathers, this he has fulfilled to us their children by raising Jesus, as also it is written in the second Psalm, "You are my Son, today I have begotten you"' (Acts 13:32, 33).

At his resurrection from the dead, Jesus Christ experienced a glorious transformation. It was like a new birth. From his condition of humiliation in which he was subjected to the abuses of men, he rose to a position of authority appropriate to his glorious person as the Son of God.

Some day the raging and the plotting of sinners will be directed specifically against you personally. It is inevitable. Paul says, 'Indeed, all who desire to live a godly life in Christ Jesus will be persecuted' (2 Tim. 3:12). Only with much suffering will you enter the kingdom of God (Acts 14:22). What should be your reaction in those kinds of circumstances?

You should begin by remembering the sonship of Jesus Christ. Contemplate him in his resurrected state, his position of power and glory. Remind yourself that even now he rules from God's right hand, and that you are seated with him in heavenly places.

Christ's resurrection is not something yet to be accomplished. According to the unchangeable, unchallengeable decree of the Lord, he already has come out from under all the humiliations and mistreatments that man could heap on him.

By faith you can benefit from his exalted position. Even while you are filling up that which is lacking in the sufferings of Christ for the sake of the spread of the gospel, you also can enjoy the benefits of his sovereignty as the Son of God.

So the first thing you should do when you suffer is to remember the glorious sonship of Jesus Christ. You benefit now from his present glory.

The power of his prayer

Secondly, you should recall the consequences of his sonship (verses 8, 9). As Son of God, he has the power of prayer, and he has the potency of God. To him the Father has said:

'Ask of me
And I will give you
the nations
as your inheritance,
and as your possession
the ends of the earth'

(verse 8).

All a son has to do is to ask his father, and the thing desired will be his. All Christ must do is ask the Father, and the rebellious nations will be subject to him.

Why are you a Christian? Why is anyone a Christian? You are a Christian because Christ prayed for you. He called your name before the Father and said, 'I want that one.' Because he prayed specifically to the Father for you, it was inevitable that you would belong to him.

Never regard anyone as beyond the reach of the transforming grace of God. If the Son asks the Father for the most hardened of sinners, he or she will belong to Christ.

Not only individual destinies, but the course of nations remains subject to the authority of Jesus Christ. We cannot understand the scourge of war when it comes on the earth. We know God cannot be blamed for the evils that come to the world. The blame always belongs to man. The sinful greed, pride and self-centredness of man constitute the point where the fault lies. Yet all the nations are subject to Jesus Christ. Nothing occurs apart from his sovereign will. He possesses the ends of the earth. With his authority he herds the nations like a shepherd using a rod of iron. As someone might smash the clay vessel of a potter, so he smashes the rebellious nations of the world (verse 9). Sinful men, though constantly offered the mercy of the Lord as it is found in Jesus Christ, are never far from being smashed in judgment. For God has appointed him to rule the nations.

As a consequence of Christ's sonship, he rules over the nations of the world. As the Son of God, he has the power of prayer, and he has the potency of God himself. When you are threatened by powers beyond your control, remember the consequences of Christ's sonship. Trust this one who is your Saviour to govern the nations in the future as he has done in the past.

4. Mighty men are charged to submit (verses 10-12)

So what should the mighty of the earth do? They should act *now*!

And now, you kings,
act wisely;
yield to correction,
you who judge the earth.

Serve the Covenant LORD
with fear;
and rejoice
with trembling.

Kiss the Son to avert his anger,
or you will perish in the way.
For his anger will consume in a moment.
Blessed are all who trust in him

(verses 10-12).

Time is running out. *Right now* kings and judges of the earth must act wisely. In every age these verses have a special application to prominent figures who stand guilty of offending the Lord Christ by their ruthless behaviour. The righteous indignation of Jesus Christ burns against those who rape and pillage other nations.

Yet at the same time, be sure that you apply this clear word from God to yourself.

Yield to correction, teenagers, or you will perish in the way. Keep rebelling against the authority-structure under which God has placed you, turn a deaf ear to their counsel, and you will suffer the same destruction as rebellious kings of the earth.

Single people and married people alike, bow before his will. Kiss the Son of God as an act of wholehearted submission to his will for your life. Receive with joy his appointment for you, or you will perish in the way.

Hear by faith the good message that the Son of God has brought to the world: 'Blessed are all who trust in him.' Whoever you are, you can be blessed if you will turn to him. No matter how long you have continued in rebellion against the Son of God, it is not yet too late. All who trust in him will be blessed.

Conclusion

This psalm is all about God's Son, the Lord Jesus Christ. He that honours the Son honours the Father.

Give to Jesus Christ the recognition he deserves. Resist all rationalizations and doubtings about his person and work. He is what the psalmist declares him to be. Enjoy the privileges and the blessings of the adopted sons and daughters of God by submitting yourself to the authority of Jesus Christ.

Psalm 8
The Measure of a Man

To the chief musician. On the *gittith*. A psalm of David.

Reader: 1 Covenant Lord, our Lord,
how majestic is your name
in all the earth!
For you have set your glory
higher than heaven itself.

1st Congr.: 2 Out of the mouth of babes and sucklings
you have determined that strength should come

2nd Congr.: in response to your adversaries,
to silence the enemy and the vengeful.

Reader: 3 When I see
your heavens,
the work of your fingers,
moon and stars
which you have ordained;

1st Congr.: 4 What is man
that you give him any consideration,

2nd Congr.: or the son of man
that you concern yourself with him?

1st Congr.: [5]You have made him a little less
than the angels;
2nd Congr.: with glory and honour
you have crowned him.

1st Congr.: [6]You have made him rule
over the works of your hands;
2nd Congr.: all things
you have set under his feet:

Reader: [7]all sheep and oxen,
as well as the cattle of the fields;
birds of the sky,
and fish of the sea,
including everything that travels the paths
of the sea.

All: [8]Covenant LORD, our Lord,
how majestic is your name
in all the earth!

The Measure of a Man—
What is Man?

Introduction

What is man? Is he from heaven? Is he from hell? Is he a decadent beast or is he a heavenly being? If you are still caught up in the spirit of the Renaissance then you believe that man is the measure of all things. What man is determines what everything else ought to be. You see man as Michelangelo's David, perfect in form and proportion, graceful in line and spirit.

But if you read the daily newspapers you may have an entirely different evaluation of man. One man mutilates the bodies of eleven other people and attempts to store their dismembered parts in his apartment. Another man seeks to develop a nuclear weapon so he can blackmail the rest of civilization. You cannot help but ask the question, what is this mystery called man?

So how is man to be measured? Clearly man himself cannot be the judge of all things. Man himself must be judged.

God's word alone unravels the mystery of man. Psalm 8 in particular deals with the question of the marvels of man. Interestingly, the New Testament takes a great deal of notice of this psalm that explains the enigma called man. Three different authors of the New Testament quote Psalm 8 at significant points in their argument.

Look at this psalm from the perspective of the New Testament and ask three questions about man. What is man—is he like the devil, or is he like God? What is man—is he mortal, or is he immortal? What is man—is he to be victor, or can he expect to be vanquished? From all three of these passages in the New Testament that reflect on the message of Psalm 8 it becomes evident that man redeemed in Christ is God's greatest instrument for praising him.

1. What is man—is he like the devil, or is he like God?

Jacob Bronowski begins his book *The Ascent of Man* with a chapter entitled 'Lesser than the Angels.' By this title he alludes to the statement in Psalm 8 that God has made man 'a little less than the angels' (verse 5). In the early pages of this book he describes the ascent of man. 'Cultural evolution' is his theme, and he looks at the wonders of man's development in the areas of art and science. He speaks of the brilliant sequence of cultural peaks that man has achieved throughout his history.

But after almost four hundred pages of recounting the supposed advance of man across the centuries, he reproduces a historic letter. Albert Einstein, the nuclear physicist, writes to Franklin Delano Roosevelt, the president. The year is 1939. Einstein says to the president, 'We have discovered a new scientific technique that may make it possible for us to develop extremely powerful bombs.' Einstein proceeds to note that one of these bombs placed in the bow of a ship and driven into a port would not only destroy the port itself but a great deal of the territory surrounding the port as well. In the next two pages of his book, the author reproduces vivid pictures of Hiroshima after the dropping of the first atomic bomb.

Then Bronowski moves on to talk about Auschwitz and the elimination of eight million Jews. 'This is what men do when they aspire to the knowledge of gods,' he says.[1]

The ascent of man? Is that a proper title for a book recounting the history of mankind over the ages? Has man ascended, or has he only become more adept at manipulating the powers inherent in creation to his own end? Is man more like a devil or more like a god?

The example of the children

One answer to this question may be found on the lips of Jesus Christ as he applies the message of Psalm 8 to a critical point in the last week of his own life. In five days he will be crucified by the political and religious authorities of the day. On Palm Sunday he enters Jerusalem

[1] J. Bronowski, *The Ascent of Man*, Boston, 1973, p.374.

and is greeted by the exclamations of the people. The blind and the lame come expectantly to the temple area, and he does not disappoint them. The man Jesus does something that no other person ever has done since the creation of the world. He makes the blind to see. Men who had totally lost their vision behold the wonders of the world once more.

Though he is a man, does not this person have the power of God within him? Is it not the work of the Creator to make the blind to see? Children gather to observe this amazing thing. They are filled with excitement. They shout, 'Hosanna to the Son of David!' (Matt. 21:15). They see in Jesus the quintessence of man. He must be the promised Messiah, the son of David anointed by God's Spirit and sent to bring salvation to men.

But a note of dissonance disturbs the chorus of children's voices. The religious leaders of the day are indignant. They accost Jesus with their complaint. 'Do you hear what these are saying?' they demand (Matt. 21:16). The implication is that Jesus must rebuke them, silence them. For these children are praising him with the hosannas that belong only to God.

Jesus responds by quoting Psalm 8: 'Yes; have you never read, "Out of the mouth of infants and nursing babies you have prepared praise"?' (Matt. 21:16).

No stronger praise can be offered to God than that which comes from the mouths of babies and infants. The sucking strength of the newborn child glorifies God for the wonder of his creation. The infant wails when he is hungry, and his expression of absolute dependence praises God, the sustainer of life. When these gathered children spontaneously praise Jesus for his intervention to save the helpless blind and lame, they are only offering a slightly more mature version of the same praise that infants and babies present by their natural expressions that give glory to God.

When man finally reaches his majority, he too can glorify God if he recognizes that his life comes moment by moment from the hand of his Creator and Redeemer. As a human being you can give proper glory to God if you will acknowledge yourself to be a dependent creature living only by God's grace.

Giving to God the praise due to him

The section quoted by Jesus from Psalm 8 is bracketed by a refrain in the psalm which exalts the glory of God far above the smallness of man:

> Covenant LORD, our Lord,
> how majestic is your name
> in all the earth!
>
> (verses 1, 8).

It is only as man gives proper praise to God that he fulfils the role in this world that God intended for him. If perfected praise comes from the lips of the dependent infant, adult man can do no better than to humble himself and follow the child's example. But when man refuses to express his dependence on God, he puts himself in a position of rivalling his Creator. Deliberately or otherwise, he makes himself God's personal adversary.

Jesus was gentle with the Pharisees who challenged the praise of the children. When he met their opposition earlier, he avoided confrontation by departing from Judea into Galilee. Explaining this action, Matthew placed Christ's ministry in the context of the work of the Suffering Servant of the Lord: 'A bruised reed he will not break, and a smouldering wick he will not quench' (Matt. 12:20). Despite their proud resistance to the advancement of God's glory by the redemption of men, Jesus responded gently when they disparaged the praise offered by the children. He did not accost them with the whole of the verse from Psalm 8:

> Out of the mouth of babes and sucklings
> you have determined that strength should come
> *in response to your adversaries,*
> *to silence the enemy and the vengeful*
>
> (verse 2).

What is man—is he like God, or is he like the devil? The answer to the question depends on the relationship a person sustains to God the Creator and his Son Jesus Christ. When a man gives strong praise to God, then he reflects the image of the God he glorifies.

But when a person determines to establish his own autonomy, he takes on the form of a devil, God's perpetual adversary.

You are a person with potential for praising Jesus Christ or opposing him. You may place your priority on satisfying personal ambitions. Or you may humble yourself as a dependent creature, giving proper praise to God and entrusting yourself to God's Son Jesus Christ.

2. What is man—is he mortal or immortal?

A second question about man arises from Psalm 8. Is man mortal or immortal? Is man subject to death, or is he freed from death's power?

This question is a complex one, and can be answered in various ways. Clearly from one perspective all men are mortal. They are subject to the termination of their present life by physical death. Made of fallen flesh and blood, man deteriorates and dies. It is inevitable.

From another perspective it may be affirmed that all men 'live' forever. The Scriptures teach that the soul continues to exist after the flesh dissolves. Whether blessed in the presence of God or cursed by banishment from his face, the soul of man continues to live. Yet continuation of existence apart from the presence of God might better be designated as eternal 'death' rather than 'life.' For separation from God is nothing less than death itself.

When Paul the apostle quotes Psalm 8 in 1 Corinthians 15, he views man's mortality from a particular perspective. He makes his point quite clearly: 'Flesh and blood cannot inherit the kingdom of God, nor does the perishable inherit the imperishable' (1 Cor. 15:50). The perishable must clothe itself with the imperishable, and the mortal with immortality before man can participate in the eternal kingdom of God (verse 53).

Paul does not intend to contrast the immortal soul of man with his mortal body. He contrasts instead man's present existence, in which he is subject to death, with the changed character of his condition after the resurrection. He says, '[Christ] must reign until he has put all his enemies under his feet. The last enemy to be destroyed is death. For "God has put all things in subjection under his feet"' (1 Cor. 15:25-27).

There is no question about it, says the apostle Paul. Psalm 8 has declared that God has put everything under the feet of man. As a consequence, the man Christ Jesus must reign until he has subdued all his enemies. Death is man's ultimate enemy, and so Christ's work must include the destruction of the last enemy, death itself.

Our Lord Jesus Christ has invested his life in the redemption of man. If a redeemed person finally is lost in death, then Christ's suffering and sacrifice are all in vain. As the apostle says, 'If in this life only we have hope in Christ, we are of all people most to be pitied' (1 Cor. 15:19). But the Scriptures assure us that Christ must continue to reign until every opposition to his work has been put down. He will reign until he has put all his enemies under his feet.

Is man mortal or immortal? Will he decay in the grave at death and never experience life with God again? Man outside Jesus Christ is mortal. His flesh corrupts in the grave, and rises again only to be sentenced forever to undergo the curse of the second death.

But man in Christ is immortal. He never dies. His body sleeps in the grave until the resurrection, while his soul goes immediately to be with Christ. At the last trumpet, the dead in Christ will rise first. Their corruptible bodies will put on incorruption, and their mortal bodies will put on immortality.

Give glory to God for complete redemption. Join with the psalmist in praising God for the perfections of his work:

> Covenant LORD, our Lord,
> how majestic is your name
> in all the earth!
>
> (verse 8).

What is man? Is he like the devil or is he like God? Everything depends on his relationship to Jesus Christ. What is man? Is he mortal or immortal? It all depends on his relationship to Jesus Christ.

What is man—is he victor or vanquished?

Finally, is man victor or vanquished? Is he a sure winner or a born loser? Consider the third quotation from Psalm 8 in the New Testament, found in Hebrews 2.

A few years ago a football player caught the attention of the media because of his size. At the age of eighteen he was six feet six inches tall and weighed over thirty-four stone (220 kg or 485 lb). They called him 'the World.'

But the largest of men cannot compare in size with a rhinoceros, a hippopotamus or an elephant. Man is by no means the biggest animal in the world, and never has been. Neither is man the most numerous of creatures on earth. The fish of the sea, the birds of the air and the insects on the ground constitute a teeming mass of life that far exceeds man in numbers.

Yet the Scriptures declare that God has made man lord of all creation. The psalmist says,

> You have made him rule
> over the works of your hands;
> all things
> you have set under his feet:
> all sheep and oxen,
> as well as the cattle of the fields;
> birds of the sky,
> and fish of the sea,
> including everything that travels the paths of the sea.
> (verses 6, 7).

When he considers man's glory, the psalmist stands in awe. But when compared with the wonder of the rest of creation, what is man?

> When I see
> your heavens,
> the work of your fingers,
> moon and stars
> which you have ordained;

what is man
  that you give him any consideration,
or the son of man
  that you concern yourself with him?

(verses 3, 4).

Consider the stars, the sun and moon that God has made. How can man compare with the majesty of those celestial bodies? Our sun is a part of that massive grouping of stars known as the Milky Way. The expanse of night-time haze created by millions of massive stars seems so distant from our sun and its satellites. Yet as remote as the Milky Way may seem, it envelops and includes our sun. At the same time, this and that glitter of light that appears to be a part of this galaxy actually may be a cluster of other star-galaxies millions of light-years away. Astronomers tell us that many of those distant points of light contain more stars than the millions to be found in our own cluster.

The world today knows far more about the expansive world of stars than did David when he wrote Psalm 8. Yet we give far less consideration to the amazing character of the universe that surrounds us.

But suppose you could be 'beamed up' on a shaft of light, travelling at 186,000 miles per second. After a few million years of journeying you would arrive at Andromeda, one of the galaxies nearest our own. Suppose you took along one of the newest, most sophisticated of our modern space telescopes. Once you had reached your destination, you might turn your telescope around to peer at Mother Earth. You might find it interesting to check out man's latest exploits. What would you see? Absolutely nothing. This world and the works of man are so small that they don't amount to a pinpoint in the vastness of the universe.

Yet the Scriptures tell us that God has made man ruler over the works of his hands. Stars remain silent over the centuries. They see nothing, they speak nothing. They have no feelings and no creativity. In all these ways man is like God. Man has been given the intelligence necessary to rule over the world that God has made.

Birds of the air, fish of the sea and all that swim in the paths of the seas are under his dominion. All things are subject to him.

But in quoting this portion of Psalm 8, the writer to the Hebrews points out a discordant fact. We do not see all things subject to man (Heb. 2:8). The intent is not to dispute the truthfulness of the assertions of Psalm 8 about man's role in the purposes of God. But it is surely correct that all things are not now subjected to humans. A woman devotes her life to working with lions. She writes a book entitled *Born Free*. But then she is killed by the very lions she has tried to subdue. (If instead she were murdered by men, then the point is made even more dramatically. Man cannot subdue his own bestial tendencies, not to speak of controlling the beasts of the jungle.) The gay sector of our cities cries out for millions more dollars to be invested in AIDS research. Why? Because man cannot control the microscopic creatures that bring death to his frame. In so many ways we do not yet see all things brought into submission to man.

But what do we see? We see something very significant. We see Jesus. For a little while he was made lower than the angels. But now he is crowned with glory and honour. As a result of his victory, all things have been subjected to man, the man Christ Jesus (Heb. 2:9).

He has become our leader, bringing many sons of God to their destined glory (Heb. 2:10). Through suffering many things to confirm his own holiness, he is able now to make others holy.

What is man? Is he victor or vanquished? What will be your experience? Will you be victorious in the struggles of your life? In the physical struggles? In the social struggles? What about your spiritual and emotional struggles? Will you triumph or will you collapse in defeat? It all depends on your relationship to Jesus Christ. If by faith you are bound to him, you will be the victor. You will not be vanquished. Through union with him you are more than conqueror. You will face many tests in life. But just because the Son of Man has suffered through trials, he is able to succour those who are tested. Even as the mouths of babies and infants give praise to God by their cries of dependence, so as you express your dependence on Jesus Christ you will find him able to strengthen you. Through the victories you achieve in his name, you will give glory to God.

Conclusion

Now compare the options. What is man? Is he mortal? Is he defeated? Is he in his essence like a devil? Or is man immortal, victorious, remade in the image of God?

It all depends on each person's relationship to Jesus Christ, Son of Man and Son of God. By trusting in him, you may experience the fulfilment of God's purposes for you as a man or woman.

Remember your unique role in God's creation. As the poetic structure of Psalm 8 indicates, all considerations of the nature and destiny of man must be bracketed by a single refrain. Man can be evaluated rightly only in terms of his relationship to the words that open and close Psalm 8:

> Covenant LORD, our Lord,
> how majestic is your name
> in all the earth!
>
> (verse 8).

The ultimate test of every man must rest in an evaluation of his capacity to give glory to God his Creator. Only man redeemed in Christ can fulfil his destiny of being God's greatest instrument for praising him.

Psalm 11
The Tried and the Trusted

For the chief musician. By David.

Reader: 1In the LORD of the Covenant I have trusted.
How then do all of you say to my soul,

Congr.: 'Flee to your people's mountain
like a bird'?

Reader: 2For behold the wicked!
They bend their bow,
they set their arrow on the string
against the just
to shoot from the thick darkness
against the upright in heart.

All: 3If the foundations be destroyed,
what will the righteous do?

Reader: 4But the LORD of the Covenant—

Congr.: He *is* in his holy temple.

Reader: The LORD of the Covenant—

Congr.: His throne *is* in heaven.

All: His eyes
test,

his eyelids
    try
        the sons of men.

Reader: 5 The LORD of the Covenant tries
    the righteous;

Congr.: but the wicked and the lovers of violence
his soul hates.

Reader: 6 He will rain on the wicked
    snares, fire and brimstone;

Congr.: and a tempest of poisonous winds
    will be the portion of their cup.

All: 7 For the righteous LORD of the Covenant
    loves righteous deeds;
    the upright
will gaze on his face.

The Tried and the Trusted—*Trusting God through Trial*

Introduction

Nobody likes a test. Or, at least, tests are not generally enjoyed by most people. But then there are the exceptions. Some tests obviously are so beneficial that people actually want to take them. Men who must drive military tanks in modern warfare understand that testing before conflict can be the key to victory. Modern tank simulators have become so sophisticated that a rigid testing programme can anticipate all the realities of battle before actual conflict begins.

Success or failure in a test often depends as much on the attitude of the person giving the test as it does on the person being tested. If the person designing a test has your best interests in view, then you are much more likely to do well in it. Psalm 11 is all about tests, and perhaps that is why it is not generally listed among people's favourite psalms. Yet Psalm 11 has a great message for the people of God. Consider today how God tests men, and how you should view his tests. This psalm is about 'the tried and the trusted'. It talks first about the God who is to be trusted, and then describes the people who are being tried.

1. The God who is to be trusted

The psalmist says:

> In the LORD of the Covenant I have trusted.
> How then do all of you say to my soul,
> 'Flee to your people's mountain
> like a bird'?
>
> (verse 1).

The psalmist trusts in the LORD of the Covenant, and in no

other. He does not make the mistake of trusting in men. As the metrical version of another psalm expresses it:

> Put no confidence in princes,
> Nor for help on man depend;
> He shall die, to dust returning,
> And his purposes shall end.[1]

Neither should a person's trust be placed in a nebulous idea of God. Trust must be directed specifically towards the LORD of the Covenant, the only one who ultimately is responsible for all the trials his people undergo.

In growing segments of the world today the phrase is being constantly chanted: '*Allahu Akbar,* God is great.' It is the confession of those who subscribe to the Muslim faith. But only one God is great. Jesus said, 'I am the way, and the truth, and the life. No one comes to the Father except through me' (John 14:6). Success or failure during the difficult times of life depends altogether on whether the God you trust is the one true, living God.

If this Lord fails him, the psalmist has no other recourse. To him this Lord, and this Lord alone, is enough and more than enough. But he is being ridiculed by those who are counselling him. They tell him to resort to flight rather than to trust in this Lord in his time of trial.

A trap set for the righteous

Two aspects of their mockery are particularly worth noting. It is not just to 'a' mountain that they urge him to flee. It is to 'your people's' mountain that he must flee. In the greatest expression of mockery imaginable, he is being told to flee to the very place where he would expect that his God would be most obviously present to deliver him. It recalls the mockery of Rabshakeh, captain of the army of Assyria in the days of Isaiah the prophet. As he stood outside the walls of Jerusalem with his conquering army, he ridiculed the people of God. 'I will give you two thousand horses,' he said, 'if you are able on your part to set riders on them' (2 Kings 18:23).

[1] Psa. 146:3, 4; *Trinity Hymnal,* 1990, No. 57

Furthermore, these 'friends' tell the psalmist to flee 'as a bird' to his mountain. A bird approaches only those places where he feels safe. The trap works only if it is located in a place where the bird expects nothing to happen. The bird lands with a sense of security, the trap is sprung, the hunter appears and the captured victim is doomed.

So these wicked people seek to trap David in the very place where he feels most secure. At Mount Zion, the place where God and his people dwell, there they expect to catch him.

So the church, the sanctuary of God, often becomes the snare of the devil. A bishop in one branch of the church of Jesus Christ publicly declared that 'Jesus Christ, as portrayed in some New Testament passages, is "narrow-minded" and "vindictive." The Gospel writers "twisted" the facts concerning Jesus' resurrection, which was never meant to be taken literally. The virgin birth of Christ is an unthinkable notion, and there is not much value in the doctrine of the Trinity, or in the belief that Jesus Christ was sent to save fallen humanity from sin. St Paul, the missionary of Christianity to the Gentiles, was a repressed and "self-loathing" homosexual. As for the Old Testament, it contains a "vicious tribal code of ethics" attributed to a "sadistic" God.'[2]

The church is supposed to be a refuge from the immorality and the unbelief that run rampant in the world. Yet here is a man within the inner sanctum of the church denouncing the very heart of Christian faith and practice.

And how will the church respond to this challenge to the very core of its beliefs? Another bishop of the same church doubts that any decisive stand will be taken against these heretical writings: 'The House of Bishops has shown itself to be impotent in the face of challenges to the core beliefs of the church … We've been paralysed by our politeness' (ibid).

Do you who are elders in the church of Jesus Christ perceive the responsibility resting on your shoulders? You must maintain a refuge for the people of God. People flee to the church, thinking they will find justice and truth in contrast to the lies and

[2] *Time*, 18 February 1991, p. 62

corruption of the world. If instead they find prejudice against the upright and partiality towards the wicked, where will they turn to find the truth? What could be more discouraging to the remnant of God's people as they seek to stand for truth and righteousness in the midst of a crooked and perverse generation?

But the psalmist trusts that no matter how far may go the schemings of the wicked in converting the sanctuary of the Lord into a trap for the righteous, the Lord will still preserve him. Actually, he is startled at the audacity of the wicked in proposing to catch him in the very presence of the Lord. How could they presume to say, 'Flee to your people's mountain like a bird'? Don't they know that God will be there in all his power and glory to defend him?

Yet the wicked do pose a real threat to the well-being of the righteous.

> For behold the wicked!
> They bend their bow,
> they set their arrow on the string
> against the just
> to shoot from the thick darkness
> against the upright in heart
>
> (verse 2).

Behold the wicked! Look at them! They have the audacity to make these plots. They shoot from the thick darkness. From the innermost sanctuary of God they seek to destroy the righteous. Using the most powerful weapons available to them, they set their foot on the bowstring and stretch it to capacity with the strength of both hands.

Remember the experience of Nehemiah? Five times his enemies tried to lure him outside the city of Jerusalem. 'Come out into one of the villages, and let us meet together,' they said. But Nehemiah perceived that it was a trap, and he refused to go (Neh. 6:2-9).

Then one day a person pretending to be Nehemiah's friend said to him, 'Let us meet together in the house of God, within the temple. Let us close the doors of the temple, for they are coming to kill you.' Nehemiah records his response: 'But I said, "Should such a man as I run away? And what man such as I could go into the temple and live? I will not go in." And I understood and saw that God had not sent him, but he had pronounced the prophecy against me … that I should be afraid and act in this way and sin, and so they could give me a bad name in order to taunt me' (Neh. 6:11-13). Can you imagine? His enemies set a trap in the sanctuary of God. But the Lord preserved him.

So don't be surprised. The very place where you put your trust may be transformed into a trap one of these days.

The shaking of the foundations

But be assured. If your faith is rightly directed towards the one true God, you will not be destroyed. Your foundations for life may seem severely shaken. But because the Lord is committed to preserving the righteous, the foundations cannot be destroyed. That is the next point the psalmist intends to make:

> If the foundations be destroyed,
> what will the righteous do?
>
> (verse 3).

Two foundations must stand firm if you are not to be shaken: the foundation of God's church on earth, and the foundation of God's rule in heaven (cf. verse 4). If these two foundations are destroyed, where can the righteous stand? The church on earth is described as the 'pillar and buttress of the truth' (1 Tim. 3:15). If it does not stand for the right, what recourse do the righteous have?

The Lord's rule in heaven provides the ultimate foundation for the maintenance of truth in the world. If God does not reign over all powers, then the truth will never stand.

> But the LORD of the Covenant—
> he *is* in his holy temple.
> The LORD of the Covenant—
> his throne *is* in heaven
>
> (verse 4).

A member of one church lost his job because of his Christian integrity. He would not sell used merchandise as though it were new. After undergoing such unjust treatment, it seemed as though the foundation of life itself had been shaken. It had been shaken, but it could not be destroyed. In the end, this man testifies that he ended up with a much better job. Furthermore, in his new job he was allowed complete freedom to share the gospel of Christ with others.

The two foundations that are a concern to the psalmist will stand. The enemy cannot overthrow either God's church on earth or God's throne in heaven. If a person flees to the Lord's mountain where he hopes to find support, he will find it. As Jesus assured his disciples, the gates of hell will not prevail against his church. Out of the gates of hell may pour forth a great army of demons and wicked men that assault God's truth, his church and his throne. But they will not destroy the foundations.

Today the temple of the Lord is not located on a specific mountain in Jerusalem as it was for the psalmist. Jesus declares to the Samaritan woman that neither in this mountain nor in Jerusalem will men worship, for God is a Spirit (John 4:21, 24). God's temple now is located in the place, wherever it might be, where men worship him in Spirit and in truth. God, with all his protecting care, will be found in that place. His royal power radiates from heaven and touches every place on earth where he is worshipped. In that place the foundations are secure, and you are safe.

Count on the fact. God can be trusted. Especially when his rule seems to be threatened, when his church seems to be overrun by his enemies, continue to exercise your faith in his sovereignty.

Many people say they believe in the providence of God. They affirm trust in his sovereignty. As long as things go well, they believe God is in control. But when the foundations appear to be shaking, they lose their confidence. But that is the very point at which you must keep exercising your trust. No matter how great may appear to be the threat, be assured that he will remain firm as a foundation for all that trust him.

So God is the one to be trusted. The Lord is worthy of your trust. Even as he brings you under the greatest of trials, he still can be trusted.

2. The people who are tried

After focusing on the object of men's trust, the psalmist depicts those who are being tried.

> His eyes
>   test,
> his eyelids
>   try
>   the sons of men
>
> (verse 4).

As a teenager I was regularly in prison. That is, along with the Salvation Army I went on Sunday afternoons to share Christ with those who were in prison. Often the Salvation Army woman would lead the inmates in a particular song. The words of the song went like this:

> There's an eye watching you;
> There's an all-seeing eye watching you.

This song was making a point with the inmates. God tests men. The psalmist says, 'His eyelids try the sons of men.' He squints. He pulls his eyelids closely together to concentrate his focus on the things men are doing, and on the thoughts they have buried deeply in their hearts.

Don't think for a moment that God does not know every thought that arises in your heart. When your motives are so mixed that you yourself cannot even tell what is driving you, the Almighty God knows.

But why? What is the point of God's scrutinizing the hearts of men? What is he expecting to accomplish when he puts them to the test? The answer to this question depends on what the Lord finds. He tries the righteous with one goal in mind, and he tries the wicked with another goal in mind. The psalmist says:

> The LORD of the Covenant tries
>   the righteous;
>   but the wicked and the lovers of violence
> his soul hates
>
> (verse 5).

See the difference? The 'trying' of the righteous is set over against the 'hating' of the wicked.

The trying of the righteous

A father begins the process of teaching his son or daughter to ride a bicycle. From the beginning, the father is constantly testing his child. First he tests to see if the child's feet can reach the pedals. Then he wants to be sure the child can balance the bike with training wheels. Then he wants to know if his pupil can turn the handlebars without flipping over the bicycle. Then with the training wheels off, he trots alongside the bike, huffing and puffing as he goes. His hand, invisible to the child, holds lightly to the back of the seat. He deftly removes and then reapplies his steadying influence as he senses the need. This whole process is designed to put the one he loves to the test. The purpose of the test is to train the child so that he or she can experience the exhilaration of riding over hill and dale unaided. It is the kind of test you want.

God gives this kind of test to the believer throughout his life. No matter how severe your current testing may seem to be, remember: it is the one the Lord loves that he puts under these kinds of tests.

His hatred of the wicked

This trying of the righteous stands in sharpest contrast with the Lord's hatred of the wicked and the lovers of violence. Hatred may seem to be a strong word, but it is in Scripture. God hates lovers of violence.

Make no mistake: God's hatred is not a passionate loss of control on his part. He does not strike out irrationally against the wicked. But whoever commits an act of brutality automatically becomes the object of his hatred. His wrath is a just, appropriate and righteous response to evil in the world. When violent, unthinkable atrocities are committed by one person against another, God's righteous indignation is stirred. He will act appropriately to bring just judgment, and no power will stop him.

The last two verses of the psalm spell out the final result of God's testing of men. The different destinies of the wicked and the righteous are described vividly.

The fate of the wicked

First, the psalmist describes the fate of the wicked. He says:

> He will rain on the wicked
> snares, fire and brimstone;
> and a tempest of poisonous winds
> will be the portion of their cup
>
> (verse 6).

All kinds of surprises will rain down from heaven on the heads of the wicked, including the snares they have set for others. The wicked may set a trap, but they will end up falling in it themselves. Snares, fire and brimstone will come down in abundance on the head of the wicked.

Abraham's nephew Lot troubled his soul every day by living in the wicked city of Sodom. God showed great patience with the sinful inhabitants of that city. But one day he rained down fire and brimstone from heaven, consuming the whole of that depraved community.

Our Lord Jesus Christ, the most compassionate man that ever lived on the face of the earth, has said, 'As it was in the days of Lot … so will it be on the day when the Son of Man is revealed' (Luke 17:28, 30). On the day the Son of Man returns, he will rain down fire and brimstone on the wicked.

According to the psalmist, the cup of the wicked will be a 'tempest of poisonous winds.' Their lot in life as measured out by the Lord will be tempestuous trials. While the cup of the righteous overflows with blessing, the cup of the wicked bubbles with trouble.

The modern world knows something about poisonous winds. It understands the horrors of having even the air you breathe filled with deadly poisons. It also knows that those who resort to poisonous gases often have those winds blow back in their own faces. A tempest of poisonous winds will be the portion of the cup of the wicked, for the Lord will see to it.

The final blessing of the righteous

But the result of the testing undergone by the righteous will be altogether different. The psalmist concludes:

> For the righteous LORD of the Covenant
>   loves righteous deeds;
>   the upright
> will gaze on his face
>
> (verse 7).

A married couple celebrating their fiftieth wedding anniversary were asked what advice they would give to a young couple just starting out. The answer was illuminating. They said that throughout their marriage each of them took an interest in what the other wanted to do. If she liked to eat out, he took her out to dinner. If he liked to watch racing-cars, she went to the track.

The Lord and his people are drawn together by similar interests. The righteous LORD of the Covenant loves the righteous deeds done by his people. He delights in seeing the right thing done. His people please him when they delight in righteousness. As a result of their common love of righteousness, the two will enjoy each other's company through time and eternity.

Do you wonder where you stand in relation to the judgment of God as described in this psalm? Does God view you as a wicked person, the object of his wrath? Or does he see you as righteous, the object of his love?

Surprisingly, the Old Testament saints seem to have had a better perspective than Christians today in this regard. God's people of old looked forward to God's judging them. They were confident of the outcome. They rejoiced in their expectation that the Lord would come to render his judgment over them.

Is that the way you view God's coming judgment? Are you looking forward to being judged? Most Christians would answer these questions in the negative. Christians are so conscious of their sin that they dread the prospect of being judged.

But you should recognize that you become the special object of God's love when you look to Jesus Christ for your righteousness. By your justification, you are guaranteed that you will be confirmed in righteousness. So you too should rejoice in anticipation of the Lord's judgment. At that moment, you will receive all that Christ has earned for you by his perfect obedience. In addition, his sanctifying power enables you to do righteous deeds. Though imperfect because of the remnants of sin in your life, your deeds done in his name are regarded by God as being absolutely perfect. You are the special object of his favour because of the righteousness of Christ in you. For that reason, you can look forward to the Lord's judgment.

The final blessing of God on the righteous is seen in the last phrase of verse 7: 'The upright will gaze on his face.' The believer in Jesus Christ has a privilege that even Moses did not experience during his lifetime. For eternity the righteous will have the privilege of gazing into the face of the Lord. Their eternal happiness will include a bliss that cannot be imagined on earth. It will involve the certainty of the Lord's favour as they look into his approving face.

Conclusion

God's testing of the righteous and the wicked goes on through every age. The wicked attempt in their perversity to turn even the place of greatest refuge for God's people into a trap.

But count on the fact that the foundations will not be destroyed. Keep putting your trust in him. In the end you will see just how much the righteous LORD of the Covenant loves righteousness.

Psalm 14
The Atheistic Fool

To the chief musician. By David.

1st Reader: 1The fool declares to himself,
'There is no god!'

All: They are depraved.
They do abhorrent things.
Not one of them does any good.

1st Reader: 2The Covenant LORD of heaven scrutinizes
the sons of men

All: to see if there are any
who understand,
who search for God:

2nd Reader: 3Every single one of them has turned away;
unitedly they have become degenerate.
Not one of them does any good,
not a single one.

4Have they no knowledge at all,
all these workers of iniquity,
who devour my people as they devour bread?

All: They refuse to call on the Covenant LORD.

1st Reader: 5 Right then and there
they become terrified with great anxiety!
For God abides
among the [assembled] generations of the righteous.

6 The perspective of the meek
all of you ridicule,
because the Covenant LORD is his only confidence.

All: 7 But let salvation for Israel
come out from Mount Zion!

1st Reader: When the Covenant LORD restores the losses of his people,

All: Jacob
will be overjoyed,
and Israel
will be ecstatic.

The Atheistic Fool—
The Folly of Atheism

Introduction

In the prevailing circumstances of today, it is not just individuals who are foolish in their way of life. Whole nations, the whole of the human race, toss this way and that as a ship of fools.

If the atheist is a fool, then a vocation that is controlled by atheism is a vocation for fools. If modern education derives its values from an atheistic perspective, then the whole enterprise is built on folly. The same principle holds for government, data management, biology, sports, news media and the arts. Each one serves as a vocation for fools, so long as the endeavour works on the assumption that 'There is no god.' Any vocation built on a supposed principle of neutrality with respect to God has chosen folly as its foundation.

An alarming slide into deeper and deeper degradation may be traced in the psalmist's picture of the fool. The atheist begins by saying *to himself*, 'There is no God.' The initial decision in favour of atheism is made in the secret chambers of the soul. But the moral consequence of this heartfelt affirmation is instant corruption. As a result of this corruption, the atheistic fool can *do no good*. But as a last twisted stab at maintaining personal goodness, the person who begins with the seemingly honest affirmation that there is no god ends by persecuting anyone who serves the one true God.

This descent into degradation by the atheist leads the psalmist to a very legitimate concern. The righteous believer inevitably suffers at the hands of the atheist. So the psalmist concludes with an earnest prayer for the Lord to deliver the righteous from the wicked and to restore all that he has lost.

The fool

The struggle between Satan's people and the people of God

The early selections in the book of Psalms express continual concern for the persecution of the righteous by the wicked. It is very important for God's people to realize the basic nature of this struggle between the seed of Satan and the seed of God. Does it catch you by surprise when the wicked constantly rise up to put pressure on the righteous? It shouldn't. The struggle between God's people and Satan's people is as old as human history, and will continue until the end of time.

This psalm is all about the atheist, and in one sense Satan is the atheist *par excellence*. From him we learn that atheism does not necessarily involve a categorical denial that there is a god. Instead, practical atheism says that there is no god *for me*. Satan knew well enough that there was a God. But he wanted to have nothing to do with him.

This psalm underscores just how permeating is the wickedness of the atheist who denies God for himself. He does no good! Not a single one of them does any good at all! This evaluation of the ethical quality of the deeds of the atheist may sound extreme. But given the divine test of goodness, it is true. The wicked may do relative good in comparison to the evil done by other wicked men. But when judged by the standard of God, the atheist does no good whatsoever.

The folly of the atheist

Now look at the Lord's explicit evaluation of the folly of the atheist.

> The fool declares to himself, 'There is no god!'
>
> (verse 1).

By a strange twist of the logic of pride, a man boasts that he is ignorant of God. He would not think of boasting that he was ignorant of virtually anything else. But by claiming that the witness to God's existence simply is not clear to him, he insulates himself from any sense of accountability to God. But as Paul says, it is as men claim to be wise that they become fools (Rom. 1:22).

The focus of the fool's denial about God is that he does not believe that a God exists who will recompense him for his evil ways. The person guilty of brutal war crimes thinks like a fool. Would he abuse defenceless prisoners if he knew that one day he would be hunted down and receive in himself the same treatment he has given to others?

But God's Word says all the wicked will be recompensed for their evil deeds. Scripture affirms: 'God considers it just to repay with affliction those who afflict you' (2 Thess. 1:6).

Be sure you are not playing the fool. If you live without any expectation that God will require an accounting of all wrongdoing both in this life and in that which is to come, you are living like a fool. Don't leave a single compartment of your life under the influence of the atheistic delusion.

Don't trust in man!

> They are depraved.
> They do abhorrent things.
> Not one of them does any good
>
> (verse 1).

A Christian can be badly hurt if he does not recognize the extent to which evil permeates the world. Remember what Jesus taught about man? At one point many people were inclined to believe on him. But Jesus 'did not entrust himself to them … for he himself knew what was in man' (John 2:24, 25).

It is not that you must always be pessimistic about what men will do to you. But you must always remember:

> They are depraved.
> They do abhorrent things.
> Not one of them does any good.

To say that the atheist is depraved, abhorrent and does no good may appear to be an overstatement. But it may be that this psalm is repeated almost identically as Psalm 53 to reinforce the truth that otherwise would be rejected by the carnal mind.

Don't you find it striking? Educated humanity says you may or may not believe in God as you choose, but you must believe in man. But God says you are a fool if you don't believe in God; and be sure you *do not* put your trust in man!

The contrast could hardly be set out more vividly! Man's wisdom says, 'Believe in the ever-increasing greatness of man, and don't worry about God.' But God's wisdom says, 'You're a fool if you don't believe in God; and be sure you never put your trust in man.'

A nation and a race of fools

To reinforce his point, the psalmist says that this evaluation about man is not his alone, but is the Lord's as well:

> The Covenant LORD from heaven scrutinizes the sons
> of men
> to see if there are any
> who understand,
> who search for God
>
> (verse 2).

It is not simply that someone who has been disappointed in personal relationships sees everything through jaundiced eyes. Instead it is the studied judgment of the Lord himself, who scrutinizes the hearts of men.

From heaven God looks. He has the advantage of putting everything in the broader perspectives of time and space. He is like the coach's assistant at a sports event who sits up high in the press-box. He can see the formations of the defence in a way that the coach on the sidelines cannot.

No one can plead in reaction to God's evaluation of men: 'But you don't understand.' God looks with his broader perspective across space and time to see if any men are truly wise, if any have the ability to discern the truth. The Lord in his generosity goes even a step further. He will look to see if there are any who even seek to know God.

You would assume a positive outcome to this search. Certainly some men seek to know God, even if they do not arrive at a perfect understanding. Aristotle and Plato, along with numerous other philosophers, were God-seekers, were they not? Certainly the heathen in the jungle, unspoiled with the materialism of the modern world, seeks to know the true God.

But the Lord answers with an unqualified 'No'! The supposed seeker has a prejudicial perspective that keeps him from wanting to find the true God. He may come with a sentimental concept about the love of God that will not allow him to affirm God's justice. Or he may imagine God to be an unfeeling, impersonal 'it' who is to blame for all the calamities that come in the world. In any case, no man in and of himself looks for a personal Lord who will rule over his life.

> Every single one of them has turned away;
> unitedly they have become degenerate.
> Not one of them does any good,
> not a single one.
> Have they no knowledge at all,
> all these workers of iniquity,
> who devour my people as they devour bread?
> (verses 3, 4).

Some interpreters would attempt to distinguish between Israel and the rest of men in this psalm. They would propose that the reference to 'my people' points to Israel in contrast to the Gentiles. Israel, according to this perspective, truly seeks after God, while the idolatrous Gentiles turn away from him. But Scripture testifies against this perspective. Israel's forefathers worshipped idols, and the nation itself turned to idolatry repeatedly, abandoning the living God despite all the favours he had showed to them.

It is an agreed-upon pact among men, Jews and Gentiles alike. In consort they deviate from the quest of the true God. Together and as individuals the story is the same. Not one of them does any good.

God himself evaluates men, and reaches the same conclusion as the psalmist. But the Lord reinforces his assertion by the additional phrase, ' … not a single one.' There is no exception. All the sophisticated religiosity of the ages is only meaningless deception. No one really wants to know God.

Paul quotes these verses in Romans 3 to show specifically that Jews are no better than Gentiles. Despite all the privileges associated with their being God's instrument for revealing himself to the world, they do not seek the true God any more than the heathen nations do. As a result, every mouth is silenced and the whole world is held accountable before God. Don't think that religious background somehow will assure that a person will be different. For 'There is none that does any good, no, not one.'

Once this fact about man has been recognized, a person is ready for the gospel of God's grace. For now, apart from a man's seeking God, a righteousness from God has been manifested in the person of Jesus Christ. As a gracious gift for sinners who were spiritually dead to the reality of God, Jesus Christ offered his perfect person as a substitutionary sacrifice for sin. By grace through faith the atheist can be changed in his heart so that he knows that God is both just and the justifier of anyone who believes in him for salvation.

Now is the time to ask yourself the question: 'Do I realize the truthfulness of the affirmations of this psalm concerning the permeation of sin in men? Am I willing to count on the righteousness of Jesus Christ alone to deliver me from the just judgment of the God to whom I am indeed accountable?'

The atheist persecutes God's people

The psalmist goes one further step in tracing the degradation of the atheist. For atheism doesn't stop simply with an intellectual rejection of the truth. Not seeking after God has a far reaching implication in terms of a person's relationship to God's people in the world.

The man who doesn't seek God becomes a ferocious, bestial persecutor of anyone who does seek after God. The atheist cannot remain neutral about religion. He devours God's people as he would devour bread. His daily fare in life becomes the consumption of the righteous.

Don't think you can play with atheism as though it were a morally neutral thing. You cannot live peaceably with atheism.

Atheism is a wild beast which gives itself over to consuming God's people.

The struggle between the seed of Satan and the seed of God plays itself out in every generation. Many of you today are being victimized in your careers, your community, and sometimes even in your church, because the practical outworkings of atheism are not so generous as men might suppose. In actual fact, the broad-mindedness of the atheist is quite narrow. Because his very essence is threatened by anyone who makes a meaningful affirmation about God, he feels the necessity to defend himself by literally consuming all Christians. He ridicules them as obscurantist. He snubs them as bores. He fires them from their jobs under the pretence of incompetence.

His refusal to call on God

And by no means will atheists join in the one activity that is most suitable for man, the dependent creature: 'They refuse to call on the Covenant Lord' (verse 4). Genesis 4:26 states that at a certain point in time, 'At that time people began to call upon the name of the Lord.' It is not that men never had prayed before. But they never had constituted themselves as a people that called on the Lord in worship.

The atheist cannot by any means come and call on the Lord of the Covenant in the assembly of God's people. He will not bow before this distinctive God of history who is the only possible source of salvation for men from their long list of insoluble problems. At certain times, even the atheist will call on some kind of god. He will acknowledge the god of chance, and hope for his share of good luck. He will look to astrology, and count on the stars to determine his fate. But he will not call on the God of history and of the covenants. He will grant no recognition to the God and Father of our Lord Jesus Christ.

When you lose your appetite for coming to church, beware! When you don't want to assemble with the people of the Lord and call on his name, take note! It may be a sign that a creeping atheism is taking over your life. You may be starting down the fatal path of the fool. Broad and populated though it may be, it leads only to destruction.

The awesome nature of true worship

> Right then and there
> they become terrified with great anxiety!
> For God abides
> among the [assembled] generations of the righteous
> (verse 5).

'At that very point' the atheist becomes terrified. He will not acknowledge it, not even to himself. But at the place of public worship, at the point where he ought to acknowledge the Lord of glory, there a strange trembling begins in the pit of his stomach and in the back of his brain. Before his conversion, Martin Luther trembled as he prepared to offer his first communion. Something about standing in the worshipping assembly sets the atheist a-trembling.

'With great anxiety' they stand among the saints. That 'angst' of which the modern existential philosophers write is an uncontrollable reaction of the atheist to his own refusal to worship the Creator.

God abides among the assembled generations of the righteous. Loyalty to the Lord is passed on from generation to generation as God's people assemble for worship. This reality awes the atheist. In the church of Jesus Christ he sees happy families living together in self-sacrificing love. These people who worship the true God manifest a kind of life that the world does not understand.

The world stands in awe. Despite all its mockery of Christianity, the world is amazed at the love that is found in the assembled generations of the righteous. Remember how Paul describes the visit of the unbeliever to the worship of the church? The unbelievers are convicted of their sin, they fall down on their faces and exclaim, 'God is really among you' (1 Cor. 14:25).

Where do you stand today? Are you a part of the assembled generations of the righteous? Have you been awakened to the reality of God by the worship of his people? Does his truth penetrate the hardened shell of your years of professed unbelief? Come. Humble yourself before him. It is not too late for you to share in the blessings of his people.

The atheist ridicules the faith of the believer

> The perspective of the meek
> all of you ridicule,
> because the Covenant Lord is his only confidence
> (verse 6).

In contrast with the proud atheist is the meek believer. The only confidence in life for the meek is found in the Lord his God. Faith is to the believer what the shell is to the turtle. He takes his faith in God everywhere he goes, and defends himself from every enemy with this faith. He has been trusting God for a long time and will continue to walk in the same way.

A newspaper article on turtles once indicated how slow this creature has been to change over the ages. According to these scientists, the turtle has persisted, largely unchanged, for two hundred million years. According to this article, turtles seem to have taken some kind of evolutionary bypath from the main path of development. As a curator at the American Museum of Natural History in New York has stated, 'We can't even imagine what a half-turtle would look like.'[1]

The humble believer in God is much the same. He doesn't fit into the pattern of the rest of humanity. For hundreds and thousands of years, believers in God have gone their own distinctive way on the path of faith. Wherever they go, whatever they encounter, the story is the same. Belief in the Covenant Lord of history remains their only confidence. Whether their problems are great or small, personal or national, they always return to a single source of constancy. As with the humble turtle, it is hard even to imagine what a half-believer would look like. Once God has been acknowledged to be true, and once he is understood to work in the

[1] *The Washington Post*, 26 January 1991, p. A9

world according to the patterns and principles of the Scriptures, a person cannot look anywhere else for his confidence.

The atheist ridicules the meek believer in God because of this unbreakable trust in the Lord. This ridiculing of the meek is not merely playing fun and games. It can become very bitter. But the effect of this persecution on the righteous is that he is thrown even more completely onto the Lord. God alone remains as his only confidence. The troubles of the world only deepen this relationship.

It may not seem to be very desirable to have only one hope in life. The world would suggest that at least a person ought to 'hedge his bets,' to diversify his investments by counting on something or someone in addition to God. But the only alternative to trusting the Lord for all of life is to be a fool who says in his heart, 'There is no god.' If there is a real God, then he must be the only object of your continual trust.

The confidence of God's people

> But let salvation for Israel
> come out from Mount Zion!
> When the Covenant LORD restores the losses of his
> people,
> Jacob
> will be overjoyed,
> and Israel
> will be ecstatic
>
> (verse 7).

Now hear this passionate plea and this confident expectation of the people of the Lord. First they express a prayer and then they declare a confidence.

They plead for deliverance to come from Mount Zion. In a new covenant context, Mount Zion represents the throne of God in heaven where Jesus Christ is seated at God's right hand. All authority in heaven and on earth has been given to him.

The people crying out to the Lord in this psalm have already suffered at the hands of the atheists. They have lost a great deal.

But if suffering continues, it will be only to the degree that Christ the Lord allows it.

In addition, they declare their confidence that the Covenant Lord will restore their losses. Inevitably the Lord will give back all that has been taken from them. At that time, God's chosen people will be filled with joy and ecstasy.

God will be faithful. He will deliver his people. Then joy will be the portion of the cup of the righteous. Forever they will rejoice in the Lord as they celebrate in the assembly of the righteous.

Conclusion

The folly of the atheist is always with us. May God grant grace to enable you to turn from the folly of the atheist. May you have strong faith in the God and Father of our Lord Jesus Christ. Then you will enjoy forever the blessings that come to the assembled generations of the righteous.

Psalm 15
Abiding Securely in Holiness

A psalm of David.

Reader:
1 Covenant Lord,
Who shall sojourn
in your tent?
Who shall dwell
in your holy mountain?

1st Congr.:
2 He who walks
uprightly,
2nd Congr.:
and does
righteousness,
All:
and speaks
truth from his heart;

1st Congr.:
3 he who does not slander
with his tongue,
2nd Congr.:
and does not wrong
his neighbour,
All:
and does not humiliate
his intimate friend.

Reader:
4 He is repulsed by
the unscrupulous;
but the person who fears the Covenant Lord
he holds in highest regard.

1st Congr.:	He swears to [his own] hurt but will not change.
2nd Congr.:	5His money he will not lend at an exorbitant interest rate,
All:	and a bribe to frame the innocent he will never accept.
Reader:	He who lives in this way will never be ruined.

Abiding Securely in Holiness—*Holiness Assures Safety*

Introduction

The book of Psalms opens with a lengthy series of contrasts between the godly and the ungodly, the righteous and their enemies. Sometimes the antagonists of God's people are described by expressions such as the 'wicked' and the 'ungodly,' defining their moral character. At other times they appear as the 'enemy,' characterizing their prevailing spirit of animosity. The psalmist frequently speaks very personally of them as 'my' enemies (cf. Psa. 3; 5; 6; 7; 9; 13). In other cases, these enemies are explicitly described as directing their animosity towards God himself (cf. Psa. 8; 10). It is interesting that the book of Psalms, often viewed sentimentally as a book of pious devotionalism, begins with this rather objective contrast between the righteous and the wicked.

In any case, life must be lived in this context. The Christian must constantly contend with real-life enemies. These enemies have various faces. They could be explicit opponents of righteousness in the community, or unsuspecting tools of Satan within the Christian fellowship itself. They could be identified with prevailing sin, oppressing sickness or calamity. But most obviously in the mind of the psalmist, the enemy is to be identified as people who oppose and oppress the servants of the Lord.

This particular psalm describes the concrete characteristics that distinguish the righteous from the wicked, the children of God from the children of Satan. Even more specifically, it concentrates on the security that belongs to those who walk in the ways of the Lord despite this constant confrontation with enemies who seek to destroy them.

Do you desire security? Are you tempted to give up on the possibility of finding a place of lasting safety in the midst of this fallen world? The psalmist tells you where unshakeable security can be found, even in a world filled with powerful opponents of righteousness. You may abide securely in holiness.

Form and outline

Psalm 15 begins with a question concerning security. The question is addressed to the LORD of the Covenant, the only source of true security. Who will abide in the safety of God's protecting presence? Who will continue uninterruptedly under the blessings of his sovereign rule? (verse 1).

The second section of the psalm provides an eleven-point answer to the question concerning security (verses 2-5a). The answer does not come with a neat set of three points, an expected total of seven points, or an orthodox list of ten points. In defiance of all theories of biblical numerology, the psalmist offers an unorthodox eleven-point description of the man who lives securely under the blessing of the Lord.

These eleven points are arranged into three groupings of threes, with an intermediate grouping of two. So although consistently arranged in an asymmetrical pattern, the answer of the psalmist to this significant query comes with a thoroughgoing fulness of concrete exposition.

The psalm ends with a summary statement of the consequence of dwelling in the presence of the Lord (verse 5b). The effect, simply put, is security. The person who dwells continually in God's presence by manifesting holiness of life will never be shaken. Ruin never will overtake him.

1. A question concerning security (verse 1)

Covenant LORD,
Who shall sojourn
  in your tent?
Who shall dwell
  in your holy mountain? (verse 1).

The question of the psalmist is neither rhetorical nor hypothetical in nature. It is a question about real life, and is posed as though it were a problem for the worshipping community now assembled in the presence of the Lord. Requiring the people to consider this basic question of security in the context of worship prepares them for going out to face the variables of life after having resolved this foundational problem of the source of their safety.

A more disturbing form of the same question is found in Isaiah 33:14:

> The sinners in Zion are afraid;
> trembling has seized the godless:
> 'Who among us can dwell with the consuming fire?
> Who among us can dwell with everlasting burnings?'

Because of the universality of the sin of men, who can expect to abide in the presence of God's consuming holiness?

The psalmist combines the images of sojourning and setting up residence, of travelling with God in his tent and residing with God on his holy mountain as the dual source of security. Life invariably consists of being tossed about from pillar to post. God's people remain throughout life as strangers and pilgrims, having no continuing city. So the cry of the heart remains, 'Who can have the assurance that God will be with him through all the changes of life?'

At the same time, God has established his kingdom in this world. He rules from the heavenly Mount Zion. Perceiving God's cause in this world exclusively from the perspective of a pilgrim could lead a person to attempt to make his own way rather than to remain faithful to the Lord. But God also has established himself as sovereign among men. The question therefore is not whether the Lord is in control of the changing affairs of life, but whether or not a person will benefit from the Lord's ruling on his or her behalf.

In response to this question the psalmist records his elevenfold answer. He begins with the positive, then turns to the negative. He then returns to the positive and finally concludes with the negative. By this method he views the question from as many perspectives as those needing constant assurance may require.

A description of those who live in security (verses 2-5a)

Who shall abide in God's presence?

A commitment to holiness

> He who walks
>   uprightly,
> and does
>   righteousness,
> and speaks
>   truth from his heart
>
> (verse 2).

A person's 'walk' encompasses his total attitude towards life. The Lord asks for a whole-souled commitment to the way of faith that affects everything a person does and says.

According to C. H. Spurgeon, 'True believers do not cringe as flatterers, wriggle as serpents, bend double as earthgrubbers, or crook to one side as those who have sinister aims; they have the strong backbone of the vital principle of grace within, and being themselves upright, they are able to walk uprightly.'[1]

When under the pressures of real life, it is easy to forget the importance of consistency in doing and saying what is right. But if you desire the stability that comes from abiding in the presence of the holy God, it is necessary to walk and to speak from a heart committed to holiness. 'From the heart' must proceed words that consistently honour the truth.

What the righteous man does not do

Having made his point from the positive side, the psalmist next turns to the negative:

> He who does not slander
>   with his tongue,
> and does not wrong
>   his neighbour,

[1] *The Treasury of David*, vol. I, p. 177.

and does not humiliate
his intimate friend
(verse 3).

This second grouping notes that the righteous man does not do certain things. 'He does not …, he does not …, he does not …' He does nothing to hurt his neighbour.

The easiest way to hurt a neighbour is by talking about him in an evil way. The closer the relationship, the more vulnerable a person will be to your evil talk. Sometimes husbands hurt wives and wives hurt husbands because they speak indiscriminately about one another. Parents can hurt their children, and children their parents by bitter or sarcastic remarks. You can put your friend at work or your neighbour next door under great stress by speaking evil of him. Be careful that you do not injure the health, family or business of another person by humiliating him or her through your words.

We also need to remember that it is possible to gossip with the ear as well as with the tongue. As the old Puritan John Trapp has stated quaintly but no less truly, 'The tale-bearer carries the devil in his tongue, and the tale-hearer carries the devil in his ear.'[2]

God does not approve of a busy tongue that tears down others. The person who does not restrain himself from speaking against his neighbour is moving out from under the protection of the Almighty. He is not abiding with the Lord. It is no wonder that the person who regularly speaks evil against others finds himself lacking in security.

His choice of friends

The next section in this psalm notes the choice of friends by a person who abides in security:

He is repulsed by
the unscrupulous;
but the person who fears the Covenant LORD
he holds in highest regard (verse 4).

[2] Quoted in Spurgeon, *Treasury*, vol. I, p. 177.

The way you choose your friends directly affects your stability in life. If you maintain a rapport with the wicked by failing to rebuke them, then you have stepped out from under the Lord's protection. Remember the example of Moses, who 'refused to be called the son of Pharaoh's daughter' but instead 'chose rather to be mistreated with the people of God than to enjoy the fleeting pleasures of sin' (Heb. 11:24, 25).

The instability of the unscrupulous is like a contagious disease. If you live in companionship with unprincipled people, you cannot expect that your life will be free of constant uncertainty.

Get closest to the people who fear the Lord. Esteem most highly the one who walks with God, no matter what may be his success or social position in the eyes of men. Give honour to whom honour is due. Reserve your greatest respect for the upright in heart. Only then will you be assured that the Lord is with you. Honour his people, and you will be honoured by the Lord. Associate with solid people who do not deviate from the standard of God's righteousness, and you will find your life resting on an unshakeable foundation.

His personal integrity

The third triplet of this psalm centres on the significance of personal integrity, particularly in the area of finances. Each element describes a person who will not be corrupted for reasons of personal gain:

> He swears to [his own] hurt
>   but will not change.
> His money he will not lend
>   at an exorbitant interest rate,
> and a bribe to frame the innocent
>   he will never accept
>
> (verses 4, 5).

The person who abides securely with the Lord will not deviate from a commitment once he has given his word. He will not back out of a bad business deal even if it means heavy loss to himself. He may look foolish in the eyes of men. But in the eyes of the Lord he proves the integrity of his heart.

According to the New Testament ethic, your word is your oath (Matt. 5:34-37; James 5:12). Don't think you can change your commitment simply because you did not formally swear an oath or sign a contract. A simple 'yes' means you are committed. Even wise and godly men make mistakes in their business dealings. The most far-sighted trader can read the trends wrongly. But if a man retains the integrity of his word, God will see to it that all other losses will be bearable. Learning the lesson of meaning precisely what you say and holding to the commitments you make is worth more than a great deal of money. The value of legal tender fluctuates greatly, but the worth of personal integrity remains constant in the eyes of God as well as men.

Personal integrity must be displayed in your relations with those less fortunate than yourself as well as with people whom you wish to impress. If you have a larger commitment to God than to your own personal advancement, you will not take advantage of the needy by demanding an exorbitant payback for any favours you might render. Lending without charging an excessive interest rate is just one concrete way of showing compassion to your needy neighbour. A desire to promote the wealth and outward state of people less fortunate than yourself shows that you are trusting God for your security rather than the money you have banked. Living in an inflationary economy may require that some interest be charged. But particularly when a poor brother has been brought to a point of need, the one who himself thrives because of the grace of Christ will be quick to manifest the same goodness to others that the Lord has shown to him.

Integrity of heart is also seen in the refusal to accept a bribe as an inducement to frame the innocent. This 'bribe' could come in the form of an actual monetary offer. Or it might take the form of gaining social acceptance through silently assenting to statements about someone else that you know to be false. By failing to defend the reputation of the innocent, you are in effect 'accepting a bribe.'

When Allen Pinkerton set up his detective agency, he refused to hire anyone who was willing to accept a bribe. His contemporaries in law enforcement said he would never get his organization off the ground if he adhered to that policy. But in the end, Pinkerton's agency became the largest in the country. At one point he had the privilege of saving president-elect Abraham Lincoln from assassination as he travelled from Philadelphia to Washington for his inauguration in 1861.

It becomes dramatically clear how much God himself hates a bribe when we consider the price he paid to save sinners. He would not clear the guilty without first sacrificing his own Son to satisfy the demands of justice. Consider the loss he was willing to suffer in order to maintain his integrity as God.

In one sense, all three of the 'tests' in this section regarding personal integrity relate to money. Beware of the love of money, which easily can substitute for trust in God. The love of money corrupts personal integrity faster than anything else. Money generally is regarded as the great stabilizer of life. But in actual fact it has a greater capacity to destabilize a person's circumstances than anything else. For trusting the stability promised by money robs a person of the stability that only God can give. Compromising personal integrity for the sake of financial gain is the quickest possible way to lose the security that comes from God, a security that lasts right through all the 'changing scenes of life.'

How do you stand in relation to this elevenfold test? Obviously faith in Jesus Christ must be perceived as the leading factor in determining a person's relationship to God. But true faith will manifest itself in the ways described in this psalm. Apart from the fruit of faith depicted in these verses, it is futile to expect stability in any area of your life.

3. The consequence of living a life pleasing to the Lord (verse 5b)

In summary, the psalmist concludes by reaffirming the security of those who walk in the way of the Lord:

> He who lives in this way
> will never be ruined
>
> (verse 5).

The person who lives according to the previous eleven criteria 'will never be ruined.' He will be like Mount Zion itself, like the dwelling-place of God, like a rock that cannot be moved (Psa. 125:1).

If a person deviates from these principles, his life will be devastated. In seeking security outside God, he will lose it. If you depart from any one, or any combination, of these principles, you will have moved out from under the protection of the Lord. If you gossip about your neighbour, eventually you will be ruined in the realm of personal friendships. If you lie, you will be ruined in the area of personal trust. If you fail to handle money with integrity, you will be ruined in the realm of material possessions. But if you follow the way of wisdom taught in the word of God, you never will be moved.

Conclusion

No greater privilege could be imagined than that of living with the Lord throughout this earthly pilgrimage. You can find stability of life in him, no matter what may be your outward circumstances. This psalm shows the blessing of abiding in his presence.

Where is the gospel in this psalm?

First, it may be remembered that Jesus Christ alone has fulfilled this description of the upright man to perfection. He alone measures up to all eleven criteria of the man who may abide in the presence of the Lord. By faith you can be one with him, and share in all his virtues. The meaning of 'justification' is not only the removal of your guilt. It also includes the legal reckoning to you of all the righteousness of Christ. You may be united with him in his holiness by faith, and you may enjoy the full benefits of his righteousness.

At the same time, the believer in Christ is being transformed daily by the power of his resurrected life. As Spurgeon says, 'In perfection this holiness is found only in the Man of Sorrows, but in a measure it is wrought in all his people by the Holy Spirit.'[3]

[3] *Treasury*, I, p.177

Let us strive to perceive more fully the significance of these practical areas of human living. Let us find our security through abiding in him.

Psalm 16
Overcoming Life's Last Enemy

A *michtam* of David.

1st Reader: 1Preserve me, Almighty God,
Congr.: for I have entrusted myself wholly to you.

1st Reader: 2[My soul], you have declared to the LORD of the Covenant:
Congr.: 'You are my Lord;
whatever good I experience
means nothing apart from you.'

2nd Reader: 3'Regarding the holy and noble ones
who live in the land,
all my delight is in them.

4'They will only multiply their griefs
who rush to find some other god.'
1st Reader: I never will condescend to pour out
an offering of life-blood to them;
Congr.: I could never even form their names
on my lips.

1st Reader: 5The Covenant LORD [himself]
is my portion and my cup;

Congr.: you keep my allotment secure.

1st Reader: 6 The boundary lines have fallen out for me
in the most pleasant circumstances;

Congr.: beyond a doubt
I have a delightful inheritance.

1st Reader: 7 I will bless the Covenant LORD
who counsels me;

Congr.: even in the darkest of nights
my inmost thoughts correct me.

1st Reader: 8 I am committed to have the Covenant LORD
face to face with me all the time;

Congr.: because he remains at my right hand,
nothing can disturb me.

1st Reader: 9 Therefore my heart is filled with joy,
and my whole being rejoices;

Congr.: this body of flesh
dwells in security as well.

1st Reader: 10 For you will not abandon any part of me
to the grave,

Congr.: you will not allow your holy one
to see corruption.

1st Reader: 11 You have assured me
of the path that leads to life;

Congr.: satisfying joys
will be found in your presence.

All: Pleasures that last forever
are in your right hand.

Overcoming Life's Last Enemy—*Preservation even in Death*

Introduction

Fyodor Dostoyevsky in his novel *The Brothers Karamazov* describes the death of a 'holy man.' When this pious saint is placed in a small room for the faithful to pay their last respects, a strange thing occurs. The windows are not opened, and the senses of the people tell them that his body has begun to decay. The rumours fly. Overnight his reputation, built up by a lifetime of selfless service to the Lord, is devastated. How could the body of a holy man decay so quickly after death? Would not the Lord preserve his holy one from this humiliation?

This superstitious criterion for holiness can be dismissed easily as unreal and irrelevant. But the problem of the death and decay of God's holy ones still rises up to haunt God's people in every generation. The dilemma is as old as Adam and as current as the latest funeral you attended. It obviously was a problem for God's people before the resurrection of Jesus Christ. It continues to be a puzzle that must be reckoned with even today.

In response to the problem of death and decay, consider this poem celebrating the defeat of death by King David. Learn from him that those who commit themselves in life to the Lord will be preserved in death by him. Even the threat of imminent death should not shake your confidence in his power to preserve body and soul.

In facing the last great enemy, the psalmist declares that he is committed to the Lord (verses 1-6) and preserved by the Lord (verses 7-11).

Psalm 16 begins with the sum and substance of the whole:

> Preserve me, Almighty God,
> for I have entrusted myself wholly to you
>
> (verse 1).

David faces death. It could be that his life was being threatened by a brutal enemy. Possibly a severe illness had struck him. Or perhaps numerous infirmities associated with ageing had overwhelmed him. But what's new? Every man eventually has the same experience. The sentence of death is in us all. For many of us, the time of our departure from this world is not far away. It may come this year.

What is David's hope and expectation? He fully expects that God will employ his almighty power to preserve him from this threat to his life. 'Preserve me, Almighty God, for I have confidence in you' (verse 1). He is certain that God will deliver him from death and all its consequences because he has entrusted himself to the Lord.

By the resurrection of Jesus Christ, great David's greater son, death has been defeated. It has lost its power to terrorize and destroy the man who trusts in God. Now death itself has undergone a transition. Instead of being a cruel enemy, it has become the pathway that leads out of the trials of this life and into the glories of the life to come.

In order to benefit fully from God's grace that overcomes the threat of death, consider first the way in which David committed himself to the Lord.

1. Committed to the Lord (verses 2-6)

When you face death, you are forced to take time to talk to yourself. You must deal with the problem personally so you will be able to cope with the reality. Whether it is your own death, or the death of someone who means a great deal to you, it is essential that you talk through the matter with yourself. What does the psalmist say to himself when he faces death?

He rehearses the fact that he has committed himself to the Lord:

> [My soul], you have declared to the LORD of the
> Covenant:
> 'You are my Lord;
> whatever good I experience
> means nothing apart from you'
> (verse 2).

The psalmist does not boast in his personal merits. He declines to list the many things he has sacrificed in order to serve others. He simply says that he has entrusted himself completely to the Lord. He indicates that he has found no good in anything except as it relates to the Lord.

David is not trying to talk himself out of the importance that life has to him. He is not attempting to trick himself into discounting the trauma of facing imminent death. Far from it. He is just putting everything into perspective. Nothing in this life means anything to him apart from God. The union, the communion, the fellowship that his soul has with Almighty God gives everything its lasting significance. Without the certainty that God is with him, nothing has any meaning.

Remember Mary and Martha? Martha was overwhelmed with a sense of purpose in life. She was busy about many things, stewing in the kitchen to prepare a meal for a dozen hungry men. But Mary chose the better thing, a single thing, and it would not be taken from her (Luke 10:42).

Mary's choice did not mean perpetual inactivity. But it represented a settling of priorities. First and foremost, integral to everything else in her life, would be sitting at the feet of Jesus and absorbing the words of life that came from his lips. All her other activities would flow from that one source of life. Is that the way you perceive your house, your car, your job, your spouse, your vacation, your health, your physique, your money, your entertainment, your life in all its parts? 'Whatever good I experience means nothing apart from you,' says the psalmist.

Only this kind of total trust in the Lord can prepare a person to face death. Even Jesus himself could endure those dark hours of death only because he had surrendered his will completely to the Lord as he struggled in Gethsemane. 'I have come to do your will,' he said to the Father, for 'A body have you prepared for me' (Heb. 10:5-7).

Adopt the same attitude towards your own life. While you have opportunity, find in the Lord your all in all. Then he will preserve you even in death by his almighty power.

The blessing of those who 'live in the land'

How does the Lord respond to the consecration of a person so wholly to him? He answers with a corresponding delight:

> Regarding the holy and noble ones
> who live in the land,
> all my delight is in them[1]
>
> (verse 3).

Abraham was the first of God's people to 'live in the land.' For him, entrance into the land symbolized a return to paradise. God originally had driven man out of the garden of Eden so that he would not live forever in his fallen state. But now he returns this man Abraham to the 'promised land,' symbolizing a restoration to paradise. Even though Abraham lived in the land as a vagrant in a tent, by faith he kept 'looking forward to the city that has foundations, whose designer and builder is God' (Heb. 11:10). All during his sojourn, he kept desiring a better country, that is, a heavenly one' (Heb. 11:16). In the land he offered up his son Isaac, the appointed heir of the promise, and received him back again as a figure of the resurrection. With resurrection faith, he reasoned that if necessary God could raise his son to life again.

In the very locale where Abraham offered Isaac, God offered his son Jesus. On Mount Moriah, the designated spot where Abraham

[1] Expositors differ regarding the identity of the speaker in verse 3. This exposition suggests that God himself responds to the commitment of the psalmist as expressed in the previous verse. This perspective fits the flow of thought naturally, and follows the pattern of many other psalms that introduce a brief statement from the Lord without formal notification that a change of speakers has occurred. For other instances, see Psalms 87, 91 and possibly 32.

surrendered his son to God, Jesus Christ was offered as a sacrifice for sin and was received to life again (Gen. 22:2; 2 Chron. 3:1). God showed his delight in his holy one by guaranteeing the possession of eternal life to him even as he passed through death.

From the days of Abraham, the land promised by the Lord as an inheritance for his people became crucial to their thinking. Both Jacob and Joseph insisted that they be taken up from Egypt at their death and buried in the land promised to Abraham.

Why? What difference would it make where they were buried? It made a difference to them because they took God at his word. He had promised that they would possess the land, and this word from the Lord had not yet been fulfilled for them. So they concluded that after they died God would raise them to life again and fulfil to them the promise he had made.

God taught the same lesson to Moses. At the bush that burned but was not consumed, God said, 'I *am* the God of Abraham, the God of Isaac, and the God of Jacob' (Exod. 3:6). God is not the God of the dead, but of the living. Yet he speaks to Moses five hundred years after the death of Abraham and identifies himself as Abraham's God.

What could that affirmation mean? It could mean only one thing. It meant that Abraham was still around, waiting for the fulfilment of God's promises to him concerning the possession of the land. Since a physical, earthly territory can be possessed in the fullest sense only by someone in the flesh, the implication of this statement is that one day God will raise up Abraham in the flesh to give him the land he promised. He will enjoy the paradise restored by the Lord.

You can share in this blessing promised to the saints of old. Declare with David that the LORD of the Covenant is your Lord, and that whatever good you experience means nothing apart from him. Then you will join Abraham in enjoying his expanded expectation that one day he would inherit not just the land but the world (Rom. 4:13). For now it is not merely a little parcel in Palestine that belongs to Abraham and his seed. It is the whole of the new heavens and the new earth that the children of Abraham by faith will possess.

The futility of pursuing other gods

What is the alternative to sharing in the blessings of those who claim God's promise of resurrection from the dead? The Lord himself explains:

> They will only multiply their griefs
> who rush to find some other god
>
> (verse 4).

If God is the only source of blessing in life, then pursuing any other god can only lead to grief. Do you really think that the gods of fame, fortune, power and public recognition will deliver you from death? Will knowledge acquired by pursuing advanced degrees deliver you from the ultimate destiny of the grave? Will family or fun deliver you from death?

No! By pursuing these things as though they have the power to save, you only multiply your sorrows and disappointments in life. They may give you satisfaction for a time. But these pleasures will fade soon enough.

Hear the word of the Lord, and you will live. 'Solid joys and lasting pleasures none but Zion's children know.' Entrust yourself wholly to the Lord, and you will find that he will preserve you even in death.

How do you avoid the pitfall of being lured into the deification of material things? The psalmist tells you to do two things: repudiate the slightest involvement in the adoration of other gods, and relish the inheritance that the Lord has given you.

Rejecting false gods

David says:

> I never will condescend to pour out
> an offering of life-blood to them;
> I could never even form their names
> on my lips
>
> (verse 4).

The theme developed in a modern novel is startling in its description of the decadence of the imaginations of modern man. A sophisticated, successful businessman suddenly discovers that he is carnivorous, feeding on female human flesh.[2]

The unending reports of tortuous brutality coming from all parts of the globe are almost as bad. Unfeeling soldiers disconnect infants from life-sustaining machines and discard their corpses in a common grave. Civilians flee the butchery of the city only to be slaughtered by their own countrymen in helicopter gunboats as they troop defencelessly along the road en masse. These actions are the equivalent of an 'offering of life-blood' intended by the brutal as a means of gaining permanency of power.

But the godly man is committed in another direction. He never will participate in the offering of the life-blood of the innocent. He will not even let the names of the gods of prestige, power, money, pleasure and possessions be formed on his lips.

Why? How can he resist the allurements of the gods of this world?

He turns from false gods because he is completely content with the inheritance the Lord has given him.

Contentment in the Lord

What is this glorious inheritance that he has already begun enjoying? It consists in possessing the Lord himself:

> The Covenant LORD [himself]
> is my portion and my cup;
> you keep my allotment secure.
> The boundary lines have fallen out for me
> in the most pleasant circumstances;
> beyond a doubt
> I have a delightful inheritance
>
> (verses 5, 6).

According to the law of Moses, the priests of Israel were not allotted any share in the land that they could claim as their own. Instead, they had a very distinctive inheritance:

[2] *Time*, 25 March 1991, pp.70f.

> And the Lord said to Aaron, 'You shall have no inheritance in their land, neither shall you have any portion among them. I am your portion and your inheritance among the people of Israel' (Num. 18:20).
>
> Therefore Levi has no portion or inheritance with his brothers. The LORD is his inheritance, as the LORD your God said to him (Deut. 10:9).
>
> The Levitical priests, all the tribe of Levi, shall have no portion or inheritance with Israel … They shall have no inheritance among their brothers; the LORD is their inheritance, as he promised them (Deut. 18:1, 2).

Though not of the tribe of Levi, David understood that he was a member of a 'kingdom of priests' (Exod. 19:6). So he did not hesitate to claim the heritage of the priesthood in Israel. The Lord himself was his appointed portion, his assigned cup, his personal allotment, his eternal inheritance. Rather than thinking himself deprived by this apportionment, he regarded the possession of the Lord himself as the ultimate privilege, the most 'delightful inheritance' he could imagine.

David's thoughts anticipate the words of Paul: 'To me to live is Christ, and to die is gain' (Phil. 1:21); for 'Whatever gain I had, I counted as loss for the sake of Christ. Indeed, I count everything as loss because of the surpassing worth of knowing Christ Jesus my Lord. For his sake I have suffered the loss of all things and count them as rubbish, in order that I may gain Christ' (Phil. 3:7, 8).

Both David and Paul were totally contented in the Lord. They understood that possessing Christ means more than anything else in life.

If you are to experience the full blessing of the Lord you must make the same commitment. Don't think that deliverance from death and all its terrors will come automatically to everyone who enters the doors of the church. You must make the commitment of your whole self to him. You must be satisfied with having him and nothing else. Then you will experience the wonders of his deliverance from death.

This deliverance from death is the theme of the second part of this psalm. First, the psalmist was committed to the Lord (verses 1-6); then, he was preserved by the Lord (verses 7-11).

2. Preserved by the Lord (verses 7-11)

David stands face to face with the 'last great enemy,' death itself. He is in the 'valley of the shadow of death.' It is no longer a matter of playing games. This time it is the real thing. One day you will be in that position. Suddenly you will realize that you are not dreaming. You are facing the 'last great enemy.' How will you respond? Will you panic?

At that critical moment, you will reap the fruit of your total trust in the Lord. Christ said it on the cross, and Stephen echoed it as he sunk under the weight of the stones that crushed his life-breath: 'Into your hands I commit my spirit' (Luke 23:46; Acts 7:59). Out of a lifetime of trusting in the Lord will flow naturally the ability to make the final commitment of the whole of your life to him. David says:

> I will bless the Covenant Lord
> who counsels me;
> even in the darkest of nights
> my inmost thoughts correct me.
> I am committed to have the Covenant Lord
> face to face with me at all times;
> because he remains at my right hand,
> nothing can disturb me
> (verses 7, 8).

The Spirit of the Lord counsels and corrects you when your thoughts go astray. Using the reservoir of the truths of the word of God stored in your soul, the Spirit applies those truths to your heart to comfort and encourage you in times of trial.

When you would be inclined to panic, you are reminded of the way Christ committed his soul into the hands of the Father and was not disappointed. Even in the darkest of nights when you face the prospect of death itself, or when you see your loved one hovering at the brink of the abyss, God will be there to console you with comforting counsel. He is different from all other counsellors because he can actually enter the secret chambers of your soul and apply the comforting reassurance that you need. Deep down in the recesses of your inmost thoughts, the Lord through his Spirit corrects your tendency to panic and flight.

Turn your thoughts to him, and you will see that he stands face to face with you at all times. He is no further than the breath of life itself. Because he remains at your right hand, nothing can disturb you.

The resurrection of the body

How far can you go with your expectation of deliverance from death and its terrors? It would be relatively easy to imagine that your inner spirit might be transported to another realm where it would experience a nebulous existence for eternity.

But Scripture urges you to have greater expectations. Not only your soul but your body as well will be delivered from death. As the psalmist says:

> Therefore my heart is filled with joy,
>   and my whole being rejoices.
> This body of flesh
>   dwells in security as well.
> For you will not abandon any part of me
>   to the grave,
> you will not allow your holy one
>   to see corruption
>
> (verses 9, 10).

Was David thinking of the patriarch Enoch when he penned these words? Enoch was translated to heaven and never saw death. Was he anticipating the experience of Elijah, who was swept up into God's presence in a chariot of fire? Elijah's body experienced instant transformation.

Perhaps David was thinking that the Lord would spare him the humiliation of ever having his body decay in the grave. But the apostle Peter points in another direction. On the Day of Pentecost he reminded the people that 'The patriarch David both died and was buried, and his tomb is with us to this day' (Acts 2:29). His body saw decay.

But David was a prophet. This promise of salvation for body and soul finds its first realization in the person of Jesus Christ. Seeing what was ahead, David spoke of the resurrection of the Christ, that he was not abandoned to the grave, nor did his body see decay (Acts 2:31).

But what does his deliverance from death mean to David? What does it mean for us today? It means that just as the head is not separated from the body, so the believer in Christ will not be separated from him. As he was raised into new life and took on the form of a new body that cannot suffer corruption, so you will have the same experience. God will not allow a single one of his holy ones to see corruption. Neither you nor your loved ones that fall asleep in Jesus will remain under the power of death and the grave.

A joyful response

How does this message of victory over death affect you? How should it affect you? It should affect you the same way as it did the psalmist. It should fill you with joy. As he says:

> Therefore my heart is filled with joy,
> and my whole being rejoices
> (verse 9).

How can you contemplate deliverance from death apart from joy? Through all the ages, God's people have rejoiced as they faced death. They have baffled the world of unbelief by the radiance of their countenances. Through all the centuries they have been joyful because they have been reassured of Christ's victory over the grave. Echoing David's joy in the face of death, John of Damascus, in the eighth century after Christ, wrote his great resurrection hymn:

> The day of resurrection!
> Earth, tell it out abroad;

The Passover of gladness,
the Passover of God.
From death to life eternal,
From this world to the sky,
Our Christ hath brought us over
with hymns of victory.[3]

With unwavering faith, David concludes his psalm of victory over death with a confident word:

You have assured me
of the path that leads to life;
satisfying joys
will be found in your presence.
Pleasures that last forever
are in your right hand

(verse 11).

There is a path that leads to life. It is the new and living way that Christ has opened by his death and resurrection. Into the very presence of God himself this pathway goes, and the Son of God clears the way. Put your complete trust in that way of access and you will experience satisfying joys that last forever. All other joys and pleasures will appear as mere illusions that endure only for the moment. They decay with death and become putrid even in this life. But the joy of resurrection faith endures forever.

Let every sabbath, as a celebration of Christ's resurrection, be a time for you to rejoice in the certainty that the living Christ can give. Praise the Lord for his deliverance of body and soul from every threat of death.

[3] *Trinity Hymnal,* 1990, No. 267.

Psalm 32
A Guidebook for the Guilty

By David. A *maskil.*

1st Congr.: 1 Oh how blessed is he

2nd Congr.: whose wrongdoing is carried away!
whose sin is covered [by the blood]!

1st Congr.: 2 Oh how blessed is the person

2nd Congr.: whom the Covenant LORD does not hold
accountable
for his iniquity;
and no self-deceit
is in his spirit.

1st Reader: 3 While I maintained my silence,
my very bones felt as if they were ageing
as I kept inwardly moaning all day long.

4 For day and night
your hand weighed me down;
my strength melted away
as in the heat of summer.

Selah

5 Then—
My sin
I made fully known to you,

and my iniquity
I no longer tried to cover.
I said,
'I will confess my wrongdoings
to the Covenant LORD,'
and you carried away
the guilt of my sin.

Selah

All:

6 Because of your gracious forgiveness,
everyone who reveres you will appeal to you
in the time when you can be found.
No, the torrent of floodwaters
will not reach up to touch him.

1st Reader:

7 You
are a hiding place for me.
From assault
you will preserve me;
with songs celebrating deliverance
you will surround me.

Selah

2nd Reader:

8 'I will make you wise and point you
in the way you should go:
I will counsel you
with my eye.

9 Let not any one of you be
as the horse—or even the mule!
He has no sense.
Bit and bridle are his ornamentation,
but only for restraint.

Otherwise you will never
get him near you.'

All: 10 Numerous agonies
invariably come to the wicked;
but the one who rests his case with the
Covenant LORD
will be enveloped in his mercy.

1st Reader: 11 Be happy in the Covenant LORD and rejoice,
all you who have been declared righteous;
Sing for joy,
everyone whose heart as been made upright.

A Guidebook for the Guilty—*The Blessedness of Sins Forgiven*

Introduction

Everyone who has become aware of his or her own sin knows the necessity of dealing with guilt in a way that fully satisfies the demands of conscience. Nothing debilitates a person more completely than guilt. Consider one fine Christian who finds himself suddenly unable to function in service to Christ. His weakness has come, not because of some gross sin, but because of a sense of failure to do certain things he felt he ought to be doing for the Lord. Although he knows the formulas for forgiveness, he cannot seem to make them work in his current situation. So he finds himself incapable of functioning as he knows he should. Guilt has crippled him.

So Psalms 51 and 32 are set in Scripture to serve as a 'guidebook for the guilty.' The prophet Nathan had pinpointed King David's sin of adultery and murder by declaring, 'You are the man' (2 Sam. 12:7). When confronted with his sin, David broke his year-long silence regarding his sin. He expressed the agony of his soul by acknowledging, 'I have sinned against the Lord.' The prophet then indicated God's mercy in his provision for sinners: 'The Lord also has put away your sin' (2 Sam. 12:13).

Every day the Christian needs fresh deliverance from a condemning conscience. He must have reassurance that he is not living far from God. Psalm 51 leads a guilt-laden sinner through the initial steps of confession and reconciliation with God. Psalm 32 follows with the much-needed rounding-off of the problem by an affirmation of the blessedness of the man who has been forgiven, thereby assuring the self-conscious sinner that God's benediction rests with him. The celebration of these psalms of forgiveness in public worship has the added therapeutic value of effecting reconciliation in the presence of God while the sinner stands in the midst of the worshipping community.

Outline

This psalm has two major sections which communicate God's truth about the pathway to pardon. An introduction and a conclusion record the spontaneous reaction of God's people to this glorious truth.

Verses 6 and 10 consist of a 'congregational response' to the truth that has been taught in the two major sections of the psalm. By this arrangement, the people of God confirm among themselves their understanding of the pathway to pardon.

An outline of the psalm is as follows: exultation over the blessedness of forgiveness (verses 1, 2); reviewing the pathway to pardon (verses 3-6); encouragement to follow the pathway to pardon (verses 7-10); the joy that comes with forgiveness (verse 11).

1. Exultation over the blessedness of forgiveness (verses 1, 2)

Benedictions are a common form of biblical expression running through the Old and New Testaments. The patriarchs Noah, Isaac and Jacob pronounced solemn, prophetic blessings over their children, and Moses similarly pronounced blessings on the twelve tribes of Israel. Melchizedek blessed Abraham as he returned from battle (Gen. 14:19, 20), Rebekah' s family blessed the bride-to-be as she departed to parts unknown (Gen. 24:60), and the aged Jacob blessed—of all people—the Pharaoh of Egypt (Gen. 47:10).

A benediction within the household of faith is not so much a petition as it is a pronouncement of faith. The one who declares the benediction expresses his confidence that God will surely bless his people in accordance with the promises of redemption. The person properly pronouncing a benediction according to Scripture does not assume that he has in himself the power to bless. Neither does he presume on God. But he speaks his blessing out of a confidence that God will be true to his word.

Numerous individuals are the recipients of blessings in the name of the Lord. But in addition, prominent benedictions in Scripture are addressed to the people of God as a whole. They include the blessings of the covenant spoken by Moses in the plains of Moab (Deut. 28) and the blessings pronounced by Christ in the Sermon on the Mount (Matt. 5).

But is there any other place in Scripture that compares to this psalm in the explicit pronouncement of God's blessing over sinners? Do you grasp just how radical the opening declaration of this psalm is? 'How God's blessing rests on sinners!' says King David. To reinforce his point, he repeats the fact of this blessedness twice over: how blessed, how blessed are sinners! He does not whisper this truth silently to himself so no one will misunderstand him. Instead, he declares it openly, preparing this psalm for public celebration in worship throughout the centuries.

Hear this word today. Repeat it to yourself and to others as often as you can. Rejoice in it especially when you come to church. God blesses sinners.

Of course, it is only a certain kind of sinner that God blesses. All other sinners can only wait for God's awesome judgment to fall on them, both in this life and in that which is to come. But a certain kind of sinner is blessed.

What kind of sinner does God bless? Is it the person who sins only a little, or only infrequently, or only unexpectedly? No, it is the sinner who repents and returns in faith to God who is blessed. Only the sinner who trusts in the provision that God himself has made for forgiveness through the blood of the Lamb will receive this spectacular benediction. Only this sinner, and this sinner alone, is blessed by God.

Consider the way this blessing affects a person's relation to God and to himself.

2. The blessed sinner's relation to God (verses 1, 2)

Three things characterize this blessed person in his relation to God: his wrongdoing is carried away, his sin is covered by the blood, and the Lord does not hold him accountable for his iniquity. He is definitely a sinner. He has done wrong. He has committed sin. He should be called to account and condemned for his iniquity. But the blessing of God delivers him from this condemnation.

David had committed adultery and murder. His sins were not merely little sins conceived in the mind. They were wrongs that hurt people. He hurt himself, his neighbour, his army and his nation. His high position as king of the land meant that his sin had repercussions for lots of good people, and for the generations to come.

Do you think you could live with yourself if you had that kind of blame to bear? It is bad enough to see the effects of sin on your own family. But what if you had to witness countless hundreds of innocent people suffering because of your personal passion and pride?

Yet David can say, 'Despite it all, I am blessed by God. My guilt is removed, my conscience is calmed, I do not fear angry retribution from the hand of God. Yes, I know that it's going to be rough. I bow my head in submission, knowing that I never will have a peaceful time in this life because of my sin. God has told me that I will have to contend with war all my days. But because my guilt has been removed in his sight, I know that the chastening judgments I receive will never be greater than I can bear. Even my toughest times will draw me closer to him, and turn out to be a blessing on all my people as well.'

Not everyone has this blessedness of the full forgiveness of all their sin. Do you? Do you live in the confidence that God is acting to bless you in everything that comes into your life? You must have strong faith in the provision made by God for forgiveness if you desire to have God's blessing on your life despite all your troubles. You must believe in the atoning blood of the sacrifice provided by God himself, and relate that sacrifice to your sins, past, present and future. Your faith must keep coming back to the focal point of God's gracious provision of forgiveness for sinners. Otherwise you will miss the blessing of the man whose sins are forgiven and whose transgressions are covered.

Seek out this blessing from God every day. Be sure you keep his benediction current in your life. Otherwise God and everything else will work against you. Even your successes will contribute to your ultimate downfall.

3. The blessed sinner's relation to himself (verse 2)

Alongside this blessed relation to God is the blessing of the forgiven sinner's relation to himself. This blessing is described in the last phrase of verse 2: 'No self-deceit is in his spirit.'

What could be worse than living with self-delusion? You might think a person who lives in the world of illusion would be very happy. He blots out all the bad, and acknowledges only the good. But think of the consequences!

What is the state of the person who deludes himself into thinking that his plastic card enables him to buy whatever he fancies? He lives with his charge card expended to the limit. He pays the minimum required each month, which is mostly interest. He never sees the debt go down. When something comes along that he really needs to buy, he is in trouble. He is a twentieth-century bondservant. He is a modern-day slave. He puts in his hours at work for others, not for himself. As the proverb says, 'The borrower is the slave of the lender' (Prov. 22:7). All this misery envelops him because he lives with a delusion.

What a blessing it is to live without self-delusion! You admit your sin. You face your wrongdoing. You stop trying to rationalize your guilt. As you make your honest confession, you put your trust in Christ. So your sin is covered by the blood and you can walk before the Lord with a clean conscience. You don't keep digging a deeper pit for yourself. You don't follow the precarious trail of one self-deceiving lie that invariably leads to another. That is the blessing. It is the beginning of the blessing of a new life that comes with the forgiveness of sin.

So how do you get to that point? The first main section of this psalm answers this question. Step by step the psalmist leads you along the pathway to pardon.

4. Reviewing the pathway to pardon (verses 3-6)

Look first at the denial and then the declaration of personal guilt. The sinner naturally begins by denying his guilt. But the grace of God leads him to declare it openly.

The denial of guilt

When a wife loses her husband, she often goes through a stage of grief called 'denial.' She will not, she cannot, accept the fact that this person to whom she has been so totally attached has died. She expects him to reappear at the breakfast table or in his chair in the study. You face an inevitable struggle of this type when a part of you dies.

Sin provokes the same kind of response. The wages of sin is death, and every time you sin a part of you dies. Your self-defence mechanism immediately goes into action. You refuse to acknowledge that a treasured part of your life is gone.

The person who commits the first act of premarital sex has killed a most precious part of himself or herself. That person never will be able to enter into the marriage relationship as an unspoiled virgin whose reservoirs of love have been stored up for a single other individual. No matter how deep may be the commitment of life once a person has entered into the marriage relationship, the gift of virginity was not there to give.

This reality is so difficult to face that the person who has stepped wilfully into sin responds by denying his guilt. It is a form of death-denial. Either he pushes it back into the recesses of his conscience, or he rationalizes the wrongness of the act itself.

Denial of sin is not a phenomenon reserved for the 'big ones.' It happens daily to everyone. You lose your temper at the children, and for a while you will not admit you have done any wrong. You conclude that either you were justified in your outburst because it was a case of needed discipline; or you submerge your sin of anger in a flurry of activity; or you break out crying, hoping for someone to make you the object of his or her sympathy.

But denial has its price. David sinned, and then denied his sin. For a year he refused to acknowledge he had done any wrong. He went in and out of church as usual. He faithfully read his bedside copy of the word of God. But inwardly he was denying his sin. For his denial he paid a price.

David describes the price a person pays for denial in terms of the inner conflict it invariably brings:

> While I maintained my silence,
> my very bones felt as if they were ageing
> as I kept inwardly moaning all day long.
> For day and night
> your hand weighed me down;
> my strength melted away
> as in the heat of summer
>
> (verses 3, 4).

David uses several figures of speech to illustrate the agony he was undergoing every moment of the day as a result of his refusal to acknowledge his sin. It was like a bad case of arthritis in which the bones never stop aching. It was like a heavy burden that cannot be set down, no matter how tired you become. It was like the experience of a prisoner of war who may be forced to labour in heat or cold, no matter how sickly or undernourished he may be. All of these feelings exerted pressure on David day and night. As a king he had all the resources of wealth, pleasure and power that a man could imagine. Yet he moaned and groaned all day long. If you could have got close enough, you would have heard him constantly sighing under his breath. Sigh, sigh, sigh—have you ever known anyone in that condition? 'Woe is me,' he seems to say constantly.

Why was David, the king, in that condition? Because he refused to acknowledge his sin.

How long did he continue in that condition? For as long as a year.

Talk about depression! Depression is not a twentieth century invention. Whenever anyone, and particularly a Christian, refuses to acknowledge his sin daily, he may expect depression.

How did David get relief from his miserable condition? What pathway did he follow to find a cure? Not by seeking a cure for himself, but by being confronted by God and his truth. A year later Nathan the prophet pointed his finger directly at the king. 'You are the man,' he declared. 'You have committed adultery with Bathsheba. And as for Uriah – God knows he wasn't just another casualty in the course of battle. Though you never laid a hand on him, you are his murderer.'

Are you guilty? Are you the man, the woman? Does God's accusing finger point at you? Of course you are. Daily in thought, word and deed you break God's law. By doing what you should not have done, and failing to do what you should have done, you are guilty.

You will be miserable until you follow the pathway to pardon. The first step is not yours but God's. He sees to it that your bones feel as if they are ageing. He weighs you down with his hand on you. He makes your spirit seem as if it is melting under the punishing rays of the summer sun.

Then God speaks to you by his word and Spirit. Make no mistake. It is his work of grace that makes you aware of your sin.

The declaration of sin

But the next step is yours. After denial must come declaration. You must affirm your sin to the Lord. Make it fully known to him. Stop trying to rationalize your guilt. Confess your wrong doings, all of them, to the Lord.

You must make a firm resolution. God doesn't do the job of confessing your sins for you. Like David, you must talk to yourself and say, 'I will …, I will …, I will confess my wrong-doing to the Lord. I will not simply acknowledge my sins to myself. I will not just talk around and about them with my closest friend. I will confess them all to God.'

As you confess them, remember that by God's blessing your sin can be covered by the blood of Jesus Christ. Only because he has shed his precious blood in suffering the punishment that sinners deserve can you come to him. But because of his death you can be assured of the covering of your sin.

> Come, every soul by sin oppressed,
> There's mercy with the Lord,
> And he will surely give you rest,
> By trusting in his Word.
>
> For Jesus shed his precious blood
> Rich blessing to bestow;

> Plunge now into the crimson flood
>   That washes white as snow.[1]

That is the only pathway to pardon, the only way to find the blessedness of the man whose transgressions are forgiven, whose sins are covered.

Join the millions that have found deliverance from a condemning conscience. Hear the corporate testimony of God's people:

> Because of your gracious forgiveness,
>   everyone who reveres you will appeal to you
>   in the time when you can be found.
> No, the torrent of floodwaters
>   will not reach up to touch him
>
> (verse 6).

God is gracious. He can be found. He forgives millions every day, and relieves them of a condemning conscience.

It cost him dearly to forgive. The blood-covering for sin, the sprinkling of an animal's life-blood on the mercy-seat in the Old Testament, did not have the power to forgive. It had power only to symbolize the provision yet to be made for forgiveness. It was like Monopoly money. It could not purchase pardon. It could only anticipate the payment of the price of pardon that would come through the life-blood of Jesus Christ.

The blood of Jesus, the Lamb of God who committed no sin, has the power to purchase complete pardon. His death can substitute for the sinner's death. By his blood all who will confess their sins to God and turn from them will be forgiven. They will be reconciled to God.

Because of this glorious provision, everybody who has true reverence for God will appeal to him. Before the sentence of the divine Judge is executed on you for your guilt, appeal to him. Before temporal judgments utterly wipe you out, before eternal banishment from God's presence becomes a reality, appeal to Jesus Christ.

[1] John H. Stockton, *Trinity Hymnal*, 1990, No. 675

Then even waters equal to the flood will not reach up to touch you. Though the righteous judgments of God should cover the peaks of the mountains, flooding all the inhabitants of the earth below, those judgments will not reach you.

You can claim this forgiveness personally for yourself. You can experience the cleansing of your guilty conscience today. Follow the psalmist in the pathway to pardon. For now he encourages you to seek personal forgiveness for yourself.

5. Encouragement to follow the pathway to pardon (verses 7-10)

The encouragement to seek forgiveness comes from two sources: from the testimony of men and from the dealings of the Lord. Consider first the encouragement that comes from the testimony of men. The psalmist says:

> You
>   are a hiding-place for me.
> From assault
>   you will preserve me;
> with songs celebrating deliverance
>   you will surround me
>
> (verse 7).

How amazing is the reconstruction of relationships between God and man as a result of the forgiveness of sin! Before repentance and confession, God's hand weighed heavily on the sinner. But now that very same God becomes the sinner's hiding-place, his protection from the assault of others. The closing verses of Romans 8 declare the same glorious message found in this psalm. Once God has justified the sinner, who shall bring any charge against him? If God has justified, who dares to condemn? (Rom. 8:33-39).

Indeed, Satan is the accuser, and he with his companions always will be busy finding fault with God's people. But the Lord himself will be their refuge, shielding them from the accusations and assaults of men.

In addition, the psalmist says that the Lord has encompassed him with songs of deliverance. In whatever direction he turns, a glorious song celebrating God's forgiveness meets him.

In this verse you have what may be called the most ancient reference to quadraphonic sound. Whether the psalmist examines his past or attempts to anticipate his future, whether he considers his points of strength or his points of weakness, he is confronted in every direction with a song that celebrates his deliverance from condemnation and guilt.

Should not the experience of David be an encouragement to you? If a king guilty of violating his solemn trust by acts of murder and adultery can find forgiveness, cannot you find pardon in the blood of the Lamb of God that takes away the sin of the world? If a tried and true saint like David can find joy in reconciliation to God through the shadow of the old covenant sacrifices, certainly you can find forgiveness in the actual sacrifice of Jesus Christ offered once for sin.

Be encouraged. Seek forgiveness for all the sins of which you are guilty. Labour no longer under the burden of a condemning conscience.

The Lord's guidance of his people

Having offered his own testimony as an encouragement to seek forgiveness, the psalmist next turns to let God himself speak his own word of encouragement and admonition:

> 'I will make you wise and point you
>   in the way you should go;
> I will counsel you
>   with my eye.
> Let not any one of you be
>   as the horse—or even the mule!
>   He has no sense.
>   Bit and bridle are his ornamentation,
>   but only for restraint.
>   Otherwise you will never
>   get him near you'
>
> (verses 8, 9).

Though the question may be debated, it appears that the Lord himself is the speaker in these verses. Only God can guide his people simply by setting his eye upon them.

How striking it is that God himself would be the one encouraging repentance and return! The offended God himself beckons, urges, commands, pleads with the sinner to return. 'Why will you die?' he exclaims. 'I have no pleasure in the death of the wicked,' he declares (Ezek. 33:11). 'Come now, let us reason together, says the LORD: Though your sins are like scarlet, they shall be as white as snow' (Isa. 1:18).

The Lord says he is ready at any moment to lead the repentant along the pathway to life. He will impart wisdom in the heart of the sinner so that the latter can avoid the traumas that inevitably come from divine displeasure. With his eye the Lord will give his counsel.

What does this last phrase mean? How will the Lord guide you with his eye? It seems best to take this phrase in the traditional sense, even though this interpretation has been rejected by most modern commentators. In contrast with the harsh restraints of a cold bit jammed in the mouth and a demanding bridle tugging at the jaw, God will guide those who are sensitive to his will with the glance of his eye. The sense of God's pleasure or displeasure, the encouraging nudge, or the shadow of a scowl, will be enough.

It was not by scathing words or battering rod that the Lord brought Peter to tears after he had uttered his three-fold denial with an ugly oath. Jesus simply looked at Peter and the tough fisherman had to flee to conceal his sobbings.

With his eye he will guide you. If you have become sensitive to his pleasure or displeasure, merely his look, communicated through your conscience as instructed by his word, will be enough. Once sin has been confronted properly, the Lord can gently communicate his approval through the constant promptings of his Spirit. Rather than overwhelming you with a stern chastening, the Lord is pleased to cultivate in you a heart that has the same desires as his own.

The positive promise of the Lord's direction must be contrasted with the negative imagery of forced control. The horse, but especially the mule, must be pulled about by his master. Do you really want to be treated like the dumb beasts? Bit and bridle may provide a decorative touch, but they add not one whit of enjoyment or power to the beast. They function only as restraints, regrettably necessary paraphernalia.

God's desire is to draw man, his highest creature, closer to himself. Shall this goal be accomplished only by the imposition of constant disciplines, curbs and restraints?

The testimony of God's people

God's people cannot fail to add their own 'Amen' to the counsel of the Lord. By their own experience they know the futility and frustration that come from delaying the confession of sin. The person who persists stubbornly in his own way will undergo one agony after another:

> Numerous agonies
> invariably come to the wicked;
> but the one who rests his case with the Covenant LORD
> will be enveloped in his mercy
>
> (verse 10).

So why should you make it hard on yourself? There is a better way. Rest your case with the Lord. Appeal to the blood sacrifice offered for sin by none other than Jesus Christ, the Son of God. Confess your wrongdoing before the Lord with genuine sorrow and repentance. Recognize that he is the Judge, and that everything in life hinges on the decision he makes regarding you.

If you turn to him in repentance and faith, you will be enveloped in his mercy. He himself encourages you to come to him and confess your sin. If you come, you can experience the unbroken happiness of the man whose transgression is forgiven and whose sin is covered.

6. The joy that comes with forgiveness (verse 11)

In echoing the beginning of this psalm at its conclusion, David twice emphasizes the joy that comes with forgiveness:

Be happy in the Covenant Lord and rejoice,
all you who have been declared righteous;
Sing for joy,
everyone whose heart has been made upright.

Two aspects of God's forgiveness stimulate great joy: a formal declaration of righteousness and an inward heart change that creates an inclination towards doing the Lord's will. Both of these conditions are a source of constant joy.

First, you can always rejoice because you have been declared righteous by God once and for all. This right standing with God despite your sin guarantees that God will order everything in your life for your good. Even the hardest, most humiliating moments you ever experience will be calculated by him to prosper your life overall.

Think of David, the author of this psalm. As a consequence of his sin with Bathsheba, the child born of their adulterous act died. Yet through that experience David came to understand more fully the comfort of hope in the resurrection of the dead. 'I shall go to him, but he will not return to me,' he said (2 Sam. 12:23).

Once you have been declared righteous by God, even your most difficult moments will be blessed by him. On the contrary, if you are not forgiven, even your most exalted hours will have a hollow, empty ring. Ask the great men of the earth and they will tell you it is true.

Secondly, you can rejoice because along with forgiveness God graciously gives a heart inclined towards him. You can do what your heart desires because you have been remade so that you love to do his will.

Make no mistake: this change of the heart's instincts will never be completed perfectly in this life. Many habits of the old, sinful nature will remain to haunt you. But great joy will still be yours because God has renewed your heart and given you a spirit inclined towards him (Psa. 51:10).

Conclusion

What a great psalm is this! What a great message of hope! What a source of daily joy! What a pivotal point for all of life! Be sure you grasp with full understanding the pathway to pardon. For then the fulness of joy can be your constant experience.

Psalm 44
A Prayer of the Perplexed

To the chief musician. By the sons of Korah. *Maskil.*

Reader: 1O God,
With our ears
we have heard,
our fathers
have told us

All: of the work you did
in their days,
in days long ago.

1st Congr.: 2You with your [own] hand
dispossessed the nations,
and planted them instead.

2nd Congr.: You troubled the peoples,
and ejected them.

1st Congr.: 3For not with their sword
did they possess the land;

2nd Congr.: and their [own] strong arm
did not save them.

1st Congr.: But your right hand

2nd Congr.: and your strong arm

1st Congr.: and your bright countenance!

All: For you found pleasure in them.

Reader: 4You [alone] are the one, my King, O God:
command conquests for Jacob.

5Through you
we will drive out
our adversaries;
in your name
we will trample
those who rise up to oppose us.

6For in my bow
I will not trust,
and my sword
will not deliver me.

7For you [are the one who] saves us
from our adversaries;
and those who hate us
you have shamed.

All: 8In God we glory
all the day,
and your name we celebrate
forever.

Selah

1st Congr.: 9But ah! You have loathed and humiliated us,
2nd Congr.: and you have not marched out with our troops.

1st Congr.: 10You make us retreat
before the enemy,

2nd Congr.: and those that hate us
ruin us.

1st Congr.: 11You have turned us over
like sheep to be devoured,

2nd Congr.: and you have scattered us
among the nations.

1st Congr.: 12You sold your people
without gaining a bit of wealth,

2nd Congr.: and you realized no profit
by their sale.

1st Congr.: 13You have made us an embarrassment
to everyone who knows us,

2nd Congr.: a scandal and an object of ridicule
to those who are closest to us.

1st Congr.: 14You have made us a taunt-word
among the nations;

2nd Congr.: the people can only shake their heads
at us.

Reader: 15All day long my disgrace
confronts me,
and the shame of my face
covers me

16because of the constant harangue and
denunciation
coming from the vengeful adversary.

Reader: [17]All this [calamity] has come on us.
1st Congr.: Yet we have not forgotten you,
2nd Congr.: and we have not been untrue
to your covenant.

1st Congr.: [18]Our heart
has not strayed,
2nd Congr.: and our walk
has not deviated from your path,

1st Congr.: [19]Even though you have broken us
in the realm of dragons,
2nd Congr.: and you have covered us
with the shadow of death.

1st Congr.: [20]If we have forgotten
the name of our God,
or stretched out our hands
to a strange god,

2nd Congr.: [21]shall not God
search out this thing?
For he knows
the secrets of the heart.

1st Congr.: [22]But it is on your behalf that we are killed
all the day;
2nd Congr.: we are regarded
as sheep for the slaughter.

Reader: [23]Awake!
How can you sleep, O Lord?

All: Arise!
  Do not despise us forever.

Reader: 24 Why do you hide your face?
  You forget our affliction and our oppression.

All: 25 For to the dust our soul
  is bowed down;
Our belly cleaves
  to the ground.

Reader: 26 Rise up
  to help us,

All: and redeem us
  to confirm your mercies.

A Prayer of the Perplexed—
The Plea of an Innocent Sufferer

Introduction

This psalm depicts God's people as suffering at a time when they can protest their personal innocence. It is not that they can claim absolute sinlessness. But they basically have been walking in the ways of the Lord. Yet they are suffering many things. The psalmist recalls past deliverances, puzzles over their tragic losses in the present, expresses confidence that the Lord ultimately will intervene on their behalf and urgently cries out for help.

This psalm points to the sufferings of the Lord's people through all the ages. Accordingly, the apostle Paul quotes the latter portion of Psalm 44 and applies it to the experience of suffering Christians in his day: 'For your sake we are being killed all day long; we are regarded as sheep to be slaughtered' (Rom. 8:36; cf. Psa. 44:22). This assertion may apply to all the various sufferings and disappointments Christians experience over the course of their lives. They are childless, they have prolonged illness, their work frustrates them. In addition, they often bear the brunt of direct assault for their faith. In their innocence and perplexity they cry out to the Lord.

Ultimately God will hear and answer their cry. But for the present the Lord's people often must endure many years of brokenness and shattered dreams.

Where is Christ in this psalm? In the history of God's people he represents the innocent sufferer in the fullest sense. He had no guilt whatsoever; yet he suffered intensely. His cry for help ultimately was answered through the full vindication of his cause that came through the resurrection. As a result of his suffering as the innocent one *par excellence*, he stands ready to sympathize, to assist and to assure all his suffering saints of their ultimate vindication, deliverance and reward even beyond their deservings.

This psalm falls into five distinct sections: recollection of past deliverances (verses 1-3); trust in God's continued help (verses 4-8); disappointment over present defeat (verses 9-16); a plea of innocence despite calamity (verses 17-22); and a prayer for God to intervene (verses 23-26).

At two points the psalm changes speakers so that instead of all the people addressing the Lord, a single individual speaks (verses 6, 15, 16). In the first of these cases, this individual appears as a warrior who will not trust in his own bow and sword but only in the Lord (verse 6). In the second case, he has suffered public disgrace because of the constant harangue of his adversary (verses 15, 16).

This representative individual speaks for more people than himself alone. His role as a warrior argues against his being a priest or a prophet. More likely he is the king of Israel, the leader of their troops and the one who suffers the greatest public humiliation at their defeat. Either this individual is the king himself, or the psalmist has put words into the mouth of someone representing the king.

1. A recollection of past deliverances (verses 1-3)

O God,
With our ears
    we have heard,
our fathers
    have told us
of the work you did
    in their days,
    in days long ago

(verse 1).

Story-telling always has been a part of the biblical tradition. Children as well as adults love to hear about the past. No stories exist in human literature that are more exciting than the narratives of the Bible. Think of the Red Sea, when God's enemies were swallowed up as the Israelites passed over dry-shod. Recall the days of Joshua, when solid walls crumbled at shout and trumpet-blast after the Israelites had silently encircled the city seven times. Remember Ehud, the left handed judge, and the boy David with his faith and his sling. God constantly intervened in wondrous ways on behalf of his people in the past. These deliverances often would come as a surprise. Suddenly the Lord would step in to accomplish his own good ends.

Remembrances of the past should encourage God's contemporary people to take heart. They should live in the hope that he will do for them as he has done for the people of long ago.

God's actions on his people's behalf

> You with your [own] hand
> dispossessed the nations,
> and planted them instead.
> You troubled the peoples,
> and ejected them
>
> (verse 2).

An emphatic '*you*' (*attah*) begins the verse, followed immediately with the underlining expression 'with your own hand.' God is the one who has done this great thing for them.

'History assumes a different aspect when seen by faith,' as one commentator notes.[1]

Then the psalmist refers to the events associated with the conquest, when the Lord gave his people their land. He divided the Jordan, he caused the walls to crumble, he allowed their ambush to work, he made the sun stand still, he sent hail from heaven. In all these various ways God ordered a great succession of victories.

Not only did the Lord establish his people in the land; he also brought judgment on the heathen because their iniquity was full. Both of these actions were great deeds done by the Lord.

[1] Weiser, *The Psalms,* p. 356.

For not with their sword
did they possess the land;
and their [own] strong arm
did not save them.

But your right hand
and your strong arm
and your bright countenance!
For you found pleasure in them

(verse 3).

The psalmist underscores once more his understanding that their deliverance was altogether of the Lord. Not by their might, but by his alone, was deliverance from their enemies accomplished.

The third of the aspects of God's personhood that is cited as bringing salvation is particularly striking. In addition to his right hand and his strong arm it was God's 'bright countenance' that delivered them. The 'shining of [God's] face' (*or paneikha*) was enough to dissolve their enemies. Almost the identical phrase is found in the second element of the priestly benediction: 'May the Covenant LORD *make his face shine* upon you' (Num. 6:25). The radiant face of God possesses enough potency in itself either to annihilate or to assure prosperity. The benedictions of the priests have taken effect. God's light has shone on the endeavours of the people, and so they have possessed the land.

The love and grace of God

The reason for the manifestation of God's power on their behalf is found in the last phrase of verse 3: 'For you found pleasure in them.' God loved them because he loved them. It is not an irrational love, but a love that finds its rationality in the sovereign grace of God. God loved them, not because they were stronger or more numerous than any other nation, but because he in himself determined that he would love them (cf. Deut. 7:7, 8).

A new covenant perspective on this principle only emphasizes all the more that salvation is all of grace. Nothing in man makes him deserve the favour of God. For it is by grace through faith that a man is saved, and not of works, so that no man can boast (Eph. 2:8, 9).

Looking back as a stimulus to faith

So God has done great things in the past. He has worked great deliverances for his people. For participants in the new covenant, his grace is even more evident and far-reaching than in the old covenant. His own Son lived a perfect life in the flesh, and suffered in himself the condemnation that sinners deserve. By God's creative power he raised from the dead Jesus Christ and all those who are in him. If you are today a believer in Christ, it is because God in his mighty working has sent someone to bring to you this gospel of God's grace. By his Holy Spirit he has awakened you to the newness of life that is in Jesus Christ.

Unless viewed from the eye of faith, the net effect of considering God's past works of salvation might tend to aggravate the problems associated with present distresses. If the Lord has done such mighty works of grace in the past on your behalf, how is it that he does not appear to be working in your present circumstances? Are you to conclude that his works of grace are to be experienced no more?

The work of faith and hope is to provide a rationale for avoiding these pitfalls of the doubting soul. Faith in the future must be awakened on the basis of God's great works in the past. The anticipation of coming deliverance stirs up the expression of trust in God's continued help that appears in the next verses.

2. Trust in God's continued help (verses 4-8)

> You [alone] are the one, my King, O God:
> command conquests for Jacob
>
> (verse 4).

Now a single individual steps forward to speak on behalf of God's people as a whole. Throughout this section there is an alternation between singular and plural speakers. But the net result is a united prayer expressing trust in God alone as their hope for deliverance.

But who is this individual who speaks for the whole of the nation? Does he represent just any individual from among the people of God? As indicated earlier, he appears to be the king of Israel, armed with bow and sword as the leader of the nation's armies (verse 6). He has as his principal concern the wellbeing of the nation whom he represents.

The king begins by joyfully acknowledging his total dependence on God for the accomplishment of any good for the nation. 'You are he, my King, O God,' as verse 4 reads literally.

The strongest possible emphasis is placed on God as the only hope for continuing victory. The king gladly acknowledges that he is not the one, but it is God alone who can lead the people into triumph over their enemies.

Pastors and elders, as shepherds of God's flock, need to make the same acknowledgement. It is not their cleverness or their skills in communicating the gospel that will advance the church. Christ alone, our King and our God, has the power to move the church forward.

A confident prayer for victory

The overriding petition is summarized at the head of this section: 'Command conquests for Jacob' (verse 4). 'Give victory over the enemies that have troubled us so greatly.' Then the psalmist expresses his confidence that the Lord will grant this request:

> Through you
> we will drive out
> our adversaries;
> in your name
> we will trample
> those who rise up to oppose us
>
> (verse 5).

The psalmist is confident that the Lord can overcome their enemies whenever he will. The parallelism places emphasis on the first portion of each phrase: 'Through you' and 'In your name' the victory will be won. All the Lord must do is give the command.

But why does the psalmist specify that these conquests should be 'for Jacob'? Perhaps it is because Jacob was the one who seemed always to be in trouble. His life was threatened constantly by his older brother Esau. For fourteen years he remained subject to the trickery of his uncle Laban. Yet God showed his ability to bless Jacob constantly despite all these distressing situations.

Victory through God alone

All the great triumphs of the church come through Christ. The experience of Jacob and Israel must remind us to look continually to God alone for victory over the threats that may arise from a secular society and a secular government.

> For in my bow
> I will not trust,
> And my sword
> will not deliver me
>
> (verse 6).

To reinforce his point, the psalmist now stresses the negative side of the source of deliverance. *Not* with our own strength is salvation to be found, but with God alone.

This repeated emphasis from every possible angle shows the importance of the principle at stake. Faith in God is the victory that overcomes the world. Trust in ourselves always will end in disaster.

It should be clear that the negative emphasis of this verse must not stand alone. If it is stated only that a person's own resources cannot save him, utter despair may be the result. An awareness of one's own weakness must be coupled with a confidence in the power of God. This expression of personal inadequacy therefore is bracketed before and after by declarations of confidence in God:

> For you [are the one who] saves us
> from our adversaries;
> and those who hate us
> you have shamed
>
> (verse 7).

God both saves from adversaries and shames those who hate God's people. King Henry VIII of England worked hard to shame the people of God in his day. Yet no name in history is more blackened than that of Henry VIII. He arranged the framing of his own wife Anne Boleyn so he could have her executed and move on to his next wife. Anne endured her shame, but it is Henry's name that remains scandalous in the light of history. The same principle holds for other names associated with the persecution of God's people like Stalin, Hitler, Caesar, Pilate and Judas.

> In God we glory
>   all the day,
> and your name we celebrate
>   forever
>
> (verse 8).

God's name causes us to 'shout Hallelujah' all day long. Both now and throughout eternity we shall have a continual celebration because of the glories of our Saviour-God. Even when trials have not yet disappeared, God can be a cause of constant celebration. What a shame it is when men fail to enter into the enjoyment of God's glories! Let us never be overwhelmed by the present distresses. Instead, let us delight in the long-term enjoyment of his glory.

3. Disappointment over present defeat (verses 9–16)

Nine different times in this section the psalmist indicates that God himself has brought great distress to his people. It is not so much that their enemies have overcome them, but that God has brought them low. This grave situation has caused serious disappointment among the people, particularly since, so far as they can tell, they have remained loyal to the Lord.

It would be an easy thing to find fault with this protest of supposed innocence. But it must be realized that many times God's most faithful servants experience devastating blows. The reason why these calamities come is not always obvious at the time. The only thing the people of God can do in such circumstances is cry out to the Lord in the integrity of their souls.

> But, ah! You have loathed and humiliated us,
> and you have not marched out with our troops
> (verse 9).

The 'Ah!' [*aph*] that begins this section expresses the heartfelt grief and puzzlement over their circumstances. It is not what they would have expected in the light of their efforts to serve the Lord. To be cast off, humiliated and seemingly abandoned by God while in the front line attempting to serve him is especially painful.

> You make us retreat
> before the enemy,
> and those that hate us
> ruin us
> (verse 10).

The enemy and the ones hating God's people must be identified ultimately as Satan and the forces of evil. They have set themselves to oppose every purpose God has made to bless his people. Yet they have been allowed to overwhelm God's people and their cause. It is no wonder that the psalmist puzzles over these developments.

Sheep without a shepherd

> You have turned us over
> like sheep to be devoured,
> and you have scattered us
> among the nations
> (verse 11).

Can you imagine anything more helpless than a sheep before wolves? The pitiful animal has no method of defence. Once it is cut off from the shepherd, it has no possibility of escape.

God's people find themselves in just that situation. They are being devoured by the wolves, scattered across the mountains like sheep without a shepherd.

Remember that when Jesus Christ saw men as sheep without a shepherd he was moved with great compassion (Matt. 9:36).

Although God may seem to be unavailable, he actually is very near to his people at all times, ordering even their sufferings for his glory and their good.

Immediately after quoting this psalm in its depiction of God's people as sheep prepared for slaughter, Paul says, 'For I am sure that neither death nor life, nor angels nor rulers, nor things present nor things to come, nor powers, nor height nor depth, nor anything else in all creation, will be able to separate us from the love of God in Christ Jesus our Lord' (Rom. 8:38, 39).

Yet this psalm says that it is the sovereign Shepherd himself who has scattered the sheep. The one to whom the sheep naturally look for protection has stretched out his hand against them. He is the one who has delivered them over for the slaughter. It is no wonder that the psalmist expresses puzzlement and distress.

Sold for no gain

> You sold your people
>   without gaining a bit of wealth,
> and you realized no profit
>   by their sale
>
> (verse 12).

Now the figure changes. Instead of being like sheep scattered by their own shepherd, they are like sons and daughters sold into slavery with no profit accruing to their father. 'Your people' you have sold, but to no personal gain.

What does God gain if his people labour under heavy burdens? Particularly if it is not evident that they have committed a sin that needs a chastening judgment, what glory does God gain from their trials?

Yes, it could be proposed that God's people will become more holy through a process of trial. But when you are the one undergoing the trial, you will not be so ready to provide a quick answer to this truly perplexing problem!

Shame and disgrace

You have made us an embarrassment
  to everyone who knows us,
a scandal and an object of ridicule
  to those who are closest to us.
You have made us a taunt-word
  among the nations;
the people can only shake their heads
  at us

(verses 13, 14).

The public humiliation of God's people is a distinctive source of pain. Both those closest to them (verse 13) and those far away from them (verse 14) treat them as an object of ridicule. Once they were seen as the nation most favoured of God. But now they stand out as a nation under divine curse.

It is one thing to be shamed in the eyes of the world, but held in high regard among those of God's people who know the truth. So long as an inner core of people support you, it is possible to endure great shame. But if that inner core of people on whom you count for support also regards you with contempt, how can you endure it?

Contrariwise, you may experience shame in the eyes of an inner circle of friends and still carry on if your shame does not become a matter of public scandal. But if you experience shame both among intimate friends and also in the eye of the public, how can you possibly be expected to survive? Everyone gossips about you, joining together to ridicule your name. How then can you stand it? Particularly if God's hand appears to be involved in bringing about this universal ridicule, the circumstance may be almost impossible to endure.

The psalmist depicts just this kind of painful situation. Like the third chapter of the book of Lamentations, he says that God is the one who has brought all this calamity and disgrace on them.

All day long my disgrace
  confronts me,

and the shame of my face
covers me
because of the constant harangue and denunciation
coming from the vengeful adversary
(verses 15, 16).

Now the psalmist returns to the first person singular. He speaks as the king, the representative spokesman for the people. Every individual included in the nation feels this shame on a personal basis. But the king in particular must bear the brunt of public disgrace at a time of national calamity.

This sense of shame overwhelming the innocent, coupled with an awareness that the Lord has ordered the bitter cup, finds its climax in the sufferings of Jesus Christ. More than any other single individual, he experienced the shame of unjust treatment both in the presence of those closest to him and before the gaping world as well. His clothing stripped from him, enduring the ignominy of the cross, he saw his disciples abandon him as he underwent the severest mockery of the world.

Do not forget that his shame, as in the case of all his sufferings, was endured vicariously. He suffered shame in the place of sinners who should have been shamefully exposed in their guilt. Concentrate on his disgrace until you see it as a way of deliverance from your own. The fact that he suffered shame for all who trust in him is just one further implication of your justification. The strength to endure disgrace before men, deserved or otherwise, comes from concentrating on the vicarious, substitutionary suffering of shame by Christ on your behalf.

So the community of God's people, along with their leader, express their sorrow over present defeat. They are deeply hurt because of their loss and their shame.

4. A plea of innocence despite calamity (verses 17-22)

From one perspective, it may seem strange to hear the people of God pleading their own innocence. Yet often calamities come on God's people just at the time when they are most deeply involved in seeking to serve him. The missionary couple denying themselves every personal convenience cannot have children. The prayer warrior of the church has a near-fatal road accident while on a well-deserved holiday. The faithful widow has her purse snatched just as she leaves the bank.

It is indeed true that God's people must be prepared to confess their personal sin and unworthiness at all times. But it would be dishonouring to God for them to deny the working of grace in their lives which has led them to give themselves to the service of the Lord. His honour would not be served by their denying the effect of the grace of sanctification in them. It is in this context that the plea of innocence on the part of the psalmist may be understood. The psalmist says:

> All this [calamity] has come on us.
> Yet we have not forgotten you,
> and we have not been untrue
> to your covenant
>
> (verse 17).

The word 'forgotten' is a keyword, since it is found here and also in verse 20. The easiest thing to do in life is to get so wrapped up in activities or pleasures that you forget God. His place of prominence in life can be set aside by simple forgetfulness.

Yet these people have not forgotten the Lord, and they have not been untrue to his covenant. How then are they to understand the cause of their calamities?

Loyalty even under the greatest trials

> Our heart
> has not strayed,
> and our walk
> has not deviated from your path,
> even though you have broken us
> in the realm of dragons,
> and you have covered us
> with the shadow of death (verses 18, 19).

In addition to not forgetting God, their heart has remained loyal to the Lord through all these perplexing trials. The point of greatest temptation to depart from the Lord often arises when someone is led to conclude that he is suffering for no just cause. But these people have remained constant in their loyalty throughout their trial. Even though they are a broken people, even though the shadow of death has covered them, they have remained true.

And what is this 'realm of dragons' where they have been broken? *'Tannim'* is the word, and it can refer to a serpent or any large marine animal. It is not necessary to posit genuine belief in a mythical 'dragon' that arises out of the sea to destroy them.

But the concept behind the term might be illustrated by British traditions about St George and the dragon. It is not that the English believe that George actually struggled with a fire breathing beast. But the story of a Christian knight fighting an evil force on foreign soil miles away from his native land in order to defend a helpless maid projects well the desired image.

So the image of an evil force arising out of the abyss of the sea threatening to consume the people of God fits the sense that Israel had in this circumstance. They are broken in the realm of dragons. They are on the edge of being consumed, dragged away into the abyss.

The same imagery recurs in the book of Revelation with respect to the last struggle between God and his adversaries. One monster after another arises out of the abyss and threatens to devour the people of God. This imagery climaxes with a reference to the person of Satan, that old serpent, the devil himself.

When God's people are cast down in the process of seeking to do the will of God, they sense a demonic, dragonlike force of evil in the world. When they conclude that God himself has cast them into this realm of dragons, they understandably experience great puzzlement and consternation.

The one who searches hearts

If we have forgotten
    the name of our God,

or stretched out our hands
    to a strange god,
shall not God
    search out this thing?
For he knows
    the secrets of the heart

(verses 20, 21).

Now the psalmist sets forth possible hypotheses to explain the tragic circumstances they face. Perhaps they have forgotten God in a crucial area of their lives without realizing it. Perhaps their prosperity has led them to immerse themselves in life's enjoyments so that they have forgotten that God was the giver of every good and perfect gift.

Or perhaps they have gone so far as to offer worship to other gods. They have been enchanted by the god of knowledge, of speed, of money, of love, of wine, of might. Are these not the very things which capture men's devotion today? For one it is education, for another sensual pleasure, for others power to control their own destiny and the destiny of others.

If God's people have fallen into these sins, then their calamity is understandable. For God will not fail to search out this kind of thing. He knows all about the 'idols of the heart.' Even unseen things cannot be hid from him, 'for he knows the secrets of the heart.'

Suffering for the Lord's sake

But it is on your behalf that we are killed
    all the day;
we are regarded
    as sheep for the slaughter

(verse 22).

As far as they know their own hearts, no secret sin has defiled them. Instead, it is for God's sake that they suffer all these calamities. They are like the two missionaries who were caught and killed in the crossfire of a coup attempt in Liberia in 1990. For decades they had laboured to bring the gospel to those people. Now in their seventies, they were shot to death by the very people to whom they had been bringing the gospel. What must have been their thoughts as they suffered the martyr's blow at the end of their lives? Very likely their responses would have followed the train of thought in this psalm: 'It is not for our sin, "But on your behalf we are killed all the day; we are regarded as sheep for the slaughter."'

In God's service and for the advancement of his saving gospel they suffer. 'All day long' they experience dying. It starts early in the morning and continues until dusk. Throughout the ages there has been this unrelenting constancy to the persecution of God's people.

By the world's estimation the people of God are reckoned as sheep for the slaughter. Their possessions are regarded as material substance to be claimed. Their helplessness against the schemings, the connivings, the lies and the dishonesties of the world makes them appear as victims fattened for the slaughter.

5. A prayer for God to intervene (verses 23-26)

But this agony cannot go on forever. God must put a stop to it. The people of God do not think they can take it any more. By the use of four bold imperatives the psalmist stresses the urgency the people feel for God to act.

> Awake!
> How can you sleep, O Lord?
> Arise!
> Do not despise us forever.
>
> (verse 23)

The first imperative comes with a shock: 'Awake!' How can God slumber through their distress? Throughout the ages this cry has gone up. When men have suffered torture for the gospel, they cry out for deliverance from this burdensome oppression. Certainly God knows, and has the power to intervene. How then can he allow it to continue?

'Arise!' says the psalmist in addressing the Lord. 'Take swift action on our behalf.'

God's failure to act is described as a 'despising' of his people. The people plead that it should not go on forever.

> Why do you hide your face?
>   You forget our affliction and our oppression.
> For to the dust our soul
>   is bowed down;
> Our belly cleaves
>   to the ground
>
> (verses 24, 25).

Now the psalmist queries God. Why does he hide the face of his beneficence? The Lord must have forgotten their affliction. Otherwise he would have acted to deliver them.

If things are as the psalmist declares, it would seem amazing that the Lord could close his ears to this prayer. And that may be just the point. Anyone who enters honestly into this prayer may expect that God will hear and answer soon. As in the case of the first Christian martyr, the Son of Man stands at the right hand of God, watching to receive his soul (Acts 7:55, 56). The 'How long?' of the suffering saints will be answered soon and quickly.

Note the lesson of this psalm well. The maltreatment of God's people has become for them the occasion of prayer, not despair. It is all too easy to succumb to depressing thoughts, particularly when injustice seems to characterize the way in which a person has been treated. But this low estate must serve as a rationale for coming to God rather than despairing over God.

> Rise up
>   to help us,
> And redeem us
>   to confirm your mercies
>
> (verse 26).

The psalmist concludes his prayer with an urgent request that God arouse himself and delay his intervention no longer. He can take no more, and he places his only hope of deliverance in the Lord.

The Lord's mercies will be confirmed by his intervention. It cannot be otherwise. God's people must wait a little longer, but they will clearly see the Lord's gracious character working deliverance for them.

Conclusion

This psalm begins with a remembrance of the way God has helped his people in the past. It moves to the present, recording a plea of innocence on behalf of God's suffering saints. It concludes with an urgent prayer that God will intervene quickly and provide the deliverance so desperately needed by his people.

In times of puzzling trial and tribulation, God's people through the ages can find the right words to say to the Lord in this psalm. In particular, they may have hope in view of the fact that Jesus Christ himself is the great innocent sufferer whose vicarious death provides a basis of confidence for the believer in every time of trouble.

Psalm 80

The Man at God's Right Hand

For the chief musician. To 'The lilies.' A testimony.
By Asaph. A psalm.

Reader: 1**Shepherd of Israel!**
Hear us,
you who lead Joseph like a flock.

Congr.: Shine forth,
you who sit enthroned among the cherubim.

Reader: 2Before Ephraim, Benjamin and Manasseh

Congr.: stir up your might
and come to save us.

Reader: 3**O God,**

All: *make us return*
Let your face shine on us,
and we shall be saved.

Reader: 4**Covenant LORD, God of hosts,**

Congr.: how long will you [pour out] smoke
against the prayer of your people?

Reader: 5You have made them feed
on tears for bread.

Congr.: You have made them drink
tears without measure.

Reader: 6 You have made us a source of strife
to our neighbours;

Congr.: and our enemies
mock us.

Reader: 7 **God of hosts,**

All: *make us return.*
Let your face shine on us,
and we shall be saved.

Reader: 8 You brought out
a vine from Egypt;
You drove out nations,
and planted her.

Congr.: 9 You made preparation for her,
you rooted her,
and she filled the earth.

Reader: 10 The mountains were covered
with her shadow;

Congr.: The cedars of God
with her tendrils.

Reader: 11 She sent forth
her shoots
to the sea;

Congr.: and to the river
her branches.

Reader: 12 Why have you broken down
her walls?

Congr.: All who pass by
have tugged at her.

Reader: 13 Swine from the wood
tear at her;

Congr.: beasts of the field
feed on her.

Reader: 14 **God of hosts,**

Congr.: return, we plead.
Look down from heaven;
see and visit this vine,
15 this shoot your right hand planted.
[Look] on the son
you have made strong for yourself.

Reader: 16 It is burned with fire,
it is cut down;

Congr.: by the rebuke of your face
they are consumed.

Reader: 17 Let your hand rest
on the man of your right hand;

Congr.: on the son of man
you have made strong for yourself.

Reader: 18 Then we shall not turn back from you;

Congr.: you will revive us,
and we shall call on your name.

Reader: **19 Covenant LORD, God of hosts,**

All: *make us return.*
Let your face shine on us,
and we shall be saved.

The Man at God's Right Hand—*Lamentation, but with Hope in God's Saving Hero*

Introduction

In this psalm not one individual but the whole community of God's people grieves over their sad circumstances. The walls of their cities have been broken down, and their entire civilization has been subjected to the ravagings of wild beasts (verses 13, 14). God's people have become a cause for mockery among neighbouring nations, and the Lord himself seems to be angry even when they turn to him in prayer (verses 5-7).

Yet despite all these discouragements, the people have not lost hope. They cry out to God for his mercy, and look to their promised Messiah for deliverance. By remembering the blessing that comes in the name of the Lord, they take heart. They rehearse his name in their assembly, hoping that the priestly pronouncement of God's blessing will bring salvation.

The tribes specifically mentioned in this psalm are the descendants of Joseph, Benjamin, Ephraim and Manasseh, who all come from Rachel, the beloved wife of Jacob. These particular tribes were the most prominent ones of the northern kingdom. So Psalm 80 depicts the circumstances of the northern kingdom shortly before 722 BC, when its capital Samaria fell before the invading army of the Assyrians. The Greek translation of the Old Testament known as the Septuagint supports this understanding of the setting of Psalm 80 by adding these words to the heading of the psalm: 'A psalm concerning the Assyrian.' According to 2 Kings 15:19, Tiglath-Pilesar III of Assyria (c. 745–727 BC) invaded Israel and forced King Menahem of the northern kingdom to pay tribute. It was this kind of devastating situation that led to the composition of Psalm 80.

This psalm meets a peculiar need of God's people in their sojourn as strangers and pilgrims through this world. Though devastation often strikes them, both as individuals and as a community, they can continue in hope because of the gracious nature of their God as it is revealed through his names.

This psalm uniquely focuses on the name of God. His personal designations stand out clearly as a consequence of the poetic structure of the psalm. Repeated allusion is made to the priestly pronouncement of God's name over the people. In view of his character as revealed through these names, he is the one who can provide hope in their desperate situation. As a consequence, God's lamenting people hope in the name of the God who sends their saving hero.

Structure of the psalm

An outline of this psalm based on the structure provided by the threefold repetition of a refrain is as follows: the people of this psalm (verses 1-3); the puzzle in this psalm (verses 4-7); the perspective of this psalm—past history (verses 8-13) and present hope (verses 14-19).

This psalm provides one of the most elaborately developed poetic structures in the whole of the psalter. An identical refrain concludes each of three stanzas:

> Make us return.
> Let your face shine on us,
> and we shall be saved
>
> (verses 3, 7, 19).

The name of God in the successive refrains progresses from 'God' to 'God of hosts' to 'Covenant LORD, God of hosts.'

In addition to this overall stanza structure with climactic refrain is a great variety of Hebrew parallelisms, including a-b-a-b (verses 5, 12, 16), a-b-b-a (verses 6, 17), and a-b-c-c-b (verse 11). Because of the difference in grammatical structure between English and

Hebrew, not all these parallels can be represented exactly in translation. But in either language, the psalm builds to a majestic climax by skilfully employing a balanced but diversified poetic structure. In short, this psalm is a magnificent composition of literary art, suitable to the message of hope it conveys.

1. The people of this psalm (verses 1-3)

Psalm 80 centres on the theme of God's renewal of life after devastation. The people of this psalm are praying for restoration. God's hand of judgment has rested heavily on them, and now their only hope rests in a saving hero whom God himself will send, a man the people can trust for the renewal of their life. Consider first the people who are praying in Psalm 80, and the reasons that led them to this prayer.

The Shepherd who reigns over them

> Shepherd of Israel!
> Hear us,
>   you who lead Joseph like a flock.
> Shine forth,
>   you who sit enthroned among the cherubim.
> Before Ephraim, Benjamin and Manasseh
>   stir up your might
>   and come to save us
>
> (verses 1, 2).

The people of God are described in this psalm as 'sheep,' animals known for having a natural propensity to stray. They have no innate sense of danger that might keep them from briars and beasts of prey. They cannot drink contentedly from the bank of a flowing stream. Instead they must wade into the water so that their saturated wool drags them downstream. The person who tends sheep must have a great deal of patience and understanding. Otherwise his flock will perish.

These people boldly designate their God as 'Shepherd of Israel.' But why should the Almighty play the part of a shepherd, trailing animals who have a special capacity for getting themselves into trouble?

God rightly may be addressed as 'Shepherd' because he has committed himself to fulfil just that role in relation to his people. He understands the peculiar needs of wandering sinners and patiently provides for their deliverance. David uses this imagery in the 23rd Psalm. 'The Lord is my shepherd,' he declares. The king understood exactly what it meant when he called God his 'shepherd,' for he himself had spent long hours shepherding sheep, risking his life to deliver them from the lion and the bear.

But the earliest reference to God as a shepherd goes back much further in Scripture. When Jacob pronounced his prophetic benediction on his sons, he blessed Joseph and said:

> The God before whom my fathers
> Abraham and Isaac walked,
> the God who has been my shepherd
> all my life long to this day …
> bless the boys
>
> (Gen. 48:15).

Jacob blesses Ephraim and Manasseh, sons of Joseph, with a prayer that God may be their Shepherd.

The tribes specified in Psalm 80—Joseph, Ephraim, Manasseh and Benjamin—are the direct descendants of the very people whom Jacob had blessed hundreds of years previously by an allusion to God as being a 'Shepherd' to his people. Jacob remembered that God had remained his shepherd through all his trials, and pronounced a blessing in hopes that this Shepherd-God would continue to tend the descendants of Joseph.

The New Testament describes just how far God will go as the Shepherd of his people. Jesus said, 'I am the good shepherd. The good shepherd lays down his life for the sheep' (John 10:11). The hireling may flee when trouble comes, but the good shepherd stands ready to surrender his life for those under his care. As the Good Shepherd, Jesus Christ has given his life for the sheep. As a consequence, you may call out to this 'Good Shepherd' and he will provide deliverance in this day and age just as he has done throughout the past.

Not only is God described as Shepherd of Israel. He also is depicted as the one 'who sits enthroned among the cherubim' (verse 1). This Lord of the covenant is not merely a shepherd who sympathizes with the needs of his people. He also is a sovereign who has the power to save his people.

If you work with wood and make a wrong cut in a beautiful piece of mahogany, there is not much you can do. You cannot restore the wood to its original condition. But God, as the Creator of all things, sits enthroned among the cherubim. He has no limitations to his power. He can revive and restore the broken so that it is better than new. A human life, an entire nation, that has been devastated because of its own sin is not without hope. For the Shepherd of Israel reigns with creative powers in his control.

Joseph as a representative of God's people

Now consider the people for whom this prayer is being offered. They represent the offspring of Rachel, including the descendants of Jacob's favoured son Joseph. In a distinctive way, Joseph was a fitting person to anticipate the experience of the people of God as described in Psalm 80. For, more than anything else, Joseph's life epitomizes the experience of a person who first is brought very low and then is lifted very high. Joseph went down into the pit where his brothers cast him. Then he went down into Egypt, having been sold to a passing caravan of Midianite traders. Next he went down into Pharaoh's dungeon as a consequence of the false accusation of Potiphar's wife, where he spent years in darkness and isolation.

But then—he is lifted up into the presence of Pharaoh himself! He rightly interprets the dreams of the Egyptian king, and provides him with an administrative plan for dealing with the famine to come. Pharaoh is so impressed that he declares to Joseph, 'You shall be over my house, and all my people shall order themselves as you command. Only as regards the throne will I be greater than you … See, I have set you over all the land of Egypt' (Gen. 41:40, 41). Ultimately Joseph appears as a world-class ruler. Representatives from all nations journey to Egypt, bowing before him and begging for grain.

So the pattern of Joseph's life epitomizes the movement of God's people from humiliation to exaltation. The people of God may sink so deeply that they are on the verge of despair. But by viewing Joseph's experience they can hope to be brought up to the point of highest glory. Jesus Christ, the one who is 'greater than Joseph,' can provide even greater encouragement in times of trouble, trial and tribulation. He went down into the depths and came back into glory, bringing his people with him.

The hope of God's people in this time of distress finds expression in the words of the refrain repeated three times in Psalm 80:

> O God,
> make us return.
> Let your face shine on us,
> and we shall be saved
>
> (verse 3).

By the intervention of the Almighty, those who have been cast down can be saved from their distress. Because he is the all-powerful one, the prospect of deliverance is always a reality.

2. The puzzle of this psalm (verses 4-7)

It was a puzzling situation. It wasn't merely 'the people,' or 'a people,' who were praying to the Lord for restoration. Instead it was '*your* people,' God's own people, descendants of the beloved tribes of Rachel, who were crying out to him. Yet it was against the prayers of his own people that God was indignant. The psalmist says:

> Covenant LORD, God of hosts
> how long will you [pour out] smoke
> against the prayer of your people?
>
> (verse 4).

The psalmist imagines a situation in which the priests offer up the sweet-smelling offering that was to be placed on the altar of incense each morning and evening. The delicate aroma was intended to drift through the curtain into the most holy place as a symbol of the pleasure the Lord received from the prayers of his people. But instead, billows of smoke pour from the other side of the veil, smothering the sweet aroma representing the prayers of God's people so that they cannot reach him.

How long can this rejection of prayer continue? Where are they to turn if he does not hear their pitiful cry? When you cry out to God for help and receive no answer, what recourse is left for you?

The psalmist vivifies the distress felt by the Lord's people:

> You have made them feed
> on tears for bread.
> You have made them drink
> tears without measure
>
> (verse 5).

The bread of life for these people has taken the form of the tears they shed in their grief over their tragedy. Instead of being nourished with bread from heaven, they have become nauseous from swallowing their own salty tears.

Yet by calling out the name of God, the people hope that his essence, as embodied in his name, will become reality for them:

> God of hosts,
> make us return.
> Let your face shine on us,
> and we shall be saved
>
> (verse 7).

This identical refrain occurs three times in Psalm 80 (verses 3, 7, 19). The only difference in each of the occurrences is the form of the name of God that prefaces the poetic appeal. The clue to the reason for this threefold repetition is found in the middle line of the refrain: 'Let your face shine on us.' The phrase is taken directly from the corresponding middle section of the priestly benediction that was revealed to Moses. The sons of Levi were to 'set' God's 'name' on the congregation of Israel with these words:

The Covenant LORD bless you
and keep you;
The Covenant LORD make his face shine upon you
and be gracious unto you;
The Covenant LORD lift up his countenance upon you
and give you peace
(Num. 6:24-27).

The middle line of this benediction matches the middle line of the refrain that occurs three times in Psalm 80. By the use of this refrain, the psalmist indicates that he intends to expand on the priestly benediction of the Old Testament. The Lord had appointed a way by which his people were to receive his blessing. Through the pronouncement of his name by the priestly mediators, all the blessings associated with that name were to be communicated to the people. As the congregation heard and received by faith the truth about God as he had revealed himself in his name, then the blessing of that name would rest on them.

What is his name? In the first appearance of the refrain in Psalm 80, his name is simply *Elohim*, meaning 'God' (verse 3). As God, he is the all-powerful one, the Creator of heaven and earth. As *Elohim* he has all the power necessary to provide deliverance for his people, even if it means re-creation.

In this second appearance of the refrain, his name is 'God of hosts' (verse 7). The myriads of angelic beings that surround God's throne are the 'hosts' standing ready to do his will in an instant. Like lightning-flashes from heaven, they can accomplish the will of God without a moment's delay. As the God of these hosts, he has not only the power to help his people, but also the means by which to enact that power on their behalf.

So God's people are in distress. They need him to intervene in their lives. They are reeling under the chastenings of his hand. Their land has been devastated, and they are overpowered by their enemies. But they can hope in the God who has revealed his nature through his names.

Christian romantics imagine that God is like an indulgent father who never would lift his voice to speak in a way that would disturb his own people. They presume that God is like David in his dotage, who never said to his son Adonijah, 'Why are you doing that?' (1 Kings 1:6). David never rebuked Adonijah, and eventually reaped the harvest of his sad mistake. When David was in his weakness, Adonijah declared himself king, leading a rebellion against his own father.

God does not make the mistake of indulging his children. As Moses said, speaking with the wisdom acquired over a long life:

> For we are brought to an end by your anger;
> By your wrath we are dismayed.
> You have set our iniquities before you,
> Our secret sins in the light of your presence.
> For all our days pass away under your wrath;
> We bring our years to an end like a sigh
> (Psa. 90:7-9).

Because we are continually departing from the way of the Lord, he constantly chastens us. He brings difficult times into our lives in order to turn us back to himself. 'For whom the LORD loves he chastens' (Heb. 12:6 NKJV), and if he chastens you a lot it is because he loves you a lot.

But what should we do when we experience the Lord's chastenings? This psalm tells you what God wants you to do. Even though he is the one chastening you, more than anything else he wants you to return to him.

If you are a dog lover, you know the difference between a good dog and a bad dog. Every puppy chews the daily newspaper. But the test comes when you lovingly administer a discouraging tap on the pup's nose. How does the dog react? If he is a 'bad' dog he will flee to the farthermost corner of the fence. But if he is a 'good' dog he will turn right back to you, the very master who has chastened him. He will nose his way between your legs, and look up pleadingly with the saddest of eyes.

When God chastens his people, he has no intention of driving them from him. He chastens as a means of bringing his people back to himself. The psalmist understands this basic principle of the ways of God with man. He leads his people in a prayer of repentance as a way of their returning to God. He asks the very one who has chastened them to hear, shine forth, stir up his might and come to save them. His prayer provides a perspective of hope for God's people.

3. The perspective of this psalm (verses 8-19)

Past experience

In developing a basis for hope, the psalmist rehearses Israel's past experience. First God richly blessed Israel. But then he brought them under his chastening judgments as a way of bringing them back.

The psalmist addresses the Lord: 'You brought out a vine from Egypt' (verse 8). God showed his tender care to his people by the way in which he brought them out of their enslavement. 'You drove out nations and planted her' (verse 8). The Lord also went ahead of them to prepare the soil in Palestine. He drove out nations before them so they could prosper in the land.

Think of all the ways that God has shown his tender, loving care for you in the past. Though you were a rebellious sinner, he sent his Holy Spirit into your soul. He turned your heart of stone into a fertile soil that would be receptive to his word. He gave you the joy of bearing the fruit of the Spirit in your life. How gracious has the Lord been to you!

But God is not like some gardeners who plant but never tend their gardens. The psalmist remembers the way God caused Israel to prosper after he had driven out the Canaanites:

> The mountains were covered
> with her shadow;
> the cedars of God
> with her tendrils.
> She sent forth
> her shoots
> to the sea;

and to the river
her branches

(verses 10, 11).

North, south, east, west—in every direction of the compass the people of God expanded their holdings. The 'mountains' refer to the southern territory of Judea. The 'cedars of God' allude to Lebanon in the north. The sea to the west is the Mediterranean, and the river to the east is the Euphrates. This tender plant was not merely stuck in the ground and forgotten. Under the blessing of God it grew in every direction so that it covered the whole land.

Sometimes the blessings of God seem almost too great. Along with the saving gospel of Jesus Christ he gives family, fellowship in the body of his church, material prosperity and physical health.

But then comes the chastening. After the blessing comes the trouble. After numerous confirmations of God's loving care to Israel, their lands and their families were devastated. They had nothing left to show for all the prosperity that once had been theirs.

This whole development was a great puzzle to them. The psalmist asks. 'Why?' (verse 12). The modern reader must feel the perplexity of that question. Why?

Why have you broken down
her walls?
All who pass by
have tugged at her.

A tender vine never should be treated with such ruthlessness.

Swine from the wood
tear at her.
Beasts of the field
feed on her

(verse 13).

The animals declared unclean by the book of Leviticus ravage the holy land, uprooting every living thing.

How could it happen? Why should this kind of thing occur? It is a piercing question, and the answer must not be given too easily.

God chose Israel while they were still in sin. Abraham, along with his forefathers, worshipped idols, and yet God called him. Israel constantly rebelled against God while they were wandering through the wilderness. Yet the nation was led by the Lord, blessed of him. Under Joshua they were not perfect as they entered the land. They failed to destroy all the Canaanites. But God continued to be with them.

Now why should God desert them? A foreign army has invaded and has broken through their last defences. The walls of their cities have been devastated, their people carried into captivity. Why?

It is a perplexing problem. Don't be a Job's comforter when you see a fellow Christian suffering. Don't say, 'I know why you're suffering. It's because you've sinned.' Remember what Jesus said and you'll be a little more cautious in explaining other people's sufferings. 'Do you think [those men upon whom the tower fell] were worse offenders than all the others who lived in Jerusalem? No, I tell you; but unless you repent, you will all likewise perish' (Luke 13:4, 5). Be careful how you judge. For with the measure by which you judge others, you will be judged.

It is a perplexing thing to see God bring tragedy, trial and trouble on one person while others who give no evidence of being better Christians remain trouble-free. Our Lord Jesus Christ himself cried 'Why?' more agonizingly than any other person who has ever lived. As he was hanging on the cross he said, 'My God, why? Why have you forsaken me?' You might be quick to answer Christ's question. You might say that God forsook him because he was bearing in himself the sins of the world. But do you really think he did not know that answer? Do you presume to think that you understand the purposes of God better than Christ himself?

He is the one who asked the question 'Why?' There is a perplexity in it. The shock of experiencing the reality of the divine curse, of descending into hell, of undergoing the wrath of God for sin, was something that even Jesus in his humanity was not able to anticipate. 'My God, why have you forsaken me?' were his chosen words, and they must be contemplated with the greatest reverence.

Sooner or later, one way or another, you will ask the question, 'Why?' Man rightly senses that he is born to be king. When reality contradicts your sense of what is right, you will not be able to restrain yourself from asking, 'Why?' Some of you will ask more intensely than others. Some will ask more frequently than others. But inevitably you will ask, 'Why is my life being shattered? How can it be? Is there any hope? Is there any place of security, refuge and restoration?'

Despite the devastations that come from God's hand, nothing can separate you who are in Jesus Christ from his good purposes as revealed in his love. For that reason, you must turn in faith and hope to the same God who has chastened you. For effective help will come only from the hand of the Lord.

Present hope

So the psalmist turns from recounting past history to calling up present hope. He says:

> God of hosts,
>   return, we plead.
>   Look down from heaven;
>   see and visit this vine,
>   this shoot your right hand planted.
>   [Look] on the son
>   you have made strong for yourself
> (verses 14, 15).

The pronouncement of the name 'God of hosts' marks a transition from considering the blessings of God in the past to a petition for this great God to act in the present. Even though he addresses the awesome Almighty, the psalmist leads God's people to use a great deal of boldness in their prayers. Employing four consecutive imperatives he says, 'Turn!' 'Look!' 'See!' 'Visit!'

God commands that his people come boldly to the throne of grace that they may find mercy and receive grace to help in time of need (Heb. 4:16). Considering the sacrifice Jesus Christ has made to clear the way, a timid approach would dishonour the effectiveness of his work. Hope, a sure hope in him, must characterize the Christian as he works through his tragedies. Modern-day Christianity has rewritten the church's favourite chapter and left out a major element. 1 Corinthians 13 has been rewritten to say: 'And now abide these two, faith and love.' But the Scripture actually says, 'And now abide these *three*, faith, *hope* and love.'

A generation that has lived in unlimited prosperity has forgotten the meaning of hope in a time of trouble. A generation that has become accustomed to having whatever it wants whenever it wants it has lost contact with the idea of living by hope in what is yet to come. It is necessary to learn again how to bear the burdens of life in anticipation of a deliverance that will come in the future.

Hope is a very tender flower. It must be encouraged through the harsh winters of life. The word of God takes great pains to recall the past in which God has shown his ability to save. It offers promises for the future, so that hope can be sustained. The Lord wants his people to call out to him with a firm hope that deliverance will come. But in our distress we tend to despair rather than to hope in his coming deliverance.

A certain man had a favourite barber who cut his hair for forty years. Shortly after the barber passed the age of sixty, he began to have serious abdominal pains. The doctor informed him that he had an advanced case of terminal cancer. The barber had to stop work immediately to put his house in order. This man talked openly about his condition. He discussed the anxieties, the uncertainties and the pain that he was experiencing. He heard for the first time of Jesus Christ and his power to save. He was urged to call on Christ for his salvation, to seek reconciliation with his Maker. That night he got on his knees and cried out for Jesus Christ to be his Saviour. In addition he said, 'And Lord, help my stomach so I can eat a little.' A peace instantly settled in this man's heart, and the fear of death left him. His wife attested that he started eating like a horse and began gaining weight again.

'For forty years I never even thought about praying,' he said. 'It never crossed my mind. Now I know the power of Almighty God to save when you call out to him.' He also testified: 'I had a friend call up the other day who was facing troubles similar to mine. I told him he ought to try praying to God.'

Call on the Lord when you are in distress. Cry out to him as a source of hope so you can see for yourself that he is a God that has the power to save.

The coming Son of Man

This psalm reaches its climax by pointing specifically to the distinctive source of help provided by the Lord. The psalmist says:

> Let your hand rest
>   on the man at your right hand;
>   on the son of man
> you have made strong for yourself
>
> (verse 17).

You know of the Messianic psalms in the Old Testament. Perhaps you can even name one or two, such as Psalms 2 and 110. These psalms specifically prophesy about Jesus Christ. But many more psalms are Messianic in character than generally are recognized.

The psalm currently under consideration specifically concentrates on one particular person who is the hope of salvation for God's people in their distressing situations. It is not God in the abstract that saves. It is not men's philosophizing about God that saves. It is the Messiah, the one whom God has sent, who saves.

Many passages of the Old Testament teach that the Messiah was to come through the line of Judah. As one of the earliest prophecies of the Bible indicates, the ruling sceptre of the Messiah never would depart from Judah (Gen. 49:10). David was born in the line of Judah, and God made a special covenant about the kingship with him. The Saviour-King of Israel would come from his descendants (2 Sam. 7:12).

But the Jewish people also developed the expectation that Messiah would descend from Joseph as an offspring of the tribe of Ephraim, Joseph's son. For Joseph was designated prophetically as 'the one distinguished among his brothers' (Gen. 49:26 NASB), and Ephraim and Manasseh were granted the positions of prominence as the firstborn in Israel in place of Reuben and Simeon (1 Chron. 5:1, 2). So Israel expected a Messiah ben Ephraim as well as a Messiah ben Judah.

But how are these two strains of prophetic promise to be reconciled? Are there to be two Messiahs, one from the tribe of Judah and another from the tribe of Joseph? No, this multiple picture of Messiah anticipates the richness of the anointed one who had been promised. His glories were so great that they could not be contained in a single image. Just as the Old Testament depicted an anointed one fulfilling all three offices of prophet, priest and king, so it also anticipated the coming of one Saviour who would be like Judah in some ways and like Joseph in others.

How are these complementary images to be perceived? For over four centuries, descendants of David ascended the throne of Judah almost without a rival. Although David himself experienced many struggles and trials even after his anointing for the kingship at an early age, he nonetheless represents the stability of a monarchy that could not be overthrown.

But Joseph in a very distinctive way depicts one who descends into the depths of humiliation and suffering before being brought up to the position of honour and regality. He is a suffering sovereign who comes to lordship only through humiliation. Joseph was humiliated, Joseph was devastated, Joseph went down into the dungeon before being brought up to glory.

Our Lord Jesus Christ followed a similar pattern. He entered into unimaginable sufferings. He was rejected by his own people, hated by his own brothers and finally crucified before the nations of the world. But from his position of humiliation our Lord Christ was lifted to the right hand of God in glory where he was given dominion over all the nations of the world.

Psalm 80 presents the image of Messiah ben Ephraim. It is the Joseph-tribe that comes into prominence throughout this psalm. First Joseph, Ephraim, Benjamin and Manasseh are brought down to the lowest point of humiliation. But then they are brought up to the highest honour, situated at the right hand of God.

The pivotal point in this psalm is located in the single word in verse 15 that is translated 'son.' The section reads:

> Look down from heaven;
> see and visit this vine,
>   this shoot your right hand planted.
> [Look] at the *son*
>   you have made strong for yourself
>
> (verses 14, 15).

Some versions understandably have translated the term in italics in the last phrase of verse 15 as 'branch.' For the immediately preceding context speaks of a 'vine' and a 'shoot' which God's right hand planted. The term in the Hebrew language is '*ben*,' as in Benjamin ('son of the right hand') or 'Ben-Hur' ('son of Hur'). The question for the translator is whether the term refers to the offspring of a vine, which would be a 'branch,' or the offspring of a man, which would be a 'son.'

In this case it appears very likely that the psalmist intends to use the term '*ben*' in verse 15 with the force of a *double entendre*. The one word becomes the pivotal point of the whole psalm by referring simultaneously to the 'vine' that has played such a prominent role in the imagery of the verses that precede, and also to the 'son,' the 'son of man' who appears so prominently in verse 17. Israel was the 'vine' that God had brought out of Egypt (verse 8). The branches of that one 'vine' had spread throughout the whole land of Palestine (verses 10, 11). But Israel also had a vital connection to the 'man' of God's right hand, the 'son' of man that God had made strong for himself (verse 17). By using the single word '*ben*' in verse 15 to refer to both the 'branch' that is Israel and the 'son' that is God's appointed Saviour, the psalmist binds the two figures together in a most intimate relationship. Whatever happens to the 'son' also happens to the nation, and whatever happens to the nation happens to the 'son.' If the nation is brought down in humiliation, the 'son of man' also is humbled. If the 'son of man' is lifted up in glory, the nation is exalted with him.

But who is this 'son of man'? You know who he is. He is the Messiah, the one sent from God to be the Saviour of his people.

The New Testament refers constantly to Jesus Christ as the 'Son of Man.' Not from the lips of others, but as his own self designation, Jesus refers to himself as 'Son of Man.' He did not speak of himself as 'Son of God' or as 'Messiah.' He was the 'Son of Man.'

Two elements stand out about the Son of Man statements that Jesus makes in the New Testament. One is that the Son of Man must be greatly humbled. He must be brought very low. 'The Son of Man will be betrayed,' said Jesus. 'They will condemn him to death and deliver him over to the Gentiles to be mocked and flogged and crucified' (Matt. 20:18, 19; cf. 16:21). Repeatedly he speaks of himself as the Son of Man who must suffer humiliation at the hands of men. Secondly, Jesus speaks of himself as the Son of Man who will appear in great glory. 'The Son of Man is going to come with his angels in the glory of his Father, and then he will repay each person according to what he has done,' he says (Matt. 16:27; cf. 25:31). With clouds of glory he will come, and every eye shall see him, the Son of Man.

These two diverse elements in the experience of Jesus centre around the 'Son of Man' sayings. By this title he identifies himself as a person who will experience humiliation and exaltation.

It is this title that designates the Saviour of the suffering saints of Psalm 80. He is the lowly branch of a vine, humbled and trailing on the ground. But he also is the man of God's right hand, the Son of Man that God has made strong for himself. What greater hope could be found for God's suffering people than this Son of Man? He is a Saviour who has experienced all the humiliation, suffering and trial that man can undergo. But he has also been exalted gloriously to God's right hand where he has all the power necessary to deliver his people. Whatever tribulation and trial you have experienced, Jesus Christ has experienced the same. Whatever power for deliverance you may need can be found in him. He has united you with himself in his suffering and his glory, so that your hope of deliverance is secure. He is the 'vine' brought out of the oppressions of Egypt, and he is the 'son' exalted to the right hand of the Father.

One of the most profound teachings of the Bible is the union between Christ and his people. Before the foundation of the world you who now believe in Christ were chosen in him. When he suffered for sin, you were in him. When he rose from the dead and ascended into glory, you were united with him. Where he now is seated in heavenly places, you are seated with him.

Because of your indissoluble union with the Son of Man, you have a hope. This present humiliation is only temporary. This trial is going to pass. Just as surely as Jesus was raised from the dead to be seated at the right hand of God, you will be delivered from your trials. If you are one with Christ you have a hope that cannot be shaken.

Conclusion

Even the most frugal of cooks will brush a few grains of spilt sugar into the sink. But once sugar has been mixed into the icing on a cake, no stray fingers dare approach that icing. Those individual grains of sugar have been blended into a single whole that must not be disturbed.

You may perceive your relationship to the Saviour, the Son of Man, in a similar way. By faith you are one with Jesus Christ, and so you are absolutely secure. God would not lose a person joined to Jesus any more than he would lose his own Son. Just as each grain of sugar becomes totally united with the wholeness of the cake, so each believer in Christ is integrated completely in life and in death with his Saviour. No matter how great may be your trials, you can live in hope because of your inseparable oneness with him. For this reason you can join the psalmist in the climactic prayer for renewal and restoration despite the severity of your trials:

> Covenant Lord, God of hosts,
> make us return.
> Let your face shine on us,
> and we shall be saved
>
> (verse 19).

Psalm 82
The Judge Judges the Judges

A psalm of Asaph.

Reader: 1God is set
among the assembly of the great;
in the midst of the gods
he renders judgment:

2'How long will you judge
in favour of iniquity,
and keep on upholding
the cause of the wicked?'

Selah

1st Congr.: 3Maintain the just cause
of the poor and the orphan;
2nd Congr.: do justice
for the needy and the destitute.

1st Congr.: 4Deliver
the poor and the penniless;
2nd Congr.: rescue [them]
from the hand of wicked men.

1st Congr.: 5They have no understanding;
they cannot comprehend.

2nd Congr.: They keep walking in darkness;
the foundations of the world tremble.

Reader: 6"I said,
"All of you
are gods;
each one of you
is a son of the Most High.
7Yet inescapably as man
you will die,
and just like one more prince
you will fall.'"

All: 8Rise up, O God!
Judge the whole earth
for you possess all nations!

The Judge Judges the Judges—
God Judges Human Authorities

Introduction

This psalm talks about judges. It also talks to judges. 'Judges' in this context should not be understood as referring narrowly to people who preside over legal disputes. This designation includes all those who exercise decision-making authority that affects the lives of others. In this broader sense, everyone has the function of a judge in some of his or her relationships.

All 'judging' that affects the lives of others should be done in the light of the fact that God is the ultimate Judge. He will bring under the scrutiny of his judgmental review all decisions of humans who judge. Psalm 82 declares that the Judge judges the judges. In it we see that: man judges in a way that is like God; man judges in a way that is unlike God; God judges in a way that is unlike man.

Be careful about the way you judge. For, unknown and unnoticed by men and nations, God the Judge judges the judges. He observes carefully the decisions men make, and renders his own judgment. His decisions encompass not only the various matters under consideration: he judges the people who make judgments. As Jesus warned, 'In the same way as you judge others, you will be judged, and with the measure you use, it will be measured to you' (Matt. 7:2).

Not only does God make his own evaluations of each and every judgment that men make, he also sets in play a chain of events, short or long, that bring about an appropriate consequence to human judgments. For he will render to every man 'what is due for what he has done in the body, whether good or evil' (2 Cor. 5:10).

1. Man judges in a way that is like God

The sun eventually brings to light everything that man does. The murderer may strike at his victim under the cover of darkness. But soon enough the morning light uncovers the evil effects of his deed for all to see.

But the sun makes no moral judgment. It renders no decision about the rightness or wrongness of all the various things it exposes. Only man is like God. Only man makes moral judgments. As a reflex action, only man carries within himself a sense that he is accountable to a higher judge for the decisions he makes.

When Cain killed his brother Abel, God reserved the right of judgment to himself. Cain was a murderer, but God warned that anyone who attempted to bring judgment on him would pay seven times over (Gen. 4:15). But in the days of Noah, God established the right and the responsibility of human judges:

> Whoever sheds the blood of man,
> by man shall his blood be shed;
> for God made man
> in his own image
>
> (Gen. 9:6).

Why is man given the solemn responsibility of judging other men? Because he is in the image and likeness of God (Gen. 9:6). One of the distinctive ways in which man displays that he is like God is in exercising judgment over other men. Since the days of Noah, the courts of men in the various nations of the world have made judgments with the authority given by God. The state does not bear the sword of justice in vain. For it functions as the instrument of God to bring judgment on the wrongdoer (Rom. 13:4).

The wise person does what he can to avoid being brought into a human court. Whether it is a case of reckless driving, or of being sued for negligence, or of process in divorce, it is best to stay out of court. But it happens. Many, if not most, people will end up in court eventually. Being in court may well come to be added to death and taxes as an inevitable experience of human beings.

But man's 'judgments' are not limited to the strictly formal settings of the courtroom. Judging is a commonplace, everyday affair. All through the day you make judgments that affect your own life as well as the lives of others. You walk into the supermarket, squeeze a head of lettuce, notice its freshness and check the price. Then you render your judgment. You may decide the shopkeeper is charging more than the lettuce is worth. If you keep finding prices that you judge to be too high, you may render a judgment about the entire shop, or even a chain of stores. You decide, 'I'll do my shopping elsewhere!' It might be good therapy for the supermarkets of the land if some of you were to formalize these judgments on some special occasion! Don a black, ankle-length skirt and march through the aisles of your local store on some designated day. Wheel your trolley to the checkout counter, pull out a wooden gavel, rap the cash register and declare your judgment: 'Too expensive!' You might get some startling results!

This judging which man does all the time is dramatized in the courts of the land. The landlord sues the tenant because he has not paid his rent for three months. The tenant claims that the landlord has not repaired the gas leak in the oven. The landlord retorts with the accusation that the tenant is the one who damaged the oven in the first place. Then the judge must decide. He must determine who is right and who is wrong, who must be repaid and who must suffer loss.

Like God, man judges. He imitates his Maker by rendering decisions. The psalmist even goes so far as to say that earthly judges are 'gods.' He quotes the Lord himself as saying:

> 'I declared:
> "All of you
> are gods;
> each one of you
> is a son of the Most High"'
>
> (verse 6).

Obviously the Bible is not promoting polytheism or suggesting that human beings actually are 'gods.' But this verse gives full recognition to the solemn character of men in God's image who judge others. What majesty resides in man! Every man is made in God's image, charged with the responsibility of having dominion over the whole creation. But particularly when you judge other men, you are godlike.

Parents, when you criticize the behaviour, language and dress of your teenage son or daughter, you perform a very serious function. Contrariwise, when you look the other way and totally ignore their patterns of behaviour, you are rendering a judgment that tacitly approves their lifestyle.

Teachers, when you offer an evaluation of a student's gifts and efforts by your grading, you are performing a godlike function. You may be setting the course of his or her life by your decision.

If you have people working for you, be aware of the impact your judgments may have on their lives. You may exclude them from one career, and push them into another.

Elders, it should be obvious that you act as gods when you render a judgment about the validity of a person's Christian confession. To you have been committed the keys that let people into the kingdom of God, and put them out.

Be fully aware of this sobering fact. Men judge like God. In his place they render their decisions many times each day.

2. Men judge in a way that is unlike God

But there is another perspective on this matter of judging. In a very distinctive way, men judge in a way that is unlike God. As much as their function is like his, a critical area still remains in which men do not judge as God judges.

How many of you have been involved in a lawsuit? Did you win? Generally speaking, lawsuits involve a lot of bitterness in which all too often no one 'wins.' Hardly ever does a human judge render a decision with perfect equity. In their efforts to be conciliatory, granting some concessions to every party in a dispute, human judges often fail to render true justice to anyone. Instead of restoring the whole baby to its true mother, human judges divide the baby, giving one half to the mother and the other half to the pretender. The righteousness of the righteous is not rewarded, and the wickedness of the wicked is not exposed for what it truly is. As the psalmist says:

> How long will you judge
>   in favour of iniquity,
> and keep on upholding
>   the cause of the wicked?
>
> (verse 2).

Repeatedly in the counsels of men, injustice is done. Instead of strengthening the cause of the right, men render decisions of compromise that reward the wicked.

The principle of injustice in the decisions of men can affect people's very lives. In the last century, a minister was preaching to people who had been enslaved in Dutch New Guinea on the northern coast of South America. The landowners tolerated his preaching of the gospel, but they didn't like it. At one point a disturbance arose among the enslaved people. Even though he had nothing to do with the disturbance, the minister was brought to trial and sentenced to death. He died in prison before he could be executed for a crime he never had committed.

Judging with righteous judgment

What should a righteous judge do? What should you do when you are in a position of authority, making decisions that affect the lives of others? God's word tells you what to do:

> Maintain the just cause
>   of the poor and the orphan;
> do justice
>   for the needy and the destitute.
> Deliver
>   the poor and the penniless;
> rescue [them]
>   from the hand of wicked men
>
> (verses 3, 4).

Render righteous judgments. Do all you can to understand the cause of the poorest suppliant. Hear him out. Be very careful that your judgments are right. Don't be influenced by people in authority over you in such a way as to keep you from deciding rightly.

At the same time, don't show partiality to the poor and the disadvantaged. Scripture warns against injustice either in the direction of showing favouritism towards the rich or the poor. Very often a person's bad conscience in one direction will lead him to attempt to compensate in another because of wrongs he has done. Obviously mercy is always appropriate. But mercy is something other than partiality. Mercy recognizes a person's need and responds in compassion. But partiality shows favouritism at the expense of someone else.

The imperfection of human judgment was made especially apparent during the time of Jesus' ministry on earth. On one occasion, the lame were leaping for joy because Jesus had made them able to walk. A man who had been blind from birth had been made to see.

The critics of Jesus could stand it no longer. They came to him and demanded, 'If you are the Christ, tell us plainly' (John 10:24).

Jesus answered them in the straightforward manner they requested. 'I and the Father are one,' he said (John 10:30). He claimed that his power to do these miraculous things came directly from God, who was uniquely his Father.

His hearers rendered an instant judgment. He had blasphemed by making himself equal to God by claiming him as his Father. They concluded that he was worthy of death, and were ready at that moment to carry out the sentence of stoning, despite all the evidence that he had the power to perform miraculous works that only God could do.

Do you see what transpired? Men presumed to make themselves the judges of the Son of God. They judged him to be a blasphemer, while God had declared him to be his Son. Rejecting the divine approval of Jesus implicit in the power granted him, these men declare their own judgment, determining that he is worthy of death.

Jesus responded by an appeal to this very psalm (cf. John 10:34-38). He urged them to judge righteously. If the Scripture in Psalm 82 declared that human judges could be called 'gods' because of the responsibilities given them, why should not someone who created sight for a man born blind be designated as 'Son of God'? Was it not the miraculous work of God that he was doing? Did he not display God's creative powers when he took clay, shaped it over the man's eyes and commanded that he wash so he could see?

Be sure you judge with righteous judgment. When you reject the standards God has established, you are rejecting God himself and the lordship of his Son Jesus Christ.

The consequences of unrighteous judgment

The consequences of unrighteous judgment are disturbing, to say the least. The psalmist says:

> They have no understanding;
>   they cannot comprehend.
> they keep walking in darkness;
>   the foundations of the world tremble
>
> (verse 5).

The order of God's creation is overthrown. Wrong becomes right that must be rewarded, and right becomes wrong that must be punished. The moral foundation that is essential for order in the world is devastated.

This principle may be illustrated by the reversal of order concerning homosexuality in modern Western society. From a biblical perspective, homosexuality is a sign of deepest depravity, described in Scripture as a degrading of the body, an unnatural relationship, an inflamed lust, a perversion (Rom. 1:24-27). Once homosexuality was a crime punishable by law. But now the person most likely to face a legal suit is the student on certain campuses who dares to say anything that might be interpreted as critical of the homosexual.

Again, the matter of abortion shows how the foundations of civil order can be turned upside down. According to the current law of one state, the person who performs an abortion is protected from legal suits of malpractice in a manner distinctive from all other medical procedures. But the physician who for conscience' sake fails to refer a patient to places where an abortion can be performed may lose his licence to practise medicine.

Be careful of the judgments you render. If you have judged Jesus Christ to be the unique Son of God, then show forth the righteousness of his judgments in all your life. Whether at work, at home, or in the marketplace, as you interact with other people, maintain the just cause of the Lord. Contrariwise, if you have made yourself the judge of God himself, his ways and his laws, don't think you will be able to carry out justice in any part of your life. Turn to the Lord. Believe the works he has done as Creator and Redeemer. Then everything else will fall into its proper place.

Man judges like God. He has a most solemn role to fill in this world. Man judges in a way that is unlike God. He makes decisions that are not correct. He favours himself and those who will favour him. As a result, he turns the foundations of this world upside down.

3. God judges in a way that is unlike man

In the end, the tables must be turned. Men may render their judgments. But ultimately God himself judges. He makes judgments now, and he will make a final judgment in the future. All judgments of men are subject to review and revision by the divine court.

God judges men now

First, right now God judges the judgments of men. The psalmist says:

> God is set
> among the assembly of the great;
> in the midst of the gods
> he renders judgment
>
> (verse 1).

The Judge judges the judges. God reviews every decision that men make. He is set right now in the assembly of the great ones of the earth. He notes their judgments, he observes where they go wrong. One way or another, at one time or another, he will correct every wrong decision. 'He got what he deserves' is a secular way of understanding what happens. A criminal thinks he has eluded the law, but he has not escaped punishment. He rushes into the supposed security of his house, he closes the door, he breathes a sigh of relief. He has escaped undetected. He leans his hand against the wall to rest his weary body, and a scorpion stings him.

The Scripture warns you: 'Do not be deceived: God is not mocked, for whatever one sows, that will he also reap. For the one who sows to his flesh will from the flesh reap corruption, but the one who sows to the Spirit will from the Spirit reap everlasting life' (Gal. 6:7, 8). God knows every secret motive behind every decision you make. He knows when you decide for your own advantage and when you decide righteously.

Every man stands always under the righteous judgments of the Lord. Neither in this life nor in the life to come will you escape the just reward for everything you have done in the body.

God will make a final judgment in the future

Secondly, God will arise some day in the future to offer his final, decisive judgment. The psalmist anticipates this day to come when he concludes with a prayer:

> Rise up, O God!
> Judge the whole earth
> for you possess all nations!
>
> (verse 8).

You may be called 'gods' because of your power to judge other men. You may have an impressive amount of authority over the lives of other humans. But just because you are human, it is inescapable that you will die. As all other princes fall, you too will fall (verse 7). 'It is appointed for man to die once, and after that comes judgment' (Heb. 9:27).

But God is not like a man. He is eternal. He possesses under his control all the peoples of the world. In the end, he will rise up to give sentence. All nations will be gathered before Jesus Christ, and he will exercise judgment over all men.

Don't despair as you see injustice in the world. Instead, pray for the return of Jesus Christ. Pray that the time will come soon for him to manifest his glory in all the earth. For God the Judge judges the judges.

> O quickly come, dread Judge of all;
> For, awful though Thine advent be,
> All shadows from the truth will fall,
> And falsehood die, in sight of Thee:
> O quickly come; for doubt and fear
> Like clouds dissolve when Thou art near.[1]

[1] Lawrence Tuttiett, *Trinity Hymnal*, 1990, No. 322.

Psalm 84
Yearning for God's House

To the chief musician. On the *gittith*. By the sons of Korah. A psalm.

Reader: 1How lovely are your dwellings,
Congr.: Covenant Lord of hosts!

Reader: 2My soul yearns, even faints,
Congr.: for the courts of the Covenant Lord.
Reader: My heart and my flesh cry out
Congr.: for the living God.

Reader: 3Even the sparrow
has found a house,
and the swallow
a nest where she may lay her young:
Congr.: right at your altars, O Covenant Lord
of hosts,
my King and my God.

Reader: 4How blessed are those
who dwell in your house!
Congr.: They will continually praise you.

Reader: 5How blessed is the man
whose strength is in you!

Congr.: In his heart is the highway
to your house.

Reader: 6As they pass through the vale of tears,
they transform it
into a place of springs;
and the autumn rains cover it
with refreshing pools.

Congr.: 7They move forward
from strength to strength;
they all shall appear
before God in Zion.

Reader: 8Covenant LORD, God of hosts,
hear my prayer;

Congr.: please listen,
O God of Jacob.

Selah

Reader: 9Look on our shield,
O God;

Congr.: look sympathetically
on the face of your anointed one.

Reader: 10For better is one day in your courts

Congr.: than a thousand days anywhere else.

Reader: I would choose to be a doorkeeper
in the house of my God

Congr.: rather than to be enclosed
in the tents of wickedness.

Reader: 11 For a sun and a shield
  is the Covenant LORD [our] God.
Grace and glory
  he freely bestows.

Congr.: No good thing will he withhold
  from those who walk in wholehearted
    devotion.

Reader: 12 Covenant LORD of hosts,

Congr.: How blessed is the man
  who trusts in you!

Yearning for God's House—*The Blessings of Worship*

Introduction

As any young scientist twelve years of age or older can tell you, a vacuum yearns to be filled. There is a God-shaped vacuum in every human heart and it yearns to be filled. Over fifteen hundred years ago St Augustine said, 'Our souls are restless until they find their rest in thee.'

The message of Psalm 84 is about the yearning of the heart of God's people for fellowship with him. They have an unquenchable thirst to be in God's house so they can know him as a friend, and be assured of his blessing on their lives. The psalmist understands that God especially blesses all those who come to fellowship in his house.

When you assemble with God's people and sing to his glory, when you present your prayers and your offerings in Jesus' name, when you confess your sin and claim God's forgiveness that comes through Christ's atoning work, when you hear the reading of the word of God and have it applied to your life by a minister of the gospel duly called and ordained, when you celebrate the sacraments of baptism and the Lord's Supper as a concrete way of being confirmed in the blessings of the covenant, you are receiving God's richest blessings that invariably will have significant effects on the whole of your life. For all these reasons and more, you should long to come to God's house.

Consider from this psalm the threefold blessing pronounced on those who worship God in his house. Three times the psalmist says how blessed, how blessed, how blessed are those who worship God in his house (verses 4, 5, 12). First he develops the blessing of being in God's house (verses 1-4). Then he develops the blessing of travelling to God's house (verses 5-7). Finally he explains the blessing of trusting the God who meets you in his house (verses 8-12).

1. The blessing of being in God's house (verses 1-4)

The psalmist begins by describing the yearning that draws his heart towards the house of the Lord. He says:

> How lovely are your dwellings,
> Covenant LORD of hosts!
> My soul yearns, even faints,
> for the courts of the Covenant LORD.
> My heart and my flesh cry out
> for the living God
>
> (verses 1, 2).

'How lovely is your house!' means 'How much I love your house!' The house of God in the Old Testament was the temple that Solomon built. It was the prescribed place where all in Israel, as well as all who were proselytes from other nations, were to come for worship and fellowship with the living God. In the New Testament God's dwelling is not located in one particular place on earth. But there are clear prescriptions about the way in which God will meet with men. 'God is spirit,' said Jesus, 'and those who worship him must worship in spirit and truth' (John 4:24). Not any seeker of God will meet him, but only those who come according to the truth about his nature and in the reality of his Spirit.

Today God's temple is located wherever God's people, as individuals and as an assembly, may be found. The humble body of every believer is the place where his glory dwells (1 Cor. 6:19). Every assembled group of Christians also is the place where he meets with men (Eph. 2:21, 22).

Can you join with the psalmist in affirming that you love God's dwellings? When you meet another believer in the Lord Jesus Christ, do you think to yourself, 'What a lovely person this is! What a blessing he (or she) will be to my life!'?

How beautiful and how beloved is each and every person in whom the Spirit of God dwells! The psalmist says, 'My soul yearns, it faints for the place where God's people assemble. For there with God's people I meet the living God.'

Sometimes Christians get so distracted by the imperfections of other Christians that they miss the blessing of seeing how lovely is every one of the saints remade in God's image. Sometimes the imperfections of the church loom so large in our minds that we overlook the unique opportunity we enjoy of being a part of a community in which God dwells. Is there any other group like this one that knows and worships the living God who dwells in their midst? Is there any other assembly of people that you can attend and expect to have your hunger and thirst for personal fellowship with God satisfied?

'My heart and my flesh cry out,' says the psalmist, 'for the living God.' His desires are not divided between body and spirit. He does not have the cravings of his flesh pulling him one way and the aspirations of his spirit drawing him in another. The whole of his being longs to be in the presence of God and his people. Nothing else in life will satisfy. Nothing else can take the place of personal fellowship with the living God and his people.

More specifically, what is it that you can expect to find in God's house and among God's people? Why is this longing so strong and so persistent?

A place of peace and security

The psalmist uses a simile to describe his expectation:

> Even the sparrow
> has found a house,
> and the swallow
> a nest where she may lay her young:
> right at your altars, O Covenant Lord of hosts,
> my King and my God
>
> (verse 3).

A mother bird soars through the sky scrutinizing the earth, looking for a place of rest where she may build her nest. She seeks a place of solitude and peace where she can lay her eggs, where she can see her young mature without fear of disturbance.

Where is a place of security to be found? Her keen eye lights on the massive brazen altar of Almighty God. There at the point of sacrifice is a place of peace.

At Solomon's temple in Jerusalem, the altar of brass stood out as the most prominent structure of the temple area. On that altar large bulls were slain for the sins of the people. In preparation for this sacrifice, the priest laid his hands upon the animal, symbolizing the transmission of the guilt of the people to the substitutionary sacrifice. The guilt of the people that caused them to deserve death and condemnation was transferred to the beast. The animal was slain on the altar, and so peace was made!

As the sparrow circles the earth it finds one place of secured peace. It is the altar where God and his estranged creation are made into one.

What could be more fitting as a symbol of peace than the altar of God? There the offended God and the rebelling sinner are reconciled. Apparently the psalmist envisages the altar after the sacrifice has been made. Peace has been established, and the birds of the air may come and make their nests in the assurance that they will not be disturbed.

We know now, even as the people understood then, that an offering of bulls and goats never could remove the judgment for sin that man deserves. Otherwise, why would they have kept making the same offerings time and time again? (cf. Heb. 10:1-4, 11). Only the death of Jesus Christ, the Son of God who died in the place of sinners, could make a lasting peace. By pouring out his life-blood he received in himself all the punishment the believing sinner deserves for his sins, and so made peace. The prophet Isaiah says,

> He was wounded for our transgressions,
>   he was crushed for our iniquities;
> upon him was the chastisement that brought us peace,
>   and with his stripes we are healed.

All we like sheep have gone astray.
We have turned every one to his own way;
And the Lord has laid on him the iniquity of us all
(Isa. 53:5, 6).

By coming through faith to the altar where Christ was sacrificed, you can have peace with God. You can know God's blessing on your life.

How lovely are your dwellings, O God of hosts! My soul longs, yes, thirsts for the courts of my God. For in those courts I am assured that I have been reconciled to God.

Many commentators who have read this psalm could not imagine a nest being built safely on an altar where sacrifices were being made. So they have proposed that places around the outer structures of the temple might have existed where birds could build their nest. Just as pigeons persist in roosting around public buildings today, so in ancient Israel birds could be found in the crevices of the temple.

But the 'temple' is not the 'altar,' and the psalmist wants to make a point. There is a place where peace can be found, and that is at the altar where man's causes for offence against God can be removed. There a nesting bird can find God's peaceable hospitality.

Now if God so houses the birds of the air, will he not much more house you, O you of little faith? If nature is reconciled at the altar of sacrifice, cannot you, the sinner, be reconciled at the same place?

See the blessing of being in God's house? It is the place of peace for which your soul yearns. Stir up your heart and your flesh to seek out this place so you can find peace with God. For apart from coming to this altar of the sacrifice of God's Son in the place of sinners, you will find no peace. Only through the death of our Lord Jesus Christ can you be assured of an abundance of peace.

Imagine the ideal holiday spot, the sort of place that you want to go back to again and again. The waves break majestically against the rocky shore. The warm sun beams against your back. The stately lighthouse is firmly planted on its promontory unthreatened by the waters roughing about. It is a place of peace to which the longing to return tugs at your soul even before you are forced to depart.

In a similar way, the psalmist longs for the house of God as a place of peace. His spirit yearns for the calming effect of its blessing. He may be showing a little jealousy for the privileges of the priesthood when he says:

> How blessed are those
>   who dwell in your house!
> They will continually praise you
>
> (verse 4).

The priests had the privilege of dwelling constantly in the Lord's presence, while the psalmist had to be content with visiting the Lord's house only at the prescribed times.

Appreciate the privilege that is yours today. The door of opportunity to come and fellowship with the living God is always open to you. Christ has made all his people priests, and has opened a new and living way that leads directly through the veil separating a holy God from a sinful man. Long for the blessing of being in God's house. For from the blessing of intimate fellowship with God flow all the other blessings of life.

2. The blessing of journeying to God's house (verses 4-7)

The second blessing pronounced by the psalmist is the blessing of journeying towards God's house. You are blessed not only when you are at his house; you will discover blessing even in being on the way. At this point the psalmist apparently sees the pilgrimage of the Israelite to Jerusalem as a picture of the larger pilgrimage of life to the house of God that will be inhabited for eternity. For he includes vivid references to the relief from life's sorrows that come to a man as he journeys towards God's house. The psalmist says:

> How blessed is the man
>   whose strength is in you!
> In his heart is the highway
>   to your house
>
> (verse 5).

Do you sometimes think it is hard to get out to church? Do you find it especially difficult in the summertime to come on Sunday evening as well as Sunday morning? The children are playing contentedly on the patio. Must you go through the wrestling match of cleaning them up and putting on their good clothes a second time?

Compare your situation to the Israelites of old. We don't know much about their weekly worship. But we know that they had a Sabbath day that was observed every week. They consecrated one whole day in seven to the Lord. In addition to this weekly Sabbath, three times a year all males and very often whole families made the long trek to Jerusalem. A week or more they spent worshipping God morning and evening. Living out of a tent, they brought their families daily to the temple of the Lord – and the psalmist says they loved it! They found a special blessing even in anticipating the trip. The psalmist says, 'How blessed are those in whose heart is the highway to your house!' They loved even the prospect of travelling along the highway leading to worship.

Remember that to the ancients a 'highway' was a 'high way'; that is, it was a road lifted above the valleys, the marshes, the rough places that might hinder the traveller. The highway provided a level, unhindered path to the destination.

Travelling to God's house is not all trouble. The way that leads to fellowship with God is not as difficult and as trackless as it may appear. Many saints have gone before to clear the road for later generations. The way to fellowship with God may be straight and narrow, as Jesus said. But it is a highway that brings great enjoyment even in the journeying.

The vale of tears transformed into a place of springs

Notice the particular blessing described by the psalmist as he anticipates his trip to God's city of Jerusalem:

> As they pass through the vale of tears,
> they transform it
> into a place of springs;

and the autumn rains cover it
with refreshing pools

(verse 6).

More than once as you pass through this world you will enter a vale of tears. You will have physical pain, or disappointment in the realm of your career. You will have struggles with other people and their strong opinions. You may have a hard time making ends meet financially and you will weep over the loss of the ones you love.

But if the highway to God is in your heart, you will see the vale of tears transformed into a place of springs. Refreshment will come right out of your deepest trials. God, without any assistance on your part, will send showers that refresh in the midst of your trials.

David the king found himself in the vale of tears more than once. Two of his sons, Absalom and Adonijah, rebelled against him. His servant Shimei had the audacity to curse and mock him when he was fleeing from Absalom. Although God had indicated that he would rule in Israel, Saul kept seeking to kill him. Like a flea in hiding, David had to move from wilderness to cave to village trying to preserve his life.

On one occasion he was huddled in a cave near his home town of Bethlehem. Reminiscing about the past, he wished for a single sip of water from the well of Bethlehem. That night three of his mighty men burst through the garrison of the Philistines. They hurled a bucket down the well, and fled into the darkness splashing water as they went. Just as David began to look for his first cup of morning coffee, the three mighty men presented their prize. David was so overwhelmed that he consecrated the water to the Lord. These men had responded to a simple longing on his part by risking their lives for him.

Surely David's heart must have been lifted far beyond the confines of his cave. The love and loyalty of these men was far more refreshing than water from the well of Bethlehem. God had turned the time of David's trial into a proof of his men's devotion to him. Clearly God would accomplish what he had promised in setting him on the throne.

God lifts the hearts of his people as they journey through the valley of tears, turning it into a place filled with surprising springs and refreshing pools. He uses the saints as his source of encouragement for those in need. But when water cannot be brought by men, the Lord himself will send rain from heaven.

Going from strength to strength

The all-encompassing promise of God's provision for those journeying to his house is stated in verse 7:

> They move forward
>   from strength to strength;
> they all shall appear
>   before God in Zion
>
> (verse 7).

God's people in their journey to worship do not move from strength to weakness. They move from strength to strength. The trip will not wear them out. Instead, as they get closer to the place of eternal fellowship with God, they will anticipate even more eagerly what God has prepared for them. This experience will characterize them all. For it is certain that 'They all shall appear before God in Zion.'

Set your heart on the journey to God's house. Not only the being there but the going there will be a blessing. With great expectations launch the lifelong quest for fellowship with God and his people that alone can satisfy the soul.

There is a blessing in being at God's house. There is a blessing in journeying to God's house. Finally there is a blessing in trusting the God who receives you into his house.

3. The blessing of trusting the God who receives you into his house (verses 8-12)

The anointed one

If you had been an Israelite at worship, your attention would have focused on two people, two anointed ones of the Lord. The king, with his crown, and the high priest, with his turban, would have caught your attention. The psalmist recognizes the central role they played in worship when he focuses his prayer on them:

> Look on our shield,
> O God;
> look sympathetically
> on the face of your anointed one
>
> (verse 9).

It is impossible to tell whether the psalmist refers to the priest as he was interceding for the people of God or to the king who had a leading role in the people's worship. Both of these figures were anointed by the Lord and would have been obvious by their presence at the temple. But from a New Testament perspective, it is clear who this anointed one is. He is the Son of God, anointed by the Father to fulfil the roles of both priest and king. He is Jesus the Christ, who lived among men that he might provide a way of access to God.

God has anointed him. God has sent him into the world. So we know that God is someone who desires to be approached through him. His Son, the Lord Jesus Christ, now functions as God's High Priest at the right hand of the Father as well as ruling King of his elect nation.

Join your prayers to the plea of the psalmist: 'Look sympathetically on the face of your anointed one.' Your prayers may be weak, but his intercessions are strong. As he prays for you in your weakness, you may be assured that God will hear him.

Blessings for the whole of life

No wonder God's people love to come and worship. As the psalmist says:

> For better is one day in your courts
> than a thousand days anywhere else.
> I would choose to be a doorkeeper
> in the house of my God

rather than to be enclosed
  in the tents of wickedness

(verse 10).

A thousand days is almost three years. Yet the psalmist means what he says. He would rather spend one day in the house of the Lord than three years on the beach. He would rather have one day in the courts of the Lord than a thousand days in the cool shade of the mountains. Why? He explains:

For a sun and a shield
  is the Covenant LORD [our] God.
Grace and glory
  he freely bestows

(verse 11).

God is both a sun and a shade. In himself are blessings better than the beach or the mountains. He provides blessing and protection for all of life. Grace and glory come freely from Jesus Christ every day we are in fellowship with him.

Conclusion

The psalmist concludes by pointing out just how great is the blessing of those who trust in him:

No good thing will he withhold
  from those who walk in wholehearted devotion.
Covenant LORD of hosts,
  how blessed is the man
    who trusts in you!

(verses 11, 12).

Your God may withhold some things from you. But he will withhold nothing that is for your good.

How blessed is the man who trusts in the Lord! Make it the principal longing of your life to be in God's house, to journey to God's house and to trust in the God who welcomes you into his eternal house.

Psalm 87
Born Again in Zion

By the sons of Korah. A psalm. A song.

1st Reader: 1His foundation
Congr.: is in the holy mountains.

1st Reader: 2The Covenant LORD loves the gates of Zion
Congr.: above all the dwellings of Jacob.

1st Reader: 3Glorious things are spoken of you,
Congr.: O city of God:
Selah

2nd Reader: 4'I will remember Rahab and Babylon
among those who know me [in love].
Behold! Philistia and Tyre with Cush—
each of these was born there.'

1st Reader: 5For of Zion it shall be said:
2nd Reader: 'This one and that one was born in her.'
1st Reader: For the Most High himself—
Congr.: he shall establish her.

1st Reader: 6The LORD of the Covenant shall recall when
he records the peoples:

2nd Reader: 'This one was born there.'

Selah

1st Reader: 7Both the vocalists and the instrumentalists
[will attest]:

Choir: 'All my outpourings originate in you.'

Born Again in Zion—
A Missionary Psalm

Introduction

This missionary psalm celebrates the conversion of the heathen. It magnifies God's glory as the King on Mount Zion whose good and gracious domain reaches to all the nations of the world. 'Being born in Zion' is the image used to depict the conversion of nations whose inhabitants become citizens of the heavenly kingdom that now is manifest on earth.

God's covenant with David centred on two promises: the permanent establishment of God's throne in Jerusalem, and the permanent maintenance of David's line on the throne. This psalm concentrates on the first of these promises. God will maintain his lordship from Mount Zion in Jerusalem, the city of David.

The first half of the psalm identifies the place of God's rule (verses 1-3). The second half of the psalm presents the people of God's rule (verses 4-6). The last verse records the testimony of the worship-leaders in Israel about the inspiration they derive from the glorious place where God has determined that he shall be worshipped (verse 7).

1. The place of God's rule (verse 1-3)

> His foundation
> is in the holy mountains (verse 1).

The opening statement of this psalm makes no effort to identify the 'his' of whom the psalmist speaks. Yet in context the pronoun must refer to God. This unidentified 'his' makes the probing mind more aware of the fact that 'God's' foundation is located in the holy mountains.

In Jerusalem God laid a solid foundation in this world from which his work could spread to the four corners of the earth. The ark of the covenant, symbolizing God's throne on earth, had trekked aimlessly through the desert for forty years. For a time it sat neglected in Shiloh, and then was captured by the hands of the unholy Philistines. Only under David did it finally come to rest in the city of Jerusalem. An established foundation for the throne of God on earth meant that his saving kingdom could begin its worldwide spread from a central base of operation.

Geographically, nothing makes Jerusalem the centre of things. All roads do not lead to Jerusalem. Even today this significant city has no major airport.

But God's 'foundation' was established there among the consecrated mountains. The 'mountains' refer to the complex of hills constituting Jerusalem and its environs. Abraham offered Isaac in this vicinity and David built his palace there. Here Solomon constructed his temple and Nehemiah came back to survey this site and no other. At this place Jesus Christ consecrated himself as the Lamb of God that takes away the sin of the world. Outside the gates of this same city he was crucified and raised from the dead to deliver men from their sins. For hundreds of years these mountains were consecrated as the holy ones, for God himself centralized his work in the world on this foundation.

But today the base of the holy mountain of heaven touches down here and here and also over there. The centre of his kingdom is not restricted to Jerusalem, or to any other earthly mountain (cf. John 4:21). Wherever he pours out his Holy Spirit to empower the truth, there God dwells. God has established his foundation for working in the world right in this place, wherever it is, that his Son and his truth are honoured.

The supremacy of Zion

> The Covenant LORD loves the gates of Zion
> above all the dwellings of Jacob.
>
> (verse 2)

Many places in Palestine were special to the saints of old. Jacob laid his head on a stone and saw a ladder reaching to heaven. He called the place Beth-el, for it was the gate to God's house. But God loves the gates of Zion more. At Shiloh God first set up his tabernacle in Palestine, and in Lebanon stood the mighty 'cedars of God.' But Shiloh and the cedars of Lebanon must prostrate themselves before the greater gates of Zion, for God loves it more. Then there was Bashan, where the rich pasturelands fattened the cows, and Hermon, where the morning dew laid heavy. But Bashan's cows must be sacrificed in Jerusalem and the blessing of Hermon's dew must rest on Zion, for there the Lord commands the blessing, even life for evermore.

In distinction from other special places, Zion alone was designated the 'city of our God.' At this place God's people consecrated themselves to him. They brought their hearts as living sacrifices to the Lord. They sang the songs of Zion. They rejoiced in God, the mighty Saviour who delivered them at the very gates of Zion from armies like the invading Assyrians.

Today God shows his sovereignty in many places in the world. He works among the governors of the nations, bringing some down and raising others up. He works on university campuses confirming his truth despite the atheistic denials of the intelligentsia. He works on the Stock Exchange making some rich and others poor.

But above all other places God loves the locations where his people assemble to consecrate their hearts to him. He loves the place where saints and sinners assemble to seek his forgiveness and blessing.

> Glorious things are spoken of you,
> O city of God. *Selah*
>
> (verse 3).

Many cities of the world, ancient and modern, have been glorified in the eyes of men. Each has its own 'claim to fame': Athens through its philosophy; Rome through its military might; Moscow through the vastness of its domain; Paris through the arts; London through culture and language; Washington through democratic initiative.

But Zion is more glorious than them all, and excels each even in its own area of strength. God's city possesses a better philosophy that makes folly of the wisdom of the wise. It displays a more beautiful, more skilful art in the final design of the temple of God, made of living stones. It offers a better democracy for its citizens in the glorious liberty of the sons of God. It houses a stronger military force in the heavenly host, prepared every moment to bring Christ's kingdom of righteousness to earth whenever the Father indicates that the hour has come.

The glories of Zion have regularly been the theme of the songs of God's people. One familiar hymn declares:

> Glorious things of thee are spoken,
> Zion, city of our God;
> He whose word cannot be broken
> Formed thee for His own abode:
> On the Rock of Ages founded
> What can shake thy sure repose?
> With salvation's walls surrounded,
> Thou may'st smile at all thy foes.
>
> Saviour, if of Zion's city
> I, through grace, a member am,
> Let the world deride or pity,
> I will glory in Thy name:
> Fading is the worldling's pleasure,
> All his boasted pomp and show;
> Solid joys and lasting treasures
> None but Zion's children know.[1]

The man who wrote this expanded paraphrase of Psalm 87 was John Newton, once a drunkard who lived a life of debauchery. As a brutal slave-trader, he epitomized the worst of the scum of the earth. But God by his grace saved him. No wonder he could write

[1] *Trinity Hymnal*, 1990, No. 345.

so gloriously of the grace of God that comes from Mount Zion, the heavenly Jerusalem.

Is that your experience? Can you speak glorious things of the city of God? The second part of this psalm describes the people that make up the citizenry of this great city.

2. The people of God's rule (verses 4-6)

A king's domain is defined most significantly by the people he rules. It would be mockery to present a king without a people. Now look closely at the people ruled by the Lord from his royal city of Jerusalem. For the composition of the citizenry of the divine city is full of surprises:

> 'I will remember Rahab and Babylon
> among those who know me [in love].
> Behold! Philistia and Tyre with Cush—
> each of these was born there.'
> For of Zion it shall be said:
> 'This one and that one were born in her'
> (verses 4, 5).

The psalmist mentions first Rahab, which is Egypt (cf. Isa. 30:7). A nation guilty of attempted genocide, drowning the infant seed of God in the Nile—this nation will be born again in Zion. Next comes Babylon. The Israelite dreaded that name. Babylon epitomizes the essence of Antichrist, both in the Old Testament and the New. Yet the psalmist joyfully proclaims that this one and that one from Babylon will be born in Zion. They will be a part of the family of God. Then there is Philistia. This neighbouring nation served as Israel's thorn in the flesh. Like a cur nipping at the heels, the Philistines constantly harassed God's people. Yet the citizens of Philistia will become fully participating fellow-heirs in the kingdom of God.

Obviously membership in God's kingdom will not be restricted to pure-bred Israelites, descendants of the twelve tribes of Israel. Furthermore, heinous sins of the past need not necessarily keep a person out of the kingdom. If citizenship in the kingdom of

God hinged on the good natures of men, where would God find members for his kingdom? All men by nature are alienated, depraved sinners.

But by the glorious transformation of the new birth, men become new creatures, subject to rule by the Christ of God. From every tribe, kindred, nation and people a great multitude, reborn by God's Spirit, constitutes the citizenry of Mount Zion. How anyone could define the people of God as a racial community in the light of this psalm is a great mystery. Egypt and Babylon are listed among those who love the Lord of the Covenant. Philistia, Tyre and Cush are identified as native-born citizens of the divine city. All these ancient enemies of God's people now are treated as a part of the elect community. The New Testament states the same truth in its own way.

The apostle Paul, a 'Hebrew of the Hebrews,' unites all the people of God into one new race by indicating that common to us all is the fact that Jerusalem is 'our mother' (Gal. 4:26).

What does Paul mean when he says the heavenly Jerusalem is mother of all who are in Christ? He means that the Old Testament image of a locale for God's dwelling on earth has been replaced by the new covenant reality. The right hand of the Father, from which Christ reigns over heaven and earth, has become the highly exalted Mount Zion, from which the Spirit of God has been poured out over all flesh. This Spirit sent from the Son regenerates first this one and then that one, first a Gentile and then a Jew. But the new birth from above makes them brothers in the family of God, citizens in the heavenly kingdom come to earth. The origin of the new birth in the heavenly Jerusalem guarantees the universal character of the kingdom and the indissoluble unity of its citizens.

This Zion the Lord of the Covenant loves. This Zion fulfils the design for a renewed mankind that has been the covenanted purpose of God since the fall of mankind.

For two thousand years the church of Jesus Christ has been a mission-minded community, reaching across social, cultural, economic and racial barriers. May it ever be so. The church will have lost her identity as the city loved of God if she ever loses her zeal for reaching the whole world for Christ. Even the most hateful enemies of the cross can be reconciled to God, born again of his Spirit, and made fully-fledged members of his brotherhood.

> The LORD of the Covenant shall recall when he
> records the peoples:
> 'This one was born there'
>
> (verse 6).

Is your name recorded on the roll of the church? It should be if you have been born again of God's Spirit. The public testimony of the church on earth should correspond to the record of the roll of God in heaven.

3. The testimony of the worship-leaders

> Both the vocalists and the instrumentalists [will attest]:
> 'All my outpourings originate in you'
>
> (verse 7).

Musicians need inspiration. The soul must be stirred by some grand theme.

What theme could be greater than the rebirth of nations that occurs in Mount Zion? This lofty vision is sufficient in itself to inspire a lifetime of great music. As the vocalists and instrumentalists attest, 'All my outpourings originate in you.' The theme of alien nations born into the kingdom of God provides enough inspiration to last through the generations.

Conclusion

Many great cities have arisen in the history of humanity. Each one has distinguished itself by its own leading characteristics. But Zion, the city of God, is known in history as the city of the rebirth of humanity. In this heavenly city descended to earth men of all nations come together as God's people to worship him. From this place and that place, from this circumstance and that circumstance men assemble to give glory to God. Kneeling before the Creator, humbly confessing their sins before their Redeemer, bringing their offerings to the Lord of heaven and earth, they give glory to God. All who have been born again of God's Spirit gladly join in the testimony of the instrumentalists and the vocalists: 'All our inspiration comes from you.' For no vision is so great as the city of God filled to overflowing with a population reborn from all the nations of the world.

Psalm 91

Abiding Safely in His Presence

1st Reader: 1 He who settles down
in the secret place of God most high
will abide
under the shadow of Shaddai.

2 I will say of the LORD of the Covenant,
All: 'My refuge and my fortress—my God!
I trust him.'

1st Reader: 3 For he shall deliver you
from the lure of the ambush,
from the lethal pestilence.

1st Congr.: 4 With his feathers
he will envelop you,
2nd Congr.: and under his wings
you will trust.
1st Reader: His truth will be
your shield and your tower for
defence.

5 You will have no fear
1st Congr.: for the terror
of night,

2nd Congr.: for the arrow that flies
by day;
1st Congr.: 6 for the plague that stalks
in thick darkness,
2nd Congr.: for the destruction that devastates
at noonday.

1st Congr.: 7 A thousand
will fall at your side,
2nd Congr.: a horde
at your right hand;
1st Reader: but it will not even come near you.

1st Congr.: 8 Only with your eyes
will you behold;
2nd Congr.: the recompense of the wicked
you will see.

1st Reader: 9 Because the Covenant LORD, my refuge,
you have firmly set
as God most high, your dwelling-place,

1st Congr.: 10 you will never suffer
evil;
2nd Congr.: and a plague
will not come near your tent.

1st Reader: 11 For he will command his messengers
about you,
to keep you in all your ways;

12 in their hands they will lift you up
so that you will not bruise your foot
against a stone.

1st Congr.: 13 On the lion and the cobra
you will tread;
2nd Congr.: you will trample
the young lion and the snake.

2nd Reader: 14 'Because he has focused his desire on me,
I will rescue him;
I will make him inaccessible
because he has known my name.

15 'He will call on me,
and I will answer him.
I will be with him
in distress;
I will deliver him
and glorify him.

16 'With long life
I will satisfy him;
and I will make him see
my salvation.'

Abiding Safely in His Presence—*Safety through Trusting God*

Introduction

This psalm provides great assurance to the believer that the Lord will protect him from aggressive enemies. The promise is not merely of deliverance from trouble in general, but more particularly of safety from opposition that attempts to destroy the believer.

No heading indicates the author or circumstance that inspired the composition of this psalm. Its origins remain unknown, but its truth applies to all ages. Since the coming of Jesus Christ, the great protector of his people, believers can derive even greater confidence from the certainty of the Lord's protection.

This psalm emphasizes the importance of trusting God, since the Lord takes great delight in protecting the people who rely on him. As you look to him in view of the various dangers that threaten your life, you will experience his deliverance from every disaster.

Abiding in the secret place

> He who settles down
> in the secret place of God Most High
> will abide
> under the shadow of Shaddai [the Mighty One]
> (verse 1).

This 'settling down' in the secret place of God Most High involves meditation, prayer and a transfer of trust from your own resources to the provisions for life that come from the Lord. With God Most High, a title depicting the Lord in his most exalted position, you can abide. You can settle down into a living union with the great and glorious God. Jesus Christ made this seeming impossibility attainable when he said, 'Abide in me' (John 15:4). The eternal Son of God has come into the world so that finite men may live in unbroken union with the infinite God. Sinners may commune constantly with him in the intimacy of his secret place.

But where is this 'secret place' of God Most High? Where is he to be found if his abode is characterized as 'secret'? His 'secret place,' from an Old Covenant perspective, is probably to be identified with the Holy of Holies. In this consecrated place, hidden from the eyes of men, the infinite God took up residence among his people. The 'secret place' is that holy chamber behind the curtain through which the limited light of the seven-branched candlestick penetrated only dimly. The high priest alone could enter this 'secret place,' only once a year. For there the Lord dwelt in his glory among the gilded images of the heavenly cherubim.

But how is it possible that the everyday saint could expect to 'settle down' in this 'secret place' of the exalted God Most High?

First of all, the believer could dwell in this holy place vicariously. Through the presence of the high priest he was present. By the blood of the lamb sprinkled on the mercy-seat behind the veil he entered the Most Holy Place. In a very real sense he was there, for the blood of the lamb was viewed as though it were his own blood.

Secondly, the ordinary saint of God could remain permanently in God's holy presence by an abiding trust in the Lord. Through trusting the divine promise for protection he could continue in the care of the Omnipresent One wherever life's journey might take him. Just as a mother would not forsake her nursing infant, so the Lord will not abandon those who implicitly trust in him.

The shadow of the Almighty

Your confidence today can be even greater than that of the saints of the Old Covenant era. By the coming of Jesus the Christ, a new and living way into the protecting presence of the Lord has been opened. By a constant reliance on the blood of Jesus Christ you can settle down permanently in the Lord's secret place. Having been justified by faith, you now live every day at peace with God. As a result, you can abide under the 'shadow of Shaddai.' What is this 'shadow of Shaddai'?

Shadows mean much more to people in Palestine than in many other parts of the world. I can remember standing along a desert road south of Beersheba, waiting for the last bus of the day. It was winter and the sun was setting. As I looked southward, my face broiled on one side from direct exposure to the sun's rays. But the other side of my face felt the chill of the desert's cold that came with the nightfall. The extremes of heat and cold in the Middle East make shade or shelter a precious commodity.

The 'Mighty One,' Shaddai himself, takes on the role of protective shadow for those who trust him. The Lord moves along with his people, wherever they might go, to shield them from the incessant rays of an oppressive sun.

The God whom we trust

> I will say of the LORD of the Covenant,
> 'My Refuge and my Fortress—my God!
> I trust him.'
>
> (verse 2).

Consider the wealth of characterization concerning God summarized in these two opening verses! A total of six names reveal the nature of the one true living God. Even the general name for God is personalized by the attached pronoun: 'my God.' This God is shown to be of a totally different character from the gods worshipped by the heathen:

God Most High contrasts with a god absorbed in the creation.

The Mighty One (*Shaddai*) contrasts with a god powerless to intervene.

Yahveh, the unchanging LORD of the Covenant, contrasts with a god who has no oathbound commitment to his people.

Refuge contrasts with a god who abandons men to their own devices.

Fortress contrasts with a god who has no power to protect.
Elohim contrasts with a god who does not even exist.

But the psalmist will not merely tell about this great God. He must add his own testimonial. 'I trust him,' he says. 'I encourage you to do no more than I do myself. I put the totality of my life into his hands,' echoing the sentiments of Job: 'Though he slay me, I will hope in him' (Job 13:15).

If you wish to help others experience the reality of this God's greatness, you must step forward in faith yourself. Every day, with every problem you face, you must manifest unbroken trust in his good purposes. Only then will you communicate to others the blessings that come from trusting him.

This trust will be tested and tried. God tested Job by removing every material blessing. He tested Abraham by directing him to offer up Isaac. Because both men trusted God through their trial, the outcome was a glorious confirmation of the gospel, and a manifestation of the power of God to place fallen man in a more secure position even than that of man as created in innocence.

Trusting God is the great thing. It is the watershed of life. All worry and anxiety, all frustration and impatience and all fear to move forward with firm commitment come from failure to trust God.

Contrariwise, a realistic perspective on life comes from trusting God. Consider him in all his various aspects as the fortress into which you can run, as the Mighty One who provides protection, as the God who has bound himself to you by a solemn oath of the covenant. As the psalmist trusts him, you must trust him.

Deliverance from dangers

For he shall deliver you
  from the lure of the ambush,
  from the lethal pestilence

(verse 3).

Throughout this psalm, the 'you' is singular. Having given his own testimony of faith, the psalmist turns to challenge his readers individually to put his trust in God as he has done.

Those who will trust God are promised deliverance from two kinds of dangers: from the plottings of men and from the curses of nature. Nehemiah's enemies constantly attempted to lure him into the temple so they could kill him, but his courageous faith in the Lord delivered him. Paul escaped the murderous schemes of the Jews only because the Lord forewarned him.

You often don't know when schemers may be planning against you. While travelling by bus to Beersheba, a very polite Bedouin invited me to spend the evening in his tent. I was all ready to accept his hospitality, even though in retrospect it may have been a foolish thing to do. But as we got off at the station, I noticed through the crowd that he was whispering to a seedy-looking fellow and gesturing in my direction. That was enough for me. God knows the plots of men. He will deliver you from the lure of the ambush.

Plagues often are the instruments of the Lord in judging the heathen. God plagued the Egyptians and sent pestilence to destroy the army of Assyria. But the Lord will deliver those who trust him from the lethal pestilence. Christians often appear immune to the plagues that come on others, even as the Lord made a distinction between the Israelites and the Egyptians during the plagues sent through Moses.

But what about the times when Christians are ill with influenza or heart disease and die from cancer or AIDS? Consider Christ and the way the plots of his enemies ultimately took him to the cross.

In such trying times it is necessary to trust God all the more. For he makes everything beautiful in its time (Eccles. 3:11). Even the death of his saints is precious in the eyes of the Lord (Psa. 116:15). As Jesus said to his enemies, 'You would have no authority over me at all unless it had been given you from above' (John 19:11). For the one who trusts God, the sting of death is taken away even though death is not taken away. The tragic nature of the trial is removed, even though the trial itself is not removed.

Trust him. His word is true. Even though you walk through the valley of the shadow of death, you need not fear any evil.

Protection

With his feathers
  he will enclose you,
and under his wings
  you will trust.
His truth will be
  your shield and your tower for defence
(verse 4).

A baby chick snuggles under the warmth of the wings of the mother hen. A child curls up like a ball in a blanket. Even grown-ups seek the comfort of a place to snuggle up in safety. The Lord offers himself as a source of living consolation for his people. The Holy Spirit is called the 'Comforter' because he is sent by the Son to enter the deepest recesses of the soul and calm the believer's worst apprehensions.

God also fulfils the role of a shield and a tower for defence in a time of war. No other instrument of defence could ward off the determined assaults of an enemy. His truth shields the one who trusts in him. The slanders of Satan cannot penetrate the truth of God so as to harm the person who has been redeemed from sin by the blood of Christ.

You will have no fear
  for the terror
    of night,
  for the arrow that flies
    by day;
  for the plague that stalks
    in thick darkness,
  for the destruction that devastates
    at noonday
(verses 5, 6).

Terror and plague stalk under the cover of darkness, while a strong and self-confident enemy may initiate a frontal assault in the brilliance of daylight. But it is all in vain. The one trusting in the Lord has no fear.

If you are moved by fear, take a moment to rehearse the promises of protection found in God's word. If you trust in Christ for your salvation, then God views you as the object of his special love. For that reason alone, you should not fear the dangers that may threaten.

> A thousand
>   will fall at your side,
> a horde
>   at your right hand;
>   but it will not even come near you.
> Only with your eyes
>   will you behold;
> the recompense of the wicked
>   you will see
>
> (verses 7, 8).

The fate of the wicked appears in sharpest contrast to the destiny of the righteous. They fall by the thousands. Standing right next to the believer, they keel over, struck down in an instant.

The tragedies that befall the wicked should not be surprising. Whatever a man sows, that will he also reap. The Lord repays the wicked according to what they deserve. But the avenging wrath of the Lord never comes near the righteous. Even their tragedies turn to triumphs.

A personal testimony

> Because the Covenant LORD, my refuge,
>   you have firmly set
>   as God most high, your dwelling-place …
>
> (verse 9).

Who is this 'I,' this person who declared earlier with such definitiveness, '*I* trust him' (verse 2)? Who is it that now speaks so confidently of '*my refuge*' (verse 9)? Obviously it is the psalmist himself who speaks. But could he be the king of Israel who provides this model of trust for his people? Or might it be a priest or prophet presiding over the worship service who interjects his personal testimony?

Very likely this distinctive individual is an anointed office holder among God's people, whether he be prophet, priest or king. The anointed one of the Lord encourages his people to trust the LORD of the Covenant just as he has done.

In a climactic way, the writer to the Hebrews presents the model of Christ as one who put himself in a position of having to trust the Lord. Since the people he came to save partook of flesh and blood, Christ took on the same (Heb. 2:14). Since he trusted God through all his trials, he can encourage his 'brothers' to do the same (Heb. 2:12, 13). Can you imagine it? Christ, the glorious Son of God, brought himself to the point of having to trust God through the severest of trials. He persevered in faith despite the rejections of men. In the end, the Lord gloriously vindicated him.

> You will never suffer
>   evil;
>   and a plague
> will not come near your tent
>
> (verse 10).

The temporary, tent-dwelling lifestyle of the people of God exposes them to all kinds of trials. They are strangers in a strange land, foreigners and pilgrims having no abiding city. But the Lord promises security even as they dwell in their fragile, temporal structures. No permanent harm will come to them.

Angelic protection

> For he will solemnly charge his angels about you
>   to keep you in all your ways;
> in their hands they will lift you up
>   so that you will not bruise your foot against a stone
>
> (verses 11, 12).

Earlier the psalmist had compared the care of the Lord to the protection provided by the mother hen who gathers her chicks under her wings. Now he notes that powerful angelic messengers are given a solemn charge to protect them. The support provided by the Lord for his people will correspond to their particular situation. If comfort is the current need, the Holy Spirit will be their 'Comforter.' If the strength of an enemy terrorizes God's little flock, then powerful messengers sent from God's throne will intervene. He has given to his angelic host a permanent charge. They must protect all those who trust in the Lord.

Contrary to the popular notion, Scripture does not teach that each believer has been assigned a single 'guardian angel' charged with protecting him or her. Obviously the protection of a single one of these powerful creatures would be enough. It took only one angel to bring God's judgment on 185,000 Assyrian troops camped outside the gates of Jerusalem (Isa. 37:36). But the psalmist indicates that the Lord has charged his 'angels' (plural) to protect his people from the slightest calamity. The whole angelic force has been assigned the task of protecting each of God's saints from harm. They are always there, even though the physical eye cannot see them. They were apparent to Elisha because of his faith, though the doubting Gehazi could not perceive them until his master prayed that his eyes be opened (2 Kings 6:16, 17).

These servants are commanded to preserve God's people so that they do not even bruise their foot against a stone. In modern urban culture, bruising the foot is a rare thing. Pavements, streets, malls and tiled floors virtually have eliminated the peril of stones in the pathway. But in biblical days, stumbling-stones lay on the hillside, across the fields, wherever a person turned. Walking in the pitch-black darkness of night without a light always was a perilous thing, but hardly could be avoided.

But God commissioned his angels to protect his people from these everyday calamities. Just as the servant of a king might delight in providing appropriate aid to a youthful heir apparent, so the angels of God stand alert, ready to lift God's people out of the reach of impending calamity.

Yet there is obviously a tension associated with these assurances. Christians often are involved in road accidents. They get scratches on their bumpers and bruises on their bodies. How, then, should this promise be understood?

First of all, appreciate the many times you are protected by the Lord from dangers and calamities. You have a near accident, but God's grace spares you. The doctor is apprehensive, but your baby is born healthy and whole. Who can know the number of times that you are spared from many troubles? Without your being aware of what is happening, God's angels are guarding you in all your ways.

Secondly, learn to trust the good providence of God in spite of the calamity you undergo. Joseph went down into prison, but it was in order that he might save many lives. Paul struggled with a 'thorn in the flesh' that would not go away, but it served a good purpose in keeping him humble.

Have you ever lain in bed with an illness and thanked God for a day off? Just when you felt the need for a little break, the Lord put you on your back. An enforced time for quietness, meditation and the reading of God's word was exactly what you needed.

Trust God in the difficult times. His powerful angels are guarding you against harm 'in all your ways.' In time you will see that it was all for your good.

Thirdly, learn not to put God to the test when you are the one being tried. In one of his temptations, Christ was transported by the devil to the pinnacle of the temple. If he would cast himself off its lofty edge, the angels of God surely would swoop down to protect him from harm. By engineering this spectacular intervention by the Lord's protecting angels, Christ could be fairly sure that the people would take him directly to the throne and crown him as their king. To lure Christ into this action, the devil quotes this very psalm, which affirms that the Lord will charge his angels to keep him from bruising his foot against a stone (Psa. 91:11, 12).

But Satan fails to quote the very next verse of this same psalm:

> On the lion and the cobra
>   you will tread;
>   you will trample
> the young lion and the snake (verse 13).

That old serpent, the devil, has no interest in hearing that God's people will tread on the cobra and trample on the snake. But he will experience that trampling nonetheless. Jesus responds to the devil's temptation by quoting God's admonition to Israel that they were not to put him to the test when he was testing them (Deut. 6:16). By rejecting Satan's suggestion that he seek the crown without the cross, Jesus turns his trial into a triumph.

God has assigned to his holy, powerful angels the task of guarding his elect people. But the confidence that comes from this assurance must never lead a person to test the Lord at the time of his testing. The struggle with Satan and the evil in this world is a very real struggle, and the cost of serving God in this present age is to 'fill up that which is lacking in Christ's afflictions' (Col. 1:24). So although divine protection is assured the believer, he must not yield to the temptation to expect freedom from trials in this life, or put God to the test by complaining when he is tried.

The promises of God

'Because he has focused his desire on me,
    I will rescue him;
    I will make him inaccessible
because he has known my name'

(verse 14).

For the first time God himself speaks in this psalm. In the opening verses, the person being threatened affirmed, 'I trust him' (verse 2). Now God responds to this earlier affirmation: 'Because he trusts me …' The person in need who focuses his trust on the Lord will be made inaccessible to all harm.

'He will call on me,
    and I will answer him.
I will be with him
    in distress;
I will deliver him
    and glorify him.

With a long life
I will satisfy him;
and I will make him see
my salvation'

(verses 15, 16).

God will deliver the person in distress who calls on him. But beyond mere deliverance, the God of all glory will glorify the one who relies on him. The person who knows the Lord will not barely escape danger. He will be brought to immeasurable glory. Instead of being brought to an early grave by his troubles, he will be satisfied with long life. He will see with his own eyes the salvation of the Lord.

Conclusion

The people who trust in God will experience many trials. On some occasions the Lord will honour their trust and intervene immediately. But even when the trial involves prolonged suffering, divine grace will lead to glory. So, 'As you have received Christ Jesus the Lord [by faith], so walk in him [by faith]' (Col. 2:6).

Psalm 95

Worshipping God Your Rock

1st Reader: 1 Come,
let us sing
to the Covenant LORD;

Congr.: let us shout
to the Rock of our salvation.

1st Reader: 2 Let us hasten before him
with thanksgiving;

Congr.: with songs
let us shout to him.

1st Reader: 3 For a great God
is the Covenant LORD,

Congr.: and a great King
over all gods,

1st Reader: 4 who has in his hand
the unsearchable deeps of the earth,

Congr.: and the peaks of the mountains
are his.

1st Reader: 5 To him belongs the sea,
for he made it;

Congr.: and the dry land,
for his hands formed it.

1st Reader: 6Come,
let us worship
and bow down;

Congr.: let us kneel
before the Covenant Lord our Maker.

1st Reader: 7For he
is our God,

Congr.: and we
are the people of his pasture
and the flock of his hand.

1st Reader: 8Today, if you will obey his voice,
do not harden your heart
as at Meribah,
as in the day of Massah in the wilderness.

2nd Reader: 9When
your fathers tried me;
they tested me
and they saw my work.
10For forty years I was disgusted
with that generation
And I said,
'A people erring of heart
are they;
and they
do not know my ways.'
11To whom I swore in my wrath:
'They shall never enter my rest.'

Worshipping God Your Rock—*Worship God Rather than Hardening Your Heart*

Introduction

The world today has lost its concept of God. It has lost its sense of the greatness, the glory and the unchangeable character of God. The consequences of this loss of the reality of God are massive.

First of all, stability evaporates when people lose contact with God. Once the reality of God is lost, everything about human existence comes to be in a state of flux. Moral standards become unstable if God does not determine the difference between right and wrong. A proper balance in priorities among work, family and obligations to society cannot be achieved if man's Creator has become absent from his life.

Secondly, all sense of accountability disappears when people lose a sense of God. Coupled with the loss of accountability is the loss of integrity. If God will not bring every work into judgment with every secret thought, then no ultimate accountability for the things people do can be maintained.

Thirdly, if God has been lost, then all sense of true acceptance is lost. God is love, which means that he is the source and sustainer of all true love. If a person is not sure that the eternal God has fully accepted him or her, then no other apparent manifestations of love will be permanently convincing.

Now today, hear the life-giving word of God that can fill the vacuum created by the loss of God in the world. Hear as God calls you to worship him, the great Creator, the great Redeemer, the Unchanging One. You have no need for someone to prove the reality of God to you. Your very nature as man made in God's image convinces you that God is real. As you are confronted with the voice of God speaking directly to you through this psalm, don't expect him to communicate his reality in abstract philosophical ideas. Instead, expect him to speak to you in practical ways, calling you to reorientate your life in the light of his reality. Remove your shoes from off your feet, for the place where you are standing is holy ground.

Three points about worshipping God are developed in this psalm: the meaning of worship; the manner of worship; and the reasons for worship.

These insights on worship crystallize in the form of an admonition: 'Worship God your Rock rather than rebelling against his word, so that you may enter his eternal rest.'

1. The meaning of worship

Worship means bowing down, kneeling, acknowledging God to be the Creator of the world. The psalmist says, 'Come, let us bow down in worship, let us kneel before the Lord our Maker' (verse 6). In its essence, worship means unconditional surrender. Unconditional surrender means withholding nothing whatsoever. It means that the person's control of himself and his properties is forfeited without any qualifying condition. It means yielding to your Creator everything you are and have. Your possessions, your health, your career are acknowledged to be God's to order as he will, even apart from your ongoing consent.

When the Communists assaulted Indochina, they came in nondescript masses. Only the recruits in the foremost ranks bore weapons for warfare. The remaining troops followed into battle without arms, planning to pick up the weapons of their comrades as they fell before them. If the hopeless cause of worldwide Communism could inspire such total surrender of life, how could God's call to worship him involve anything less in terms of total submission?

For young people who still have their lives before them, worship means surrendering career plans to God unconditionally. God cannot be expected to honour a certain timetable in the achievement of goals. Personal plans must yield to his. Wherever he would have you to go, you must go. Genuine worship of Almighty God means unconditional surrender of life-plans to him.

This call to unconditional surrender does not address only the younger generation. One of the greatest untapped resources of the church today is the growing community of the retired. People of maturing age have accumulated the wisdom of years, and consequently have a greater stewardship to discharge before the Lord. For God never recognizes a time for simply sitting back and coasting through life. No, God continually calls to unconditional surrender. In life's maturity you have a special obligation to re-evaluate the possibilities of your service to God. Before beginning that analysis, the commitment must be made. Whatever he wants you to do, that you must be prepared to do. Wherever he wants you to go, there you must be prepared to go. As you assemble to worship God, surrender unconditionally. Come before him kneeling, bowing, submitting all to him. True worship can involve nothing less.

2. The manner of worship

In 1980, a mountain in the western part of the United States affected the weather patterns of the entire continent. Mount St Helen's sent its ash-clouded messengers across the country. Out of curiosity someone might have decided to visit the mountain. But without a doubt the smouldering volcano would have had something to say about how anyone might visit it, how close he could come and how long he might linger. So in your coming before Almighty God, do not presume to dictate the circumstances under which you will approach him. He will let you know exactly how you may come to him in worship. He has made his will known in this area quite plainly through his word.

One of the great problems of the church today is the presumption displayed in devising means of worshipping God. But genuine submission to him begins with approaching him in the way his word declares. The psalmist indicates several aspects of a proper approach to God in worship.

Worship in the assembly of God's people

First of all, worship must be offered in the assembly of God's people. God directed Moses to assemble the people before the rock. In a similar fashion, the psalmist says, 'Come, let *us* sing with joy to the Lord, let *us* shout aloud to him … let *us* come before him with thanksgiving, let *us* bow down in worship, let *us* kneel before him …' (Psa. 95:1, 2, 6). It is not in accordance with God's word for a person simply to watch a worship service at home on television when he could be present among the assembly of God's people. Indeed, physical incapacity may require some people to stay at home. But if there is any possible way for you to gather with God's people to hear God's word, you should be there.

Why does God make this demand on his people? Why must God's people come corporately before him in worship? God's word demands corporate worship because of the way in which he has determined to work among his people. God has poured out his Spirit on every believer. When people who have been filled with the Spirit come together they form a living temple designed for worshipping God. They are living stones united into a single structure. When God's Spirit-filled people come together, the saving grace of God is transmitted from one person to another in a way that does not happen within the solitary soul. Not even a gathering of family and friends can duplicate this experience.

If you are serious about surrendering yourself unconditionally to God, you must come to the assembly of God's people. You must not forsake the assembling of yourselves together, as has been the habit of some (Heb. 10:25). True worship must be offered in the midst of the community of God's people.

Sing for joy

Secondly, when you come to worship, you are expected to sing for joy to him. You are to 'shout aloud' your praise in worship, to extol him in music and in psalms. The psalmist says:

> Come,
>   let us sing
>   to the Covenant LORD;

let us shout
  to the Rock of our salvation

(verse 1).

Some people think of their participation in the music of worship as an optional element. They assume the trained and the talented are the ones summoned to sing. But this scripture does not say, 'Let the choirs sing beautifully in worship.' Neither does this word charge the soloist to extol the Lord in music and psalms. Instead, God's word directs all worshippers to praise him if he is the Rock of their salvation.

There is no such thing as a person without music in his soul. God has made all human beings so that they respond to rhythm and song. Knowing this basic aspect of man, the Lord has ordained that his worship will include the offering of a sacrifice of praise through singing. A person who has difficulty staying 'on key' is still summoned to make a joyful noise to the Lord in worship. In recognizing the place of this principle in the community of the new covenant, Paul indicates that people who are filled with the Holy Spirit will sing and make melody to the Lord with all their heart (Eph. 5:19).

When a congregation unites as one soul to sing 'The Lord's my Shepherd, I'll not want,' or 'Immortal, invisible, God only wise,' something happens to the whole body of believers. Employing the physical frame as a musical instrument for the praise of God has an effect on the whole soul of man that cannot be duplicated in any other way. What and how people sing has a profound effect on who they are. Worshipping God always should include a pouring out of the depths of man's soul through body, mind and emotions. Making music is one of the most effective ways of offering the living sacrifice of the whole man before the Lord.

In addition to blessing God and being blessed yourself as you sing to the Lord, you will bless others as well. As you are filled with the Spirit, you will edify one another in worship through psalms, hymns and spiritual songs. A singing church manifests the blessing of the Spirit. The psalmist is jubilant in his admonition, but intends to be taken seriously when he repeats himself: 'Come, let us sing to the Covenant LORD … with songs let us shout to him' (verses 1, 2).

Listen rightly to the word

A third crucial aspect of worship involves listening to the word of God with a softened heart. The psalmist says:

> Today, if you will obey his voice,
> Do not harden your heart
>   as you did at Meribah,
>   as in the day of Massah in the wilderness
>
> (verse 8).

Essential to the true worship of God is hearing his word with a prepared heart. It is not the daily newspaper that is being read at worship. It is not the latest opinions of men that are being rehearsed. It is the unchanging word of the Almighty God that is being declared before the congregation. His word must be given all the respect it deserves. God's word cannot be treated as though it were one more opinion with which you might agree or disagree according to your own personal inclinations. Coming to worship means submitting your opinions to his infallible, inerrant word.

One of the saddest moments recorded in Scripture is the event to which Psalm 95 refers. Even Moses, the man of God, sinned against the Lord's word when the people assembled in rebellion, making a mockery of worship. Contrary to the Lord's instructions, Moses twice struck the rock before which the people were assembled (Num. 20:11, 12). He did not treat God's word as holy. He made the commandment of the Lord a commonplace thing, and presumed to add to the word of God. Even though he was God's chosen leader, he was denied the privilege of entering the land of promise because he did not sanctify the Lord's word in worship. He would be allowed only to see the land that had been promised. For God's name must be sanctified among men. Since that day, generation after generation had been reminded of the fall of the mighty man Moses. God made his word holy when Moses failed to make it holy.

As you come before the Lord's presence in worship, be sure you do not come with a hardened heart. Years of previous service to the Lord cannot be substituted for a current commitment to stand under the Lord's word. Be careful that your heart does not resemble the hard-crusted pathway that rejects the word, or the rocky soil that receives the word with joy but soon causes the young shoot to wither. Make sure you do not approach God in worship with a heart crowded with the thorns and thistles of the cares of this world that choke the word. Rid your mind and heart of all distractions. See to it that your heart is like the good soil that hears God's word and with patience brings forth fruit unto life everlasting. True worship always will involve a softened heart ready to receive the word of God as it speaks on that specific day.

You have nothing to lose and everything to gain from hearing God's word with a prepared heart. His commandments are not burdensome. They are your life.

3. The reasons for worshipping God

Beyond the essential obligation to the Creator, there are a number of reasons why the redeemed should approach God in worship. The psalmist gives three good reasons for worshipping God, all three of which are related to God's basic nature. But rather than describing the Lord in abstract terms, the psalmist displays a healthy bent towards practicality. He might have spoken of God's incommunicable attributes, his omniscience or his omnipresence, his immortality or his invisibility. But instead he presents concrete images easily understood. He says, 'God is your Shepherd, God is your Rock and God is your Maker.' Because of these roles that God fulfils in relation to men, he deserves their worship.

God is your Shepherd

First of all, worship God because he is your Shepherd. The psalmist says:

> Come,
> let us worship
> and bow down …

For he
    is our God,
and we
    are the people of his pasture
    and the flock of his hand

(verses 6, 7).

Have you ever fed a little lamb? The experience might surprise you. That fluffy, frolicsome creature is not as delicate in its appetite as you might suppose.

If you ever get the opportunity, take a bottle with a nipple to the farmer's fence. Lose a little of your dignity and say, 'Here, lamby, lamby, lamby!' Across the meadow the dainty creature comes. But be prepared for instant action when you thrust the nippled bottle through the fence. In five seconds or less the bottle is drained. Then the little lamb looks at you with pleading eyes that beg for more.

God is the 'Good Shepherd' who delights for you to look to him for more. He wants you to come in worship, longing for an abundance of his blessings. How instructive are the examples in Scripture of those who boldly declare to God, 'I will not let you go until you bless me.' The apostle Paul re assures those who seek large blessings from the Lord: 'Now to him who is able to do far more abundantly than all that we ask or think' (Eph. 3:20).

As your Shepherd, the Lord delights in providing abundantly for all your needs in life. Worship God your Shepherd. Having given his life for the sheep, he will not withhold from you any good thing.

God is your Rock

Not only is God your Shepherd, he also is your Rock. The psalmist says:

Come,
    let us sing
        to the Covenant LORD;
    let us shout
        to the rock of our salvation. (verse 1).

Rocks generally were noteworthy in the Near East for the refuge they provided. But the psalmist is probably referring to a specific rock. He recalls the rock in the wilderness by which Israel was refreshed during its pilgrimage. The nation was thirsting in the desert. No streams watered the arid sands. No refreshing oases could be found. There were only the rocks. The people complained in their hearts, sinned against God and rebelled against Moses. But God endured their complaints against him and directed Moses to assemble the people before the rock. For on this rock the Lord himself would stand before the people. Then Moses was directed to smite the rock with the rod of God that he had in his hand. That rod—the same rod with which Moses smote Pharaoh's people with the plagues in Egypt —should have fallen on the Israelites for their rebellion. The blow of the rod should have struck the people. But the rod came down on the rock instead. God stood before the people on the rock, and Moses struck the rock. From the smitten rock came forth water in the wilderness. In his grace the Lord received in himself the blow that should have fallen on his people.

Come and worship before God your Rock. From that smitten rock flows the water that gives life to a perishing people. Christ the Saviour bore the just judgment for the sin of his people in his own body on the tree. So he can provide complete deliverance for his people. Come, let us worship God our Rock. Come with expectation and delight, for Christ has been smitten for the sin of those who will trust in him. He can provide abundant refreshment to the pilgrim wandering through this life.

God is your Maker

Worship God your Shepherd. Worship God your Rock. Finally, worship God your Maker. The psalmist says:

> Come,
> let us worship
> and bow down;
> let us kneel
> before the Covenant LORD our Maker
> (verse 6).

After working intensely on a project, you are glad to take a break and enjoy the finished product. Even if your workmanship is not perfect, it is enjoyable to contemplate what you have been able to accomplish.

God is your Maker, your Creator. Contrary to the feeble efforts of men, the Lord's handiwork is perfect. Though man has marred the beauty of God's creation, the outlines of his perfect work still remain. Because God is your Maker, take time to admire him for his handiwork.

The worship of your Maker should not be viewed as a burdensome task. For worship is, as a matter of fact, entering into his rest. After finishing his work of creation, the Lord rested. The psalmist indicates that by worshipping him, you enter into this same rest. Refusing to worship your Maker is a form of hardening your heart against his voice. He invites you today to come and find rest for your souls. As our Lord Jesus said, 'Come to me, all who labour and are heavy laden, and I will give you rest. Take my yoke upon you, and learn from me … and you will find rest for your souls' (Matt. 11:28, 29).

But if you harden your hearts and refuse to worship your Creator, then God already has taken an oath. God has sworn that the people who harden their hearts against him will never enter into his rest. Unless you give him the honour he deserves, you never will enter the eternal rest that still remains for the people of God.

Conclusion

God is your Shepherd, abundantly supplying all your needs. God is your Rock, providing shelter from the judgment you deserve. God is your Maker, the craftsman who now invites you to enter his rest.

Come and worship him. Kneel before the Lord. But be assured: if you fail to worship him, you never will enter his rest.

Psalm 96

A New Song about the Old Story

Reader: 1 Sing to the Covenant LORD
1st Congr.: a new song;
Reader: sing to the Covenant LORD,
2nd Congr.: all the earth;

Reader: 2 sing to the Covenant LORD,
All: bless his name.

Reader: 3 Tell the good news of his salvation
day after day;
1st Congr.: declare among the nations
his glory;
2nd Congr.: among all peoples
his wondrous works.

Reader: 4 For great is the Lord
and greatly to be praised.
1st Congr.: He should be feared
above all gods;

2nd Congr.: 5 for all the gods of the nations are impotent,
but the Covenant LORD made the heavens.

Reader: 6 Grandeur and glory radiate from him;

All:	might and elegance mark his sanctuary.
Reader:	7Ascribe to the Covenant LORD
1st Congr.:	O families of nations;
Reader:	ascribe to the Covenant LORD
2nd Congr.:	glory and strength;
Reader:	8ascribe to the Covenant LORD
All:	the glory his name deserves.
Reader:	Bring an offering, and come into his courts;
1st Congr.:	9bow before the LORD of the Covenant in the splendour of holiness.
2nd Congr.:	Tremble before him, all the earth.
Reader:	10Announce to the nations, 'The LORD of the Covenant reigns!'
1st Congr.:	Indeed, the world is firmly established, it cannot be moved.
2nd Congr.:	He will judge the nations with uprightness.
Reader:	11The heavens will be glad, and the earth shall rejoice;
1st Congr.:	the sea will cheer, along with its teeming mass.
2nd Congr.:	12The field will be joyful, and all that is in it.

Reader: Then all the trees of the forest
13 will sing for joy before the Covenant LORD,
for he comes!

All: For he comes to judge the earth;
he will judge the world in righteousness,
and the nations with his truth.

A New Song about the Old Story—*Singing a New Song to the Lord*

Introduction

The singing of a song to the Lord is an old tradition among God's people. At the Red Sea Moses and the Israelites sang this song to the Lord:

> I will sing to the Lord,
>   for he has triumphed gloriously;
> The horse and his rider
>   he has thrown into the sea.
> The Lord is my strength and my song,
>   And he has become my salvation
>
> (Exod. 15:1, 2).

Not only do God's people sing a song to the Lord; the Lord is their song. In himself is the reason for their singing.

After the singular event of the exodus, references to a 'new' song are found in a number of places (cf. Psa. 33:3; 40:2, 3). Psalm 96 declares that God's people should forever be singing a 'new' song. This psalm was used to celebrate the bringing up of the ark to Jerusalem, as indicated in 1 Chronicles 16:23-33. That occasion clearly marked a 'new' thing the Lord had done which merited a 'new' song.

In the book of Revelation the 144,000 represent the elect of all the ages. They 'sang a new song' (Rev. 14:3). Once, long ago, the people of God arrived on the other side of the Red Sea with their enemies defeated and sang for the first time the song of the redeemed. Now at the end of the age, all those who have been redeemed sing this last 'new song.' No one can learn this song except the 144,000, representing the elect number from every nation on earth.

But throughout the present era, God continues to perform his great wonders of salvation. In response, God's people are to sing continually a new song. Psalm 96 is designed to aid God's people in this enjoyable task.

This psalm falls into two sections, each beginning with a three-fold admonition: 'Sing … sing … sing …' (verses 1-6); 'Ascribe … ascribe … ascribe …' (verses 7-13).

1. 'Sing … sing … sing …' (verses 1-6)

> Sing to the Covenant LORD
> a new song;
> sing to the Covenant LORD,
> all the earth;
> sing to the Covenant LORD,
> bless his name
>
> (verses 1, 2).

Some people live for music. To them it is the language of the soul. They go to work and put in their eight hours, but real life waits until the time when the music begins.

Christians need to recognize the universal role of music. It speaks to every man's soul. It should not be surprising that God has established music as a vital part of the worship of his people. This psalm does not leave the matter of music up to your inclinations or your talents. Three times you are summoned to sing. 'Sing … sing … sing …'

Some people don't sing at all. In their minds it is easy to justify this omission. They feel they have no talent. But three times over, God tells you to sing. Believe it or not, however poor your efforts may sound in your own ears, your singing glorifies God, encourages others and strengthens your own soul.

People with special talent may make a theatrical performance out of their singing. But the psalmist says you are to sing to the Lord, not to men.

Some people like to sing only the songs they know. But the psalmist says you are to sing a 'new' song. The working of God's grace is always new, and always demands a fresh response.

The psalmist tells you what ought to be the message of your song. You should sing about what the Lord does and who the Lord is.

Sing about what the Lord does

First, sing the good news about what God does:

> Tell the good news of his salvation
> day after day;
> declare among the nations
> his glory;
> among all peoples
> his wondrous works
>
> (verse 3).

When you hear good news about a rise in salary, or the birth of a baby, or the healing of a sick friend, you rejoice greatly at that moment. Then life moves on, and the good news fades into the background of more current activities. But the good news of the gospel lasts and lasts. It sounds better every day. 'Sweeter as the years go by,' is the way it used to be sung.

'Tell the good news of his salvation day after day,' says the psalmist. Let not a day pass that you do not talk to someone about the goodness of God and his works of salvation. Think about what the Lord does. He forgives all your iniquities, he heals all your diseases, he spares you from the adverse effects of sin. He treats you as his child, and blesses everything that occurs in your life.

But note the full scope of what God tells you to do. You are to speak not just to the members of your family or your church about the wondrous works of the Lord. You are to 'declare his glory among the nations' and tell of his wondrous works 'among all peoples.' This great missionary psalm anticipates the gospel age of today. As the early Christians first experienced persecution, the book of Acts says that except for the apostles who stayed in Jerusalem, they all went out 'preaching the word' (Acts 8:4).

But be careful that you observe the order of the psalm. First you must come together in worship, singing the new song that praises the Lord. Then you will be ready to go and declare his wondrous works among the heathen. It is like serving homemade apple pie to your guests: first you peel the apples and bake the pie; then you serve it to your friends. First warm your soul in the fellowship of the brothers as you sing to the Lord in worship. Rehearse his wondrous works. Then you will be ready to share the good news with the rest of the world.

Sing about who the Lord is

Secondly, you are to sing about who the Lord is. The psalmist says:

> For great is the Lord
>   and to be greatly praised.
> He should be feared
>   above all gods;
> for all the gods of the nations are impotent,
>   but the Covenant LORD made the heavens
> (verses 4-5).

Other gods? They are 'godlings,' little nothings. Whether you are talking about the god of the knowledge explosion, or the god of computer power, or the god of 'I'll do what I want, when and how I want'—all these gods are little nothings. These godlings may tell you to do what pleases you, but you cannot even be sure what will give you pleasure. Do what you want, and one thing is sure: you will be a miserable person.

But the LORD of the Covenant—he made the heavens! Only as you recognize him as the Creator of all things will you be able to go through life singing.

It all makes sense. God is the Creator. He made you to be what you are. So he alone knows what is best for you. As the psalmist says, 'Grandeur and glory radiate from him; might and elegance mark his sanctuary' (verse 6).

Notice where you meet this one true God. It is 'in his sanctuary' that you see his greatest glory. Come to the place where his word speaks. Come to the assembly of his people. There you will see his grandeur and glory, his might and his excellence.

When you travel through Europe, you may be impressed by the large cathedrals built centuries ago. But the blessing of God on a people cannot be measured by the size of their cathedrals. For God does not dwell in temples made with hands. His holy place is to be found in the assembly of his people. Where the word is preached and the people of God assemble, there is the Lord. The hour is coming and now is, said Jesus, when people will worship neither in Jerusalem nor Samaria. True worshippers concentrate on worshipping the Father in spirit and in truth, for the Father seeks such to worship him (John 4:21-24). In the midst of his worshipping people is his grandeur and glory.

So you are summoned to sing, sing, sing. Sing in the sanctuary of his peoples. Sing to the Lord a new song. Rejoice in the deliverance that has come to you.

2. Ascribe to the Lord of the Covenant (verses 7-13)

But the psalmist has another admonition. Three times he repeats this second command: 'Ascribe to the Lord … ascribe to the Lord … ascribe to the Lord …' Give to him the glory due to his name. Recognize his greatness and honour him for who he is.

As the capital city of the United States of America, Washington D.C. holds distinctions in a number of areas. But one outstanding characteristic is this city's capacity for gossip. It likes to glamourize its political heroes, but it also finds a twisted pleasure in tearing them down. The exaggeration in one direction is more than balanced by the defamation in the other. This gossip cycle of bloating and then deflating chosen individuals invariably must consume its subjects, because it begins by ascribing glory to the wrong person. Inevitably it must destroy the idol it creates.

To God belongs all the glory. You cannot exaggerate his greatness. It is, as a matter of fact, your duty to ascribe to him glory and strength, giving him the honour he deserves.

This giving of glory to God is not the responsibility of only one group of people. Instead, it is the duty of the entire 'family of nations.' God has made all the peoples of the world from one family. The 'families of nations' are only sub-divisions of the one human race. It is the duty of all the nations of the world to come together and give glory to this one true God, the God and Father of our Lord Jesus Christ.

What specifically should be ascribed to the Lord? Ascribe to him two things: glory and strength.

Ascribe glory to the Lord

First, ascribe glory to the Lord. But what concretely does ascribing 'glory' mean? This word 'glory' in the Old Testament sometimes refers purely and simply to money (cf. Hag. 2:7-9). A person's 'glory' is his money. Whether you have a little or a lot, your glory is your money.

The psalmist is very specific when he says, 'Ascribe glory to the Lord.' He says:

> 'Ascribe to the Covenant Lord glory and strength …
> *Bring an offering*, and come into his courts'
> (verses 7, 8).

Bring your money to church. Whether you have a little or a lot, your money is a major manifestation of your glory. Bring a generous offering and give glory to him.

The word for 'offering' describes the 'tribute' that a conquered king presents to a conquering lord. According to 2 Kings 17:4, the King of Assyria became angry when the King of Israel stopped 'paying him tribute.' He was no longer bringing an offering to him.

God is not like the petty, perishing kings of this world. But he does expect a proper tribute. He wants you to give glory to his name in a very concrete way. He wants you to bring an offering worthy of him and come into his courts.

Are you giving God the glory due to his name? Do you find it easier to spend twenty pounds (or dollars) on a Saturday night out than to give the same amount of money on Sunday morning to the Lord?

Bow down to the LORD. Pay him the tribute he deserves. Our Lord Jesus Christ sacrificed all he had for you. He made himself poor for your sake as a way of giving glory to God. Since he had no money, he gave to the Lord his body as an offering. Should you respond to the Lord by doing any less? Give to the Lord the glory due to his name. Bring an offering and come into his courts.

Ascribe strength to the LORD

Secondly, you should ascribe 'strength' to the LORD. That is, testify before the world that you believe God has power, great power, greater power than any other ruler in the world. Announce to the nations of the world, 'The LORD of the Covenant reigns!' In particular, acknowledge two things. Acknowledge that the world holds together because of his strength, and acknowledge that the nations will be judged by his strength.

The psalmist says:

> Announce to the nations,
> 'The LORD of the Covenant reigns!'
> Indeed, the world is firmly established,
> it cannot be moved
>
> (verse 10).

It takes a great deal of might to hold the world together. Governments and nations rapidly rise and fall. But you are to announce to the nations:

> 'The LORD of the Covenant reigns!'
> Indeed, the world is firmly established,
> it cannot be moved.

All authority in heaven and earth has been given to Jesus Christ, and he holds the world together. By him all things are sustained in heaven and in earth.

In addition, the world will be judged by his strength. As the psalmist says,

> He comes!
> He comes to judge the earth;

> He will judge the world in righteousness,
> and the nations with his truth
>
> (verse 13).

The year 1990 always will be remembered in Eastern Europe as a time when the impotence of the strongest, the most oppressive of human governments was displayed before the world. Overnight, regimes toppled that had held their people captive for decades. In Romania, East Germany, and Poland, long-standing powers crumbled in short order. In what was then Czechoslovakia, over a million people stood in the public square demanding the end of an oppressive government, and got their demand in a matter of days.

One day the Lord will topple all existing nations even more quickly. For he comes, he comes to judge the earth in righteousness, and the nations with his truth.

On one occasion, an unruly mob devastated portions of a major city. The mayor and chief of police did what they could to stop the rioting in the streets. Eventually neighbourhoods were quieted, and order was restored. But a bus valued at $160,000 was charred beyond recognition. Over thirty stores had been looted in a matter of hours. Who is to mediate justice in this kind of situation? Who will pay to restore people's losses?

The Scriptures say that the Lord is coming. He will come, and he will demand a reckoning. That which human justice could not hope to achieve, he will bring about in a moment, in the twinkling of an eye, at the last trumpet. He will call every violator and every perpetrator of injustice to account. He, by his power, will restore everything lost to those who have suffered unjustly. He has a strength that will bring absolute justice to the whole of the earth.

How should you respond to this coming judgment? If you have been walking in unrighteousness, this news may strike fear into your heart—and well it should. For God will bring into judgment every secret thing that you have done. He has the power to bring back the record of those old sins and to render righteous judgments.

But if you are a believer who has been declared righteous by faith in Jesus Christ, you should respond to the coming of the

Lord as does the rest of creation. You should look forward to the last judgment with joy! At that day you will stand at the right hand of God. He will not recall any of your past sins. But he will reward you for every good deed you have done in the power of Jesus Christ. Because of the nature of the last judgment, you should rejoice! As the psalmist says:

> The heavens will be glad,
> and the earth shall rejoice;
> the sea will cheer,
> along with its teeming mass.
> The field will be joyful,
> and all that is in it.
> Then all the trees of the forest
> will sing for joy before the Covenant LORD,
> for he comes!
>
> (verses 11-13).

If thoughts about God's coming make you glum, then you have a problem in your relationship to God! The heavens are glad over the news that the Lord comes in judgment, and the waters covering the earth rejoice.

These waters have been described by the poet as:

> Mystery of waters—never-slumbering sea!
> Impassioned orator with lips sublime.[1]

The sublime lips of this sea, together with its teeming multitude, delight in announcing the glory of the God who is coming. As Romans 8:19 says, all of creation waits with eager longing for the return of Christ.

Why? Why is the created world so anxious for the Lord to return as Judge? Because his coming means the correcting of all disorders. No more cyclones, no more famines, no more riots will scar the surface of the earth. Both in man and nature a new order will prevail. In righteousness and in justice he will rule the world.

[1] Robert Montgomery, cited in Spurgeon, *Treasury of David*, II, p. 190.

Man will return to his pristine innocence, and the garden of Eden will expand to cover the globe. So you should rejoice.

Conclusion

This psalm begins with singing and it ends with singing. Nature surely will sing when the Lord returns to manifest his glory, his strength and his righteousness.

You should sing along with the rest of the world. For he is coming, and when he comes he will complete the work of salvation he has begun. As the poet has declared:

> Church of Christ, awake, awake!
> 'Thy God reigneth!'
> Forward, then, fresh courage take:
> 'Thy God reigneth!'
> Soon, descending from His throne,
> He shall claim thee for His own;
> Sin shall then be overthrown:
> 'Thy God reigneth,
> Thy God reigneth.'[2]

[2] *Trinity Hymnal*, 190, No. 69.

Psalm 99
'Holy, Holy, Holy'

Reader: 1 The Covenant LORD is crowned King,
Congr.: the nations tremble;
Reader: he sits enthroned among the heavenly host,
Congr.: the world shakes.

Reader: 2 The Covenant LORD is great
in Zion,
Congr.: he is exalted
over all the nations.

Reader: 3 They shall praise your great and awesome
name,
All: for holy is he.

Reader: 4 The King with all his might
has shown his love for justice;
you
have confirmed just judgments.
Congr.: Justice and righteousness
you have done in Jacob.

Reader: 5 Exalt the Covenant LORD our God,
and bow at the stool of his feet,
All: for holy is he.

Reader: 6Moses and Aaron were among his priests,
Samuel among those who called on his name.

Congr.: They called to the Covenant LORD
and he answered them.

Reader: 7In the pillar of cloud
he spoke to them;

Congr.: they kept his ordinances
and the statute he gave them.

Reader: 8O Covenant LORD, our God,
you answered them;

Congr.: a forgiving God
you were to them,
though repaying them for their deeds.

Reader: 9Exalt the Covenant LORD our God,
and bow at his holy mountain;

All: for holy is the Covenant LORD our God.

'Holy, Holy Holy'
Practical Effects of God's Holiness

Introduction

This psalm falls into three clear sections, each ending with the assertion that God is holy. The sections are uneven in length, and develop the concept of God's holiness from different perspectives. Each portion of the psalm sees his holiness affecting a different part of God's relationship to man.

At its root, God's holiness conveys the idea of his separateness. Holiness involves moral uprightness, but embraces much more. It is a larger concept, describing the uniqueness, the separateness of God. 'Holiness' has at its essence the classic Creator/creature distinction. Because of his holiness, God forever remains entirely separate from his creation. In exercising authority over the nations, in establishing justice in the earth, in responding to men's cries for help, God acts differently from all the creatures of the world.

The three sections of the psalm, each of which concludes with a refrain, are as follows: the Covenant LORD reigns in holiness (verses 1-3); the Covenant LORD judges in holiness (4, 5); the Covenant LORD answers in holiness (verses 6-9).

1. The Covenant Lord reigns in holiness (verses 1-3)

> The Covenant LORD is crowned King,
> the nations tremble;
> he sits enthroned among the heavenly host,
> the world shakes
>
> (verse 1).

One critical school of biblical studies interprets this statement to mean that as a consequence of the cultic drama enacted in worship, God becomes King just at that moment. This viewpoint errs by interpreting Scripture in terms of theories of mantic magic found in other ancient religions. But from the biblical perspective, God always has been King. He always rules over the nations. His lordship is never threatened by the vagaries that effect human sovereignty.

Yet the significance of God's people giving public recognition to his lordship should not be underestimated. Public recognition of God's lordship has a dramatic effect on men's view of reality. It is like a salute to the flag, or the singing of the national anthem. The symbolic ceremony unifies the spirit of a people.

The nations tremble

In this case, the impact of a recognition of God's lordship over heaven and earth causes 'trembling' and 'shaking.' Why? Why should God's lordship create terror? Because he is holy! God is not a man. His standards are not man's standards. He brings awesome judgments on nations when they contradict his holiness. Look at what he did to Egypt in the time of Moses. When they oppressed God's people, he plagued them until their fields, their flocks and their firstborn were destroyed. He drowned their army beneath the waters of the Red Sea. He has done it before and he will do it again.

When the report of what God had done in Egypt reached Canaan, the heathen kings trembled. This God was no local deity, ruling over only a segment of the earth. As Rahab the harlot testified, 'The Covenant LORD your God is God in the heavens above and on the earth beneath' (Josh. 2:11). He is the same today.

At the beginning of the 1991 Persian Gulf War, the editor of *Time* magazine interviewed Robert McNamara, designated as the architect of the earlier Vietnam War. Explaining the debacle of that encounter, McNamara declared, 'Bush and Powell and Cheney are doing a superb job, but I tell you Jesus Christ himself can't keep one of these things under control.'[1] With all due respect, the Jesus Christ of Mr McNamara is not the Jesus Christ of the Scriptures. He rules over the nations. Every nation who has repudiated his rule invariably suffers devastation and defeat.

[1] *Time*, 11 February 1991, p. 70.

Let us pray for the day when the nations will once more tremble at the holiness of the one true and living God. Let us testify fearlessly to his role as holy Lord of the nations, that men may come to understand why things happen the way they do.

The Lord is great in Zion

The psalmist also indicates that the Covenant LORD is 'great in Zion.' It is from this position that he is exalted over all the nations. This one God is the LORD of the Covenant, and the place from which he reigns is Mount Zion.

The old Mount Zion in Jerusalem was only a shadow, a figure depicting God's place of rule in the midst of his people. But just as the Old Testament temple made with stones has been replaced by the New Testament church as the living temple of the Holy Spirit (Eph. 2:21, 22), so God's place of rule has been transported from the earthly mountain in Jerusalem to the permanent heavenly prominence at God's right hand (Heb. 12:22). Today in a very distinctive sense it may be said with the psalmist:

> The Covenant LORD is great
>   in Zion,
> he is exalted
>   over all the nations
>
> (verse 2).

How should God's people respond to the exaltation of their Covenant LORD as Lord over all the nations? 'They shall praise your great and awesome name, for holy is he' (verse 3). Because God is separated from his creation as its Lord, he must be praised. No other response would be fitting. The proper way to acknowledge God's sovereignty is to lift up his name in praise.

2. The Covenant LORD judges in holiness (verses 4, 5)

A second area in which the holiness, the separateness of the Lord, becomes manifest is his role as Judge. In the first stanza, the Covenant LORD is set apart as the Lord of the nations. He is so exalted that his separateness, his holiness, must be praised. Now things come closer to home. As Judge, the Lord gets close to each and every man. He must intermingle with their affairs, he must hear their cases, he must get involved in their everyday problems.

The justice of the Lord

The old saying goes, 'Power corrupts, and absolute power corrupts absolutely.' This is true among men. Even good and godly men are corrupted by too much power. But it is not true with the LORD of the Covenant. According to the psalmist:

> The King with all his might
> has shown his love for justice;
> you
> have confirmed just judgments.
> Justice and righteousness
> you have done in Jacob
> (verse 4).

Three times in a single verse the point is made. Justice, justice, justice is the way of the Lord. The psalmist gives full recognition to the 'might' of the Lord. He has unlimited power. He could do whatever he wished. But he never abuses that power as he exercises it among men. Always he dispenses it with justice.

The perfect holiness of God is displayed in his punishment of all wickedness and in his rewarding of all righteousness. Because of his holiness, God cannot do otherwise. He cannot be like a man and allow evil to go unpunished. Otherwise he himself would be like the perpetrators of evil.

God addresses the wicked in another psalm to make this very point. First he lists the sins of the wicked:

> What right have you to recite my statutes
> Or take my covenant on your lips?
> For you hate discipline,
> And you cast my words behind you.
> If you see a thief, you are pleased with him,
> And you keep company with adulterers.

You give your mouth free rein for evil,
And your tongue frames deceit.
You sit and speak against your brother;
You slander your own mother's son

(Psa. 50:16-20).

Then the Lord exposes the erroneous conclusion of these wicked people to whom he has shown such longsuffering despite their sin. They have misread his patience:

These things you have done, and I have been silent;
you thought I was one like yourself.
But now I rebuke you and lay
the charge before you

(Psa. 50:21).

If God did not punish sin he would resemble the sinner. If God were to fail to show that sin deprives man of enjoying the blessings of his kingdom, then he would appear to condone sin. But the Lord declares that he will rebuke the sinner and accuse him to his face. The certainty of the punishment of the wicked and the rewarding of the righteous are founded in the holiness of God. While many questions may remain about the reality of justice and its presence in this world, God ultimately will make all things clear. The holy God will see to it that in the end all the scales of justice balance out perfectly. All wickedness will be punished, and all doing of right will be rewarded. When it appears that the LORD's saints are suffering injustice, this must be seen as his way of advancing his people to a higher position. For particularly it is 'in Jacob,' among his own people, that the LORD of the Covenant manifests his holiness.

The believer's response

With this confidence, the believer must show unwavering trust in the outcome of all events. As the psalmist says:

Exalt the Covenant LORD our God,
and bow at the stool of his feet,
for holy is he

(verse 5).

The right response to the Lord's holiness must be worshipful submission. Because he is holy in all his dealings among men, he must be exalted. All his people must bow before him.

Now the question is before you. Do you accept the providential ordering of your life as a manifestation of God's holiness? Do you recognize that there is absolutely no impurity or injustice whatsoever in the things he brings into your life? If you know yourself to be the sinner that you are, then you will appreciate more fully the reliance you must have on the righteousness of Jesus Christ, given graciously to you as the basis for God's merciful treatment.

How could you stand otherwise? Do you really think that your righteousness has earned the multitude of favours that you enjoy in life? Do you blind yourself to your own sin in such a way that you think you deserve better? Do you really think you are better than Job, declared by Scripture to be a righteous man? Remember how he responded to the devastation of all possessions, the loss of his family and the ruination of his physical health? 'The LORD gave, and the LORD has taken away; blessed be the name of the LORD' (Job 1:21). Are you really better than Joseph, who languished in an Egyptian prison for years because of the false accusations of Potiphar's wife? Remember his response to his brothers: 'God sent me before you to preserve life' (Gen. 45:5). Both Job and Joseph worshipped at the footstool of the Lord's holiness.

Is it not time for you to bring your restless spirit before him and acknowledge his holiness in dealing with you? Put your trust in the certainty of his just dispensings. In the long run, you will not be disappointed. If you are in Christ by faith, you cannot fail to rule with him even as you now suffer with him. Do you remember the latter end of Job, or how things turned out for Joseph? Worship at the stool of his feet, for he is holy.

3. The Covenant Lord answers in holiness (verses 6-8)

Seven times in this psalm the Lord is identified by his covenant name. The name occurs in each of the three sections of the psalm, but four of the seven times it occurs in this last stanza. The psalm begins with an affirmation of the holiness of the God of the covenant as it is manifested in his rule over all the nations of the world. It concludes by focusing on the holiness of God as it is seen in the special care he shows to those who are in redemptive covenant with him.

How is this special care shown to be holy? The holiness of the Covenant LORD is displayed in his answering the prayers of those with whom he is in covenant. Because of the perfections of his holiness, he could do no other.

In this perspective on prayer is a great truth. Answered prayer is a function of the holiness of God. Because God is holy, he will answer the prayers of his people.

Often the believer gets the mistaken idea that answer to prayer depends on his personal fervency. If he is emotional enough in his prayers, God will have to answer him. But answering prayer is a function of the holiness of God. Sometimes his answer will be 'No.' His holiness exposes the imperfections of the prayer. But do not be discouraged. A 'No' answer is not a non-answer. Next time his answer may be 'Yes.' But in any case, you can trust him. For answered prayer is a function of the holiness of God.

This responsiveness of the Lord to the cries of his people is seen in three respects: firstly, in his answering those appointed to mediate the covenant (verse 6); secondly, in the full revelation of his will to his people (verse 7); and, thirdly, in his combining forgiveness with chastening for the health and well-being of his people (verse 8).

He answered the mediators of the covenant

First, consider the holiness of the Covenant LORD as displayed in his answering those appointed to mediate the covenant:

> Moses and Aaron were among his priests,
> Samuel among those who called on his name.
> They called to the Covenant LORD
> and he answered them
>
> (verse 6).

The holy God separated for himself holy ones to be his priests. Both Moses and Aaron were of Levitical descent, and so were qualified for the role of covenantal mediators. But in addition, Aaron was set apart as the high priest who wore special garments for beauty and for holiness. He alone was able to enter into the Most Holy Place on the Day of Atonement. Standing before the very presence of God, he was able to intercede for the people, and the Lord heard him. The sins of the people were washed away.

Moses, though not functioning as priest in the same sense, was the representative head of the covenant people, set apart by God for this role. His pleas for the people caused them to be spared from total annihilation after the incident of the golden calf. To Moses the Lord said, 'This very thing that you have spoken I will do, for you have found favour in my sight, and I know you by name' (Exod. 33:17).

Samuel's name means 'asked of God,' and it was in answer to the pleas of his mother that he came into the world. In childhood he was consecrated to the service of the temple. In his maturity he showed that he understood the significance of his intercessory role when he demonstrated the power of his prayer by asking and receiving thunder and rain from the Lord in the middle of the dry season of the year. Then he declared to the people, 'far be it from me that I should sin against the LORD by ceasing to pray for you' (1 Sam. 12:23).

These Old Testament intercessors anticipate Jesus Christ, the new covenant mediator. He is now at the right hand of the Father making continual intercession for us (Heb. 7:25). He is able to offer these prayers only because he himself is holy, and has presented before the Father his own atoning blood for the sins of the people for whom he pleads. Through the atoning blood of Jesus Christ you are made perfectly holy.

You also have been appointed by God to be a mediator of the covenant. For now we are in the era of the priesthood of all believers. We are a 'kingdom of priests' (1 Pet. 2:9). You should have a 'holy boldness' in approaching the throne of grace (Heb. 4:16). God forbid that you should sin against the Lord in ceasing to pray for one another.

The Lord has made his will known

Secondly, God in his holiness answers us when we cry to him because he has made his will known to us, enabling us to walk according to his ordinances. The psalmist says:

> In the pillar of cloud
>   he spoke to them,
> they kept his ordinances
>   and the statute he gave them
>
> (verse 7).

Whenever Moses went into the tent of meeting to receive a revelation from the Lord, the pillar of cloud would come down and remain at the entrance to the tent (Exod. 33:9). The people would see the pillar of cloud, and they all would stand and worship, each at the entrance to his own tent (Exod. 33:10). The people recognized the solemnity of the hour. God was revealing his will to his people. By being the recipients of this revelation, they were set apart from all the other peoples of the world.

The holiness of the people was confirmed by their keeping the ordinances that God revealed to them. In this way, their whole pattern of life set them apart from all the other nations of the world.

This same response to the holiness of God is expected of the Lord's people today. As the apostle Peter says, 'As he who called you is holy, you also be holy in all your conduct, since it is written, "You shall be holy, for I am holy"' (1 Pet. 1:15, 16).

As a believer in Christ, you must not succumb to the unholy desires that controlled your life while you lived in ignorance of God's will (1 Pet. 1:14). Resist the impulse to manipulate people to your own ends. Reject the love of money, which is the root of all kinds of evil. Set aside jealousy that puts you at odds with your brothers. Kill the remnants of pride and self-seeking. The holy God has communicated his will to you. Show yourself to be holy, set apart from the rest of men. Walk in a way that is worthy of your calling.

Where are you today in your call to a holy walk with the Lord? Are you living according to the light of God's truth that has come to you? Or have you begun to show too much tolerance towards your own desires?

Holiness cannot tolerate the slightest pollution of its purity. Just because it so happens that absolute holiness cannot be achieved in this life, you have no right to tolerate evil desires in your heart. Having received the revelation of God's holiness in his word, act to put aside all sin. Walk in holiness as he is holy. Then you will rejoice in seeing your prayers answered.

He combines forgiveness with chastening

Thirdly, the Covenant LORD shows his holiness through answering prayer as he combines forgiveness with a healthy dose of chastening:

> Covenant LORD our God,
>   you answered them;
> a forgiving God
>   you were to them,
> though repaying them for their deeds
>
> (verse 8).

God will do no other than answer the prayers of his people. Why? Because he is a holy God. He will not deviate from the commitments he has made by his word.

But in answering the prayers of his people, the Lord carefully balances two things. First, he forgives sin so he can listen to their prayers. But secondly, he chastens them when it is for their good. He never lets his people misunderstand his mercy so that they end up presuming on his grace. He forgives, but he also repays them for their deeds.

Remember David? God forgave him for his sin the instant he confessed it. But the Lord also declared that he never would have peace in his kingdom.

Men, remember this outworking of the holiness of God the next time you are tempted to look to lust. You are running the danger of never again having peace in your life. Women, the next time you are tempted to covet the pretty things that please your eyes, remember Sapphira, the wife of Ananias. She was struck dead in the presence of the apostles because she lied to conceal her love for money (Acts 5:9, 10). As a result of this manifestation of God's holiness, 'Great fear came upon the whole church and upon all who heard of these things' (Acts 5:11).

What a blessing it is to participate in the holiness of the Lord! Your prayers are answered, God judges righteously on your behalf, and he rules over all the nations in a way that advances your good. Believe in the provision of God's grace as it is found in Jesus Christ, and you can live as a beneficiary of his holiness.

But take care that you never presume on the Lord's goodness. For he chastens those who violate his holiness.

Conclusion

Holy, holy, holy is the Lord God Almighty. The whole earth is filled with his glory.

How should you respond to the holiness of God? Respond as did Moses when God spoke to him from the burning bush. He recognized that because of God's holiness he was standing on holy ground. Respond as did Isaiah when he saw the Lord Christ seated on his throne of glory. Humble yourself with the prophet and cry out,

> Woe is me! For I am lost;
> for I am a man of unclean lips,
> and I dwell in the midst of a people of unclean lips;
> for my eyes have seen the King,
> the Lord of hosts!'
>
> (Isa. 6:5).

Exalt the Lord our God. The mountain from which he reigns is holy, and that holiness radiates from heaven to touch every place on earth and every event of human history. Bow before him wherever you are and whatever may be the circumstances of your life.

For holy is the Covenant Lord our God.

Psalm 106

Trust and Obey

Reader: 1Hallelujah!
All of you give thanks to the Covenant Lord,

All: for he is good;
his compassion lasts forever.

Reader: 2Who can adequately declare
the noble deeds of the Covenant Lord,
or make people understand
all the reasons he deserves praise?

All: 3How blessed are those
who maintain justice,
who do the right all the time!

Reader: 4Remember me, O Covenant Lord,
when you show favour towards your people;
include me
when you act to save,

5that I too may experience
the well-being of those you have chosen,
that I may rejoice
in the joy of your nation,

that I may say 'Hallelujah!'
with the people you have claimed as your own.

All: 6[But] we have sinned along with our forefathers;
we have acted crookedly and done the wrong.

1st Congr.: 7Our forefathers in Egypt
gave little consideration
to your wondrous miracles;

2nd Congr.: they kept forgetting
your numerous acts of mercy.

1st Congr.: So they rose up in rebellion
at the sea,

2nd Congr.: when they faced the Red Sea.

Reader: 8But despite it all he saved them
to maintain the glory of his name,
to make people recognize his power to save.

9He rebuked the Red Sea,
and it dried up;
he made them walk in its depths
as though they were trekking across a desert.

10He snatched them from the hand
of the one who hated them,
and freed them from the grip
of the enemy.

11 Water completely covered
  those who had distressed them;
  not one of them survived.

12 Then they shouted 'Amen'
  to his promises,
and they sang
  his praise.

1st Congr.: 13 How quickly they forgot
  his works!

2nd Congr.: They could not wait
  for his advice.

1st Congr.: 14 They had strong cravings
  in the desert,

2nd Congr.: so they put God on trial
  in the wilderness.

1st Congr.: 15 He gave them
  exactly what they asked,

2nd Congr.: but sent leanness
  into their soul …

Reader: 43 Time after time he rescued them
  but they kept rebelling against their counsel.
They were weakened
  by their constant sin.

44 But he saw their distress,
  and heard their outcry.

45 He remembered his covenant with them,
and showed leniency according to his boundless love.

46 He made all those who had taken them captive
treat them with mercy.

All: 47 Save us, O Covenant LORD our God!
Gather us from the nations
so that we may give thanks to your holy name
and joyfully shout, 'Hallelujah!'

Reader: 48 Blessed be the Covenant LORD, the God of Israel,
forever and ever.
Let all the people say:

All: 'Amen!
Hallelujah!'

Trust and Obey—
Summoning the Disobedient to Trust and Obey

Introduction

Psalm 106 may be classified as a psalm of 'historical recollection.' God's works in the past are recalled to inspire his people to serve him more faithfully in the future. In this case, the psalmist urges the people to trust and obey as a way of praising and giving thanks to the Lord.

This psalm is the first of the 'Hallelujah' psalms which begin and often end with the admonition, 'Hallelujah!,' meaning 'All of you, praise the Lord' (cf. Psa. 111-113; 117; 135; 146-150). If verse 48 is included in the body of this psalm, it would begin and end with 'Hallelujah!'

The psalmist first summons the people to praise the Lord (verses 1, 2). Then he lays down his principle that properly praising the Lord must involve obeying him (verse 3). Next he offers a personalized prayer that the Lord will remember him when he acts to save (verses 4, 5). The bulk of the psalm reviews the nation's past history, with its many failures despite the faithfulness of the Lord and the ministries of Moses and Phinehas his servants (verses 6-46). The psalmist concludes with a prayer that the Lord will keep showing mercy so the people will give thanks and praise him as they should (verse 47). Verse 48 appears to be a coda rounding off Book IV of the Psalter, as may be seen by comparing the similar endings of the other four 'books' that divide the psalm collection.

What should you do when the Lord continues to bless you instead of devastating you for your sins? You should join with the psalmist and declare 'Hallelujah!' You should turn once more with resolve to do the right, and praise the Lord for his compassion to sinful men.

So the psalmist summons God's people to praise him for his grace and goodness.

1. A summons to praise the Lord (verses 1, 2)

> Hallelujah!
> All of you give thanks to the Covenant LORD,
> for he is good;
> his compassion lasts forever
> (verse 1).

Eventually the psalmist will provide a long list of many acts of faithfulness performed by the Lord. But he begins with a summary statement of the basic reason why the Lord should be thanked. He is good, and his compassion lasts forever. God is not bitter towards us. His mercy never exhausts itself. Because of a guilty conscience, the sinner often envisages God as maintaining an attitude of displeasure towards his people. But his compassion continues in an unbroken pattern.

Because of the limitless love of the Lord, the psalmist expresses his inadequacy in the task of praising God:

> Who can adequately declare
> the noble deeds of the Covenant LORD,
> or make people understand
> all the reasons he deserves praise?
> (verse 2).

Have you ever felt this sense of frustration? It is impossible to thank the Lord properly, or to make people understand all the reasons why he deserves praise. As John Calvin says, 'There is no man who has ever endeavoured to concentrate all his energies, both physical and mental, in the praising of God, but will find himself inadequate for so lofty a subject ...'[1]

But though our abilities as sinful mortals may fail us in our attempts to praise him properly, even the most feeble effort is

[1] *Psalms,* IV, p. 207.

pleasing to the Lord. Simply listing the most obvious blessings he has brought to your life appears to him as a sweet-smelling sacrifice.

The psalmist, however, understands the best way to display to God gratitude for his faithfulness. To thank him properly, you must do what he asks you to do (verse 3).

2. Obedience as the proper way of praising the Lord

How blessed are those
    who maintain justice,
    who do the right all the time!

(verse 3).

At first this verse seems out of context. It doesn't appear to fit the flow of the psalm. But the psalmist is offering his answer to the frustration of finding an adequate way to praise the Lord: to honour him properly, maintain justice and do the right all the time. In season and out of season, stand for what is right. Only in this manner will the Lord receive the recognition he deserves. The person who always does the right shows publicly his appreciation for all that God has done for him.

3. A personal prayer

Then there follows a personal prayer by the one who wishes to be included among those the Lord saves:

Remember me, O Covenant LORD,
    when you show favour towards your people,
include me
    when you act to save,
that I too may experience
    the well-being of those you have chosen,
that I may rejoice
    in the joy of your nation,
that I may say, 'Hallelujah!'
    with the people you have claimed as your own

(verses 4, 5).

This psalm records the mighty acts of the Lord in saving his people. It shows how he delivered them even though they kept sinning against him. But at the outset the psalmist indicates that the individual must claim this experience for himself. To join in this chorus of Hallelujahs, a person must participate firsthand in the Lord's salvation.

This whole prayer is premised on the understanding that God has claimed a people for himself, and that he shows saving favour towards them. Three different phrases describe this people that are blessed of the Lord: 'your chosen'; 'your nation'; 'your inheritance.' Men do not initiate this favourable relationship with the Lord. Instead, his initiative brings salvation to his people.

The consequence of being a part of God's chosen, God's nation and God's inheritance is described by the psalmist as well-being, joy and an ability to say 'Hallelujah!' Possessing these three blessings from the Lord clearly would mean living life to the fullest.

Enter with earnestness into this prayer to participate personally in the blessings of the Lord. All enjoyment of life hinges on your being a part in his ongoing work of salvation.

4. A review of the nation's past history (verses 6-46)

The main part of the psalm recounts the nation's past history of failures and contrasts this record with the faithfulness of the Lord and his servants Moses and Phinehas.

We should be praising the Lord constantly for all he has done for us. The most convincing praise that can be offered is a life lived in conformity to his will.

But what have we done instead? 'We have sinned!' (verse 6). Along with our forefathers we have sinned. We have acted crookedly and done the wrong. Not just once, but over and over again. As a pattern of our lives, we have sinned. Instead of learning our lesson by seeing what happened to our forefathers when they rebelled against the Lord's will, we have gone right on doing the things that displease him.

How ungrateful we are! The Lord loads us down with benefits, and we revolt against his will.

The sin of complaining

> Our forefathers in Egypt
> gave little consideration
> to your wondrous miracles;
> they kept on forgetting
> your numerous acts of mercy.
> So they rose up in rebellion
> at the sea,
> when they faced the Red Sea
> (verse 7).

Remember how the forefathers behaved in Egypt? When Pharaoh made things more difficult for them, they threatened to kill God's servant Moses. Instead of relying on the Lord to give them freedom in his time, they blamed him for their distressing situation.

A little griping may not seem to be the worst thing in the world. But complaining is equivalent to the sin of rebellion. Complaining against God and forgetting his acts of mercy can only lead to further sin.

God had shown his favour towards Israel by treating them differently from their oppressors during the plagues of Egypt. Not one of them died when the angel of death passed through the land. But when they faced the Red Sea, they panicked. They rebelled once more. Instead of praising the Lord by trusting him, their contorted faces offered only ugly complaint.

The faithfulness of God

How did God respond to the distrust of his people? Did he give them what they deserved? Did he turn them over to the hands of their enemies? No. In consistency with his own self revelation, he delivered them once more:

> But despite it all he saved them
> to maintain the glory of his name,
> to make people recognize his power to save.

He rebuked the Red Sea,
    and it dried up;
he made them walk in its depths
    as though they were trekking across a desert
(verses 8, 9).

At the burning bush God revealed himself to Moses as the great 'I AM.' He is the unchanging one. Even when the people rebelled at the Red Sea, he carried through with his purposes to save them.

This great deliverance at the Red Sea shows how God can transform the hour of greatest threat into the hour of greatest victory. Instead of serving as a trap for God's people, the Red Sea became the instrument of destruction for the Lord's enemies. The water completely covered the ones who had brought them into such distress. None of their enemies survived.

Israel responded by shouting 'Amen' to his promises. They broke out into singing. But they would have honoured him more if they had not complained earlier, and had waited patiently for the Lord's salvation.

Show your faith today despite your distress. Declare your 'Amen' to God's word, and sing in anticipation of his work of salvation. Then you will be praising him as you should.

The danger of forgetfulness

How quickly they forgot
    his works!
They could not wait
    for his advice.
They had strong cravings
    in the desert,
so they put God on trial
    in the wilderness.
He gave them
    exactly what they asked,
but sent leanness
    into their soul (verses 13-15).

Do you know how long it was after the deliverance at the Red Sea before the people began doubting the good intent of the Lord once more? Three days! Less than half a week, and they were at it again! (cf. Exod. 15:22-24). It was as though they had set themselves to hurry and forget all the Lord had done for them.

Is that the way to praise the Lord? Yet sadly this forgetfulness of the Lord's faithfulness becomes the pattern of our lives week after week. We praise the Lord with a full heart and soul on Sunday, but by Wednesday or Thursday we are moaning and groaning, griping and complaining, cursing God and man all over again.

Two things tripped up God's people in the past: their forgetfulness and their desires. These two deficiencies are an integral part of the sinful human frame. Men's unconscionable forgetfulness and their endless desires for more and more things keep them in trouble. To live to God's glory, you must remember his undeserved faithfulness and restrain your personal wants. But just as in the past, God's people today keep forgetting his goodness. Their desires rather than his praise take the priority.

The next time you find yourself fretting, make a disciplined effort to remember what God has done for you in the past. Start with the works of creation. Look at the fascinating things he has made. Consider the stars and the sea, the sunflowers and the snowflakes. Each of these elements in the world represents an infinite amount of care on the part of the Creator. The rising wave, drawn by the moon, reaches upward, foams white and dashes onto the sand. The country garden, filled with its endless variety of flowers, spreads heaven's rainbow in a lower arch across the earth.

Then recall his work of redemption. He humbled himself, this Son of God. With delight to do his Father's will he set his face to go to Jerusalem. Neither friend nor foe could stop him. To free you from pain he endured anguish without measure. Next remember the blessing from God that comes through church, family and friends. Can you recall just one problem from which he has delivered you through these appointments of his grace? Just one? Or is it not many, so many that you cannot recall them all?

Don't forget his wondrous works.

Count your many blessings,
 Name them one by one
And it will surprise you
 What the Lord has done.

Then you will not be so quick to fall into the sin of complaint.

Desires that lead to discontent

Their 'strong cravings' in the desert also got God's people into trouble. God promised them a land flowing with milk and honey. They wanted it right then. Their impatience drove them to ignore the calming counsel of the Lord.

If you are like most people, you can endure pain or inconvenience for a short stretch. But steady suffering over a prolonged period brings people to the brink of despair. But a 'patient' must learn 'patience.' The patient in the hospital is so called because of his need for 'patience.' He is not in a position to demand that all his desires be fulfilled here and now.

God counsels his people to get patience at any price. They need to learn that man does not live by bread only, but by every word that comes from the mouth of God. Even the word that deprives of bread means life if it is received rightly. Besides, what good would it do to gain the whole world and in the process lose the soul that alone makes it possible to enjoy the wonderful things that God has made?

What would you have done if you had been with Israel in the desert? Would you have complained about the lack of water, about the flat-tasting manna? Or would you have lived contentedly, anticipating the apostle Paul's inspired perspective: 'For the kingdom of God is not a matter of eating and drinking but of righteousness and peace and joy in the Holy Spirit' (Rom. 14:17). It is so much simpler to seek satisfaction in things that please the flesh rather than in righteousness, peace and joy in the Holy Spirit. How easy it is to forget the true substance of the kingdom of God!

How does the Lord respond to this endless craving of his own people? God gives them their desires, but sends leanness into their souls. He shows them the emptiness of it all by causing discontent to rest in their spirit. They had all the food and drink they desired, but their souls were starving. God made manna and quail into junk food. They ate all they wanted, they satisfied their desires, but they got no true nourishment from their surfeiting.

Do you think the Lord handles human discontent the same way today? Have you experienced satiation without satisfaction?

Repeated rebellion and the intercession of Moses

The central section of this psalm recounts seven sins of the people, including sins related to food, power, beauty, lack of faith, sex, irresponsibility and idolatry. The book of Numbers speaks of the 'ten times' that the nation rebelled against God (Num. 14:22). It is not so difficult to imagine: a perfect ten in sin!

As a consequence, God says he will consume Israel. He will replace them by making a great nation out of Moses. It is not that he will give up on his stated purpose to redeem a people from the seed of Abraham, for Moses comes from Abraham through Levi. But this people have provoked him so severely that he will start all over again with Moses.

But Moses 'stands in the breach' (verse 23). Their priestly mediator intercedes, pleads for the glorification of God's name among the nations, and recalls the Lord's promise to the fathers. Moses acknowledges their great sin and offers himself as the sacrifice to be consumed in their place. 'Blot out my name if you will not forgive them,' he says (Exod. 32:32).

He offers up his life in order to bridge the gap. His willing proposal finds its fulfilment in the self-offering of Isaiah's Suffering Servant, who alone was capable of standing in the breach. That which Moses could only offer to do, Jesus Christ has done.

Even the magnanimous offer of Moses their mediator does not bring the people to their senses for long. Yet the Lord continues to show his constancy:

> Time after time he rescued them
>   but they kept rebelling against their counsel.
> They were weakened
>   by their constant sin.

But he saw their distress,
 and heard their outcry.
He remembered his covenant with them,
 and showed leniency according to his boundless love.
He made all those who had taken them captive
 treat them with mercy

(verses 43-46).

This summary statement of the psalmist concentrates not on the persistence of the people's sin, but on the pattern established by God's gracious response. 'Time after time' he delivers them, despite the fact that they keep on rebelling against the wise counsel he offers. Each new sin weakens them. But the Lord keeps hearing their cry for help, remembering his covenant and responding in mercy according to his boundless love.

Amazing! To protect the well-being of his people, he turns the wolf into a lamb. The cruel and barbarous enemies that have devastated his people learn to show pity on those they had formerly persecuted. Only the Lord's mercies could have accomplished these things.

The well-established pattern of the past provides the basis for a bold prayer for the future.

5. A prayer for salvation that leads to praise

Save us, O Covenant Lord our God!
 Gather us from the nations
so that we may give thanks to your holy name
 and joyfully shout, 'Hallelujah!'

(verse 47).

So the end of the psalm echoes the Hallelujah of its beginning. The opening admonition to praise the Lord is balanced by a closing prayer that gives all glory to God.

Let God's people now be delivered from their current oppressors, set over them because of their sin. When this deliverance occurs, they will be able to praise the Lord and joyfully shout their own 'Hallelujah!'

Psalm 110

The Glories of Our Priestly King

By David. A psalm.

1st Reader: 1The Covenant LORD solemnly said to my Lord:

2nd Reader: 'Sit at my right hand
until I make your enemies
a footstool for your feet.'

1st Congr.: 2The LORD of the Covenant will extend from Zion
your mighty rod;

2nd Congr.: rule
in the midst of your enemies.

1st Congr.: 3Your people will be a freewill offering
in the day of your strength;

2nd Congr.: in the majesty of holiness
from the womb of the morning
your youth will arise for you like the dew.

1st Reader: 4The Covenant LORD has sworn
and never will change:

2nd Reader: 'You are a priest forever
after the pattern of Melchizedek.'

1st Congr.:	5The Lord at your right hand shall crush kings in the day of your wrath.
2nd Congr.:	6He will judge the nations, heaping up corpses;
1st Congr.:	he will crush heads across the breadth of the earth.
2nd Congr.:	7From the brook along the way he will drink.
All:	So he will lift high his head.

The Glories of Our Priestly King—*The Messiah as Priest and King*

Introduction

If you should think of the most glorious people in the history of the world, who would come to mind? Would you think of the caesars of Rome, the kings and queens of Europe, the czars of Russia? Perhaps even one or two presidents of the United States of America would be given a little thought.

Ultimately serious consideration would have to be given to the kings of God's people under the old covenant. For God chose them, set them apart and gave them the responsibility of being head over his own people. Among the kings of Israel David and Solomon stand out most prominently.

Yet in Psalm 110 David speaks about someone more glorious than himself. He refers to this glorious person as his 'Lord,' one concerning whom God himself took a solemn oath. This person is unique in that he occupies not only the office of king. He also is priest. In him is combined the two offices of priest and king. Consider more carefully this distinctive person who is higher than David, uniquely holding in himself the two offices of king and priest.

Three features stand out about this glorious person described in Psalm 110: this glorious one is your King; this glorious one is your Priest; this glorious one is your Priest/King.

1. This glorious one is your King

> The Covenant LORD solemnly said to my Lord:
> 'Sit at my right hand
> until I make your enemies
> a footstool for your feet' (verse 1).

David reports what the LORD of the Covenant said to his 'Lord.' But who is this person, who could be 'Lord' over David, to whom the Covenant LORD speaks? David as king holds the highest office in Israel. Who beside God himself stands above the King of Israel as his Lord, and deserves to receive the homage of all those who have opposed him?

If a high-ranking army officer arrives at a banquet, the first enlisted man who spots him calls everyone else to standing attention until the officer has been seated. The same principle holds when a judge enters his courtroom. The office of the person demands honour.

But in this case it is the Covenant LORD of Israel who bestows unprecedented honour on this person who is David's Lord. To him the LORD of the Covenant says, 'You remain seated while I, Almighty God, render service to you.'

How exalted can this person be? He remains seated while God works on his behalf. It is not surprising that some modern commentators have treated the scene in Psalm 110 as mythological. To whom could God afford to pay such honour except another god?

The Covenant LORD furthermore says, 'Be seated at my right hand.' The position at the right hand symbolizes power, authority and dignity. While David's 'Lord' remains seated in this symbolic place of honour, God himself will be busy subduing all his enemies, making them the footstool of his feet.

Who is this person? He is exalted above David, seated at God's right hand and told to remain seated in his place of honour until God has subdued all his enemies under his feet. Is he a real figure of history, or a fiction of human imagination?

Messiah, son of David and Son of God

The ancient pre-Christian title of this psalm indicating that it was written 'by David' suggests that Jewish interpreters living before Jesus Christ had deduced that the 'Lord' of this verse must be the Messiah to come.[1] For who else could be so much greater than

[1] cf. A. Weiser, *The Psalms*, 1962, p. 692.

David, presented as David's Lord in verse 1? This person could be none other than the Messiah, the promised Saviour of Israel. He alone might be expected to stand above David and receive such distinguished treatment from the LORD of the Covenant. This conviction of the Jews that David's 'Lord' in Psalm 110 was their Messiah played a significant role in the life of Jesus Christ. Because he spoke with authority, Jesus often was opposed by the Pharisees. This conflict came to a head during the last week of Jesus' life. The Pharisees had asked him many questions, and Jesus finally responded by asking them a question.

'Whose son is Messiah?' he enquired.

To this question they had the obvious answer. 'He must be the son of David,' they replied.

Jesus had one more question: 'If Messiah is David's son, how then could David, speaking [in Psalm 110:1] by the Holy Spirit, call Messiah his "Lord"?'

How would you answer Jesus' question? A son cannot in his essence be greater than his father. A father cannot in any meaningful sense remain a father and also be enslaved to his son. How then could Messiah as David's son also be David's Lord?

From that point on, no one asked Jesus any more questions (see Matt. 22:41-45).

There is a proper answer to Jesus' perplexing question. But it means recognizing the deity of the Messiah. It means accepting the record of the incarnation to be true. As David's son, Messiah must be born of men. But as Lord over King David, he must be Son to God. This is the testimony of the Holy Spirit in Psalm 110:1.

This Messiah who is son of David but also Son of God is named Jesus. He has been given the name that is above all other names. He is the exalted one seated at the right hand of the Father, higher than all angelic beings. For never to an angel did God say, 'Sit at my right hand until I make your enemies a footstool for your feet' (Heb. 1:13, quoting Psa. 110:1). The exaltation implicit in these words applies only to Jesus.

His people's response

How should you respond to this exalted Lord Jesus Christ? He sits in the place of highest authority above the kings of the earth. This psalm tells you how to respond:

> Your people will be a freewill offering
> in the day of your strength
>
> (verse 3).

That is how you should respond. You should present yourself as a freewill offering, ready to be consumed for this one who is your Lord and King. The psalmist doesn't say that you will *bring* a freewill offering. He says, 'Your people will *be* a freewill offering.' Not because someone is cracking a whip over your head, but because of your own free will, you give yourself to Jesus Christ your Saviour, Lord and King.

The psalmist says more about the response of Messiah's people to his summons to service:

> In the majesty of holiness
> from the womb of the morning
> your youth will arise for you like the dew
>
> (verse 3).

Holiness has a majesty that suits the servants of God's Messiah. Don't think you can walk in self-centred patterns of life and serve Jesus Christ just as well. You do him a dishonour if you call yourself his servant and walk in a way that contradicts the purity of his kingdom.

Perhaps you have known some people who have acquired genuine holiness of character over the years. They walk in ways that please the Lord. Their spirit manifests the fruit of righteousness. They do not boast in their own greatness. Their holiness does not drive you from them. Instead, it attracts you to them, because in their holiness are reflected the attributes of love and compassion that characterize the kingdom of the Messiah.

Respond to the greatness of your Messiah by serving him willingly in the majesty of holiness. Set aside sin, that you might give him the honour he deserves as your Saviour and 'Lord.'

One further element in the response of God's people to the glories of the Lord Jesus Christ should be noted:

> ... from the womb of the morning
> your youth will arise for you like the dew
>
> (verse 3).

Look across a field glittering with dewdrops early in the morning. When the sun first strikes the meadow, every blade of grass glistens with the shimmering vitality of life embodied in the drop of dew.

The psalmist imagines the darkness which precedes the earliest moments of morning as an opening womb which gives birth to thousands upon thousands of dewdrops. The response of millions of Messiah's servants to his radiant glory should be like the reaction of the dewdrops to the sunlight. They dedicate themselves to him in the freshness and vigour of their youth. Their only desire is to magnify his glory.

Respond with a similar enthusiasm to the glories of your Messiah. Make yourself a freewill offering. Present yourself in holiness before him. Let Christ be exalted as Lord in your life.

2. This glorious one is your Priest

But Christ is presented in this psalm as something more than a king. He also appears as priest. Consider Christ not only as he exercises authority at the right hand of God. See him also in his glories as priestly mediator, one whose heart is constantly moved with compassion and tenderness for the needs of his people.

Kingship over the world would be a fairly adequate job for most people. But the man described in Psalm 110 not only is exalted as King of the world; he also is established as the supreme Judge and Mediator of men. If any person anywhere in the world wishes to have his prayer to be presented favourably before Almighty God, he must go through Jesus Christ. He is the one and only mediator between God and men. The psalmist says:

> The Covenant LORD has sworn
> and never will change:

'You are a priest forever
after the pattern of Melchizedek'

(verse 4).

The Lord has sworn

The word of a man often proves not to be true. Living among frail human beings, a person can become disillusioned from the disappointments that come from broken pledges. Perhaps you can remember the first time your father's word fell to the ground. He made a promise, and for one reason or another, good or bad, he did not keep his commitment. This kind of experience can lead to great disillusionment.

But when God speaks, he always carries through to fulfil his commitments. Never has his word failed. When God adds an oath to his word, he does it for your sake, not his own. Because men so regularly experience the uncertainty of words, God adds a further note of assurance by taking an oath.

Now what is it that the Lord has sworn in this psalm? He has sworn that Messiah will be 'priest forever.' The one who has been designated 'Lord' will also be priest forever after the order of Melchizedek.

The teaching of the book of Hebrews

The significance of the priesthood of Melchizedek for the ministry of Jesus Christ is developed extensively in the book of Hebrews. Following his standard pattern of weaving an Old Testament reference throughout the fabric of his argument, the writer first introduces a quotation from Psalm 110 about Melchizedek in Hebrews 5:6. He alludes to the same passage again in 5:10. But then he interrupts his consideration of the passage until 6:20, attempting to deal first with the immaturity of his hearers, which would make it difficult for them to grasp the rich truth about Jesus' priesthood. Having dealt with that problem, he develops in chapter 7 one of the most extensive expositions of an Old Testament text to be found anywhere in the New Testament. The whole of the seventh chapter of Hebrews embodies a profound treatment of every phrase in Psalm 110:4:

'The LORD has sworn … :
"You are a priest forever,
after the order of Melchizedek."'

The exposition of this passage in Hebrews 7 proceeds according to the following order:

1. Hebrews 7:1-10 explains the significance of Melchizedek. He was 'King of Salem' or 'King of Peace.' Receiving tithes from Abraham established him as a priest as well as a king. The fact that Levi was in the loins of Abraham indicates that Melchizedek's priesthood was more excellent than Levi's because of the honour that Abraham paid to this mysterious man. The absence of any record of Melchizedek' s genealogy symbolizes the eternal nature of his priesthood.

2. Hebrews 7:11-15 explains the significance of the phrase, 'according to the order of' Melchizedek. The prophecy about a Messianic priesthood that will function 'according to the order of' Melchizedek, coming centuries after the law had established the priesthood of Levi, shows that a new order of priesthood 'according to the order of' Melchizedek was to replace the Levitical order.

3. Hebrews 7:16-19 explains the meaning of the phrase 'a priest forever' as it occurs in Psalm 110:4. Because the law that governed the Levitical priesthood could make nothing perfect, a better priesthood was needed. This priesthood is founded on the indestructible life symbolized by the absence of any genealogy for Melchizedek. This different priestly order produces a priest who lives 'forever,' as realized in the resurrected Jesus Christ.

4. Hebrews 7:20-25 explains the meaning of 'The Lord has sworn.' God has taken a solemn oath that Christ's priesthood will last forever. Since he lives forever to make intercession for them, he is able to save to the uttermost those who come to God by him.

5. Hebrews 7:26-28 explains the meaning of 'You are a priest.' In the case of Jesus, priesthood means high priesthood, since he is the Son of God who has the perpetual right of access to his Father. As the blameless Son, he has no need to offer sacrifices any more, having offered himself once. He is the sinless one whose mediation does the priestly work perfectly.

What this means for the believer

Jesus Christ is your priest forever according to the order of Melchizedek. As Son of God, he has made the perfect sacrifice once for all. There is no need of further sacrifice to make the sinner right with God. He lives to make continual intercession for you. As the beloved Son of the Father, all his prayers on your behalf will be answered. Because of the perfections of his priesthood, no possibility exists for a change of the law affecting the believing sinner's relation to God in the future. You can rest secure in the sacrifice for sin offered by Christ as priest, and his continual intercession as priest.

Do you remember the first time you came to Christ and confessed your sin before him? Can you recall the tremendous relief you felt when you understood your sins were forgiven because his blood was shed once for all to deliver sinners from the curse of God? He has not changed. He is the same. Draw near to him without fear. Draw near because he is a priest forever, and his compassions are always the same. Christ is exalted as Priest as well as King.

3. This glorious one is your Priest-King

Finally, and perhaps most significantly in this psalm, Christ is exalted as your Priest-King. As one person he combines both these offices in himself.

Turn a board so that its grain runs in the opposite direction from another board. Glue the two pieces of board together, and you have produced plywood. A piece of plywood is much stronger than a single board of the same thickness. The joining of the two increases the strength of both. In a similar way, the two offices of priest and king now joined in Christ are much stronger than the two offices ever could be separately.

Psalm 110 stresses the combination of these two offices in a number of ways.

He abides in the presence of God

Verse 1 says the Messiah should sit at God's right hand until he makes his enemies 'the footstool of your feet.' Messiah at God's right hand shares the Lord's own 'footstool.' But God's footstool is not merely a figure for the place where his enemies are humbled. It is associated more specifically with the ark of the covenant. When David describes his plan to build a place of rest for the ark of the covenant of God, he parallels this phrase with a reference to his building a place of rest 'for the footstool of our God' (1 Chron. 28:2). By this allusion, it becomes evident that God's footstool is identified with the ark of the covenant and located in the Most Holy Place of the tabernacle. God dwells between the cherubim, with the ark of the covenant serving as his footstool.

The high priest of Israel stood before this ark of the covenant once a year to sprinkle the blood of atonement on the mercy-seat, which provided a covering for the ark. God's footstool on earth symbolically was the place where the blood of the atoning sacrifice was sprinkled.

Now our Lord Jesus Christ sacrificed his life-blood, taking upon himself the judgment of God for his people's sins. Then he entered the Most Holy Place by his own blood, standing before the footstool of God's throne (cf. Heb. 9:12).

What does Christ's appearance before the throne of God mean for you? It means that God on his throne will never order anything with respect to your life apart from consideration of the blood of our Lord Jesus Christ that has been shed for your sins. Jesus Christ lives in God's presence not only as your King ruling over you, but as your Priest interceding for you, having presented his own blood on your behalf. Because he abides in God's presence as your Priest-King, you can be absolutely confident that you will receive continual blessing from his hand.

He is both Priest and King forever

Psalm 110:4 also stresses the perpetual merger of these two offices in Jesus Christ. This verse affirms that 'The Lord has sworn and will never change.' It could be supposed that God might change his mind about combining the two offices of priest and king in one person. The merger of these offices was not allowed in the past.

When Uzziah the king presumed to himself the priestly office, he was struck with leprosy in his forehead.

But the Lord has sworn and never will change his mind on this matter. Jesus is both your King and your Priest, and forever will be both. The one who has died for you is the one who enforces God's law in your life.

Since there were four boys in our family, it should not be surprising that occasionally one of us would lead the others astray. At that point Mother would go outside to prepare for battle. Off the bordering hedge would come a nice switch. Mother would run her fingers down the switch to remove all the leaves so there wouldn't be any padding. Back she would come into the house ready to do battle. By that time we boys had our strategy all worked out. Peeking around the corner of the hall, we would slip into the bedroom when we saw Mother and her switch heading through the dining room. By the time she reached the hall, we were headed for the living room. If she went in one direction, we headed in the other. After about the third time round the house, Mother would begin to giggle between her threats. Then we knew we were safe. Her good-naturedness would take over, and we would be off the hook.

Our Lord Jesus Christ, though never indulgent, is certainly good-natured. He already has made reconciliation between you and your God. He will chasten you at times for your own good. But he never will lose his good-natured spirit. As your Priest, he pleads for you even as he decides what shall be your fate. Praise God that one person is forever both your Priest and your King. The one who rules over you is, and forever will be, the same as the one who pleads for you.

The 'order of Melchizedek'

The psalmist underscores the unity of the two offices still further by noting that Jesus is a priest forever 'after the order of Melchizedek.' Jesus Christ is not a priest according to the order of Levi. He is a priest according to the order of Melchizedek, and that fact underscores the unity of the offices of priest and king in him.

Did you realize that the first time the word 'priest' occurs in the Old Testament it describes a man who also is a king? The term 'priest' first appears in Genesis 14:18, describing the mysterious figure of Melchizedek, King of Jerusalem who also was priest of God Most High. Melchizedek, lord over Jerusalem, also was a priest who made offerings on behalf of Abraham.

Melchizedek, in his merger of the offices of priest and king, was a most unusual figure. Subsequently the laws of Moses made the clear distinction between priesthood and kingship. But these two offices are clearly merged in Psalm 110 despite the centuries of prohibition that preceded it. The Lord Messiah of David would be quite distinctive in reinstituting the union of these two offices in his own person.

Now consider the significance of the fact that the Lord Jesus Christ inherits the pattern of Melchizedek. Your King is also your Priest. He combines these two offices for a good reason.

It is because he has a higher position arising out of his essence that Jesus was designated as priest according to the order of Melchizedek. That higher position is embodied in the word 'Son.' Because he is the Son, he has access to the Father as a priest. Because he is the Son, he inherits the authority of king that belongs to his Father.

Because of his sonship to the Father, his position as both priest and king is completely understandable. It is not accidental that the writer to the Hebrews, in developing so fully the priesthood of Jesus Christ, begins his epistle by establishing the unique sonship of Jesus Christ. Once that relationship has been rightly perceived, Jesus can be seen in all his glory as the Priest/King.

Conclusion

But what are the practical implications of this combination of offices? Sometimes a king may seem threatening. His authority can intimidate the weak who need his help the most. But consider that simultaneously with his kingship Jesus is your Priest, the one who takes the part of the weak. Even as he rules at the right hand of the Father he also intercedes on the basis of the sacrifice he has made for your sins. Now you can come with confidence and joy to the very throne of grace, no matter how much your conscience would condemn you. His blood pleads on your behalf. The Son himself intercedes most earnestly for you, even more earnestly than you might plead for yourself. But all the time he pleads for you, he also rules over you.

Give glory to this one man who is more glorious than all others. No king, queen or potentate in times past or present can compare with him. He is Jesus, he is the Christ, he is the Lord. He is King and he is Priest—forever.

Psalm 113
'Hallelujah!' for God's Help to the Humbled

Reader: 1Hallelu Yah!
Praise,
all you servants of the Covenant LORD!

Praise
the name of the Covenant LORD!

1st Congr.: 2Let the name of the Covenant LORD be blessed
from now
to eternity.

2nd Congr.: 3From the rising of the sun
to its going down
let the name of the Covenant LORD be praised.

Reader: 4High
above all nations
is the Covenant LORD;

All: above the heavens
is his glory.

Reader: 5Who
is as the Covenant LORD our God?

1st Congr.:	Who makes [himself] high to reign;
2nd Congr.:	6 Who makes [himself] low to see
All:	in the heavens and in the earth.
Reader:	7 He raises the poor from the dust;
All:	he exalts the needy from the dunghill.
Reader:	8 To make them sit with princes,
All:	with the princes of his people.
Reader:	9 He makes the barren woman dwell in her home as a mother of sons rejoicing.
All:	Hallelu Yah!

'Hallelujah!' for God's Help to the Humbled—
Give Praise to the Lord for His Help

Introduction

One of the most difficult things to do is 'just praise the Lord.' It is much easier to rush into the Lord's presence and dump all your troubles, anxieties, cares and desires into his hands. Praising the Lord seems to be such an abstract thing that it is hard to get a handle on how to begin.

Yet in a few short verses, this psalm reaches from the highest heavens to the simplest domestic scene, all as a means of lifting the heart in praise to God. All creation is summoned to join in a universal 'Hallelujah!' for the great God's help to the humbled. Let us listen to this word from the Lord so that our hearts may join with all creation to offer our own personal praise of our Creator and Redeemer.

This psalm naturally falls into two sections: the summons to praise (verses 1-3); and the subjects of praise (verses 4-9).

1. The summons to praise (verses 1-3)

It is a good thing to begin your prayers with praise on a regular basis. It will help in all your other communication with God. If you start by praising him for the fact that he is the same yesterday, today and forever, then when you ask for help with a problem, you will have the confidence to believe that the God who helped you in the past will be able to help you in the future.

Praise him for his justice. Then when you confess your sins, you will not treat them too lightly. Praise him for his omnipotence, recognizing that he has at his disposal all power in heaven and in earth. Then you will have a basis for trusting that he can do the difficult things you ask.

Even if praising God doesn't come easily to you, heed the admonition of the psalmist and do it just the same. Stretch the capacities of your soul with a regular exercise of offering praise to God. You can do far more in the way of giving glory to him for who he is than you realize. It is like a singer stretching the limits of his voice. He can sing a lot higher, lower, softer and louder than he might at first imagine. In the same way, you can give a lot more glory to God than you realize if you will only exercise your soul daily in praising him.

Who is to praise the Lord?

God's word is specific about who is to praise the Lord. It is not only the eloquent and the super-saints that are called to give glory to him. Instead, it is any who identify themselves as servants of the Lord that should praise him. If you desire to serve the Lord, respond wholeheartedly to this summons of God's word. Praise him as he says!

More precisely, the psalmist summons you to praise him as a group, and not just individually. 'All of you, praise the Lord,' communicates more exactly the intent of the psalmist.

From the perspective of the new covenant, it is particularly God-glorifying to praise the Lord in the context of the universal church of the Lord Jesus Christ. Under the old covenant, the Jewish people were a single nation with centuries of customs, traditions and language that bound them together. United praise to their Covenant LORD was a natural outflowing of their identity as a people. But today, the church of Jesus Christ consists of an international community representing every language, culture, race and nationality. When the church today unites to praise the Lord, it is a testimony to God's power of reconciling men to himself and to one another that the world must admire. Paul makes this point strongly in his letter to the Christians in Rome:

> May the God of endurance and encouragement grant you to live in such harmony with one another, in accord with

Christ Jesus, that together you may with one voice glorify the God and Father of our Lord Jesus Christ. Therefore welcome one another as Christ has welcomed you, for the glory of God. For I tell you that Christ became a servant to the circumcised to show God's truthfulness, in order to confirm the promises given to the patriarchs, and in order that the Gentiles might glorify God for his mercy. As it is written,

> 'Therefore I will praise you among the Gentiles,
> and sing to your name.'

And again it is said,

> 'Rejoice, O Gentiles, with his people.'

And again,

> 'Praise the Lord, all you Gentiles,
> and let all the peoples extol him'
>
> (Rom. 15:5-11).

Paul quotes from Psalm 117, a companion psalm to Psalm 113. But he certainly could have quoted from Psalm 113. When people of various backgrounds are united in Christ, they can praise God in a unique way. The hope of the Old Testament was that the Gentile community would join with Jewish believers so that together they might praise the Lord. That hope has reached fulfilment in the universal church of Jesus Christ today.

You have a distinctive opportunity to give glory to God. Because you are joined together by faith in Jesus Christ, you can unite with others to give praise to him. Lift up your voices in praise to God for the wonderful work of redemption he has done.

When is he to be praised?

When are you to praise him? The psalmist has a ready answer:

> Let the name of the Covenant LORD be blessed
> from now
> to eternity
>
> (verse 2).

Right *now* as a congregation say, 'Hallelu Yah!' God receives glory whenever his assembled people give praise to him. Beginning now and going throughout eternity, join your voices in praise to him.

Where is he to be praised?

Where is it appropriate to praise the Lord? Is it necessary to make a pilgrimage to some 'holy place' to give glory to God? The psalmist answers that question directly:

> From the rising of the sun
> to its going down
> let the name of the Covenant LORD be praised
> (verse 3).

From the most extreme point towards the east to the farthest point westward people should assemble to praise the Lord. Anticipating this very day, the Lord declared through the prophet Malachi: 'From the rising of the sun to its setting my name will be great among the nations, and in every place incense will be offered to my name, and a pure offering. For my name will be great among the nations, says the Lord of hosts' (Mal. 1:11).

Things happen when people praise the Lord. It is not just an idle, expendable exercise. God receives glory, nations are united, truth is advanced, righteousness is proclaimed, mercy is experienced, faith is increased and victory is secured. Hear and obey this summons to praise the Lord.

2. The subjects of praise (verses 4-9)

But what in particular should be the subjects of praise to the Lord?

This principle should be understood from the outset: if praise is not rightly directed, it can become an insult rather than a compliment to the Almighty. God's word must instruct his people in the proper way to praise him, just as it teaches the right way in every other area of life. A proud new father wheeling his beautiful but bald newborn daughter through the supermarket will not be pleased by remarks about the 'cute little boy.' Such misdirected praise will be treated as an insult rather than a compliment.

God will not be pleased with praise that misrepresents him. A sentimental soul may seek to honour the Lord by affirming that he is so loving that he never would bring men into judgment for their sins. But the expression of these sentiments will give God no pleasure whatsoever.

Two particulars in this psalm are noted as proper subjects of praise: God's glory above the great (verses 4-6); and God's help to the humbled (verses 7-9). These things are true about the Lord, and are proper objects of praise.

His glory is above the great

First, praise God, for his glory is above the great. The psalmist says:

> High
> above all nations
> is the Covenant LORD;
> above the heavens
> is his glory
>
> (verse 4).

Men derive a distinctive delight from exercising authority over one another. Human ambition guarantees that there will always be an abundance of candidates for presidents, prime ministers and potentates. No matter how many assassinations, bombings and mental breakdowns occur, more men will rise to seek positions of power.

But without struggle or misplaced ambition, the Covenant LORD is exalted to a position that is high above all the nations of the world and all their rulers. He is not over them merely because he is located in heaven rather than on earth. He is over them in concrete authority, controlling circumstances and events that affect the course of nations. He orders the actions of men even as they exercise the freedom of their own wills. Always he orders all things for the good of his people and for his own glory.

When the first Russian cosmonaut returned from circling the globe in space, he made a triumphant affirmation. He declared that he had been to heaven and had not seen God anywhere. He concluded that God must not exist.

How would you respond to that rather bold assertion?

The psalmist might answer by challenging the basic assumption of the space traveller: 'You say you journeyed into the heavens and didn't see God? Well, your problem is that you didn't go high enough! For the Scriptures clearly state: "*Above* the heavens is his glory."'

Obviously a person has a problem when he conceives of God as an entity that can be seen. In contrast with the arrogant astronaut, ask the youngest child in a congregation that has studied the *Child's Catechism* and he will give you the right answer:

> *Question*: 'Can you see God?'
> *Answer*: 'No, I cannot see God, but he always sees me.'

Praise God for his greatness. The fact that he cannot be seen by the eye of men must not dissuade you from belief in the reality of his presence and power in this world. He controls the course of the nations, and he does all things well.

The psalmist also explains that a part of God's greatness is his humility. God takes the trouble to order the meandering speck of dust drifting across the sunbeam just as he guides the course of wandering stars dubbed by the ancients as 'planets.' His exaltation in power does not limit him to making only the 'big' decisions about the universe. He is above the great, but he also helps the humbled. The psalmist says:

> Who is like the Covenant LORD our God?
> Who makes [himself] high
>   to reign;
> who makes [himself] low
>   to see
>   in the heavens
>   and in the earth
>
> (verses 5, 6).

God's greatness and humility are set side by side. He is higher than heaven and earth. Yet his surpassing greatness is also seen in his readiness to humble himself before men. Everywhere else in the Old Testament the Scriptures speak of God's making other people low. He brings down the proud. King Nebuchadnezzar is driven out of his luxuriant palace and roams the open fields like a wild beast. He crawls on all fours, with his hair dishevelled and his beard dragging the dust. God has brought him low because of his pride.

But now the psalmist says, 'Praise God for making *himself* low.' Not as a judgment for his own pride, but as a manifestation of his humility, God has come down to identify with men on this earth.

This humble position the Lord willingly took himself. No one forced him. He did it on his own, manifesting a greatness that men cannot imagine.

Do you see our Lord Jesus Christ? He humbled himself. He left the ivory palaces. He became a man. He took on the form of a servant. Being found in fashion as a man he humbled himself and became obedient unto death, even the death of the cross.

Praise God for his greatness—a greatness seen in his humility as well as in his power. His greatness exceeds the imagination of men just as much as the stars of heaven are higher than the tallest structures on earth.

His help to the humbled

There is a second reason why the Lord should be praised. Praise him for his help to the humbled (verses 7-9). The Lord's humbling of himself was not an end in itself. It was a means to the end of helping people in desperate need.

Consider God's help of the needy as described in this psalm:

> He raises the poor
>   from the dust;
> he exalts the needy
>   from the dunghill
>
> (verse 7).

Being bowed to the dust and sitting on a dunghill are images that depict man in the extremities of humiliation and weakness. He is stuck in the ghetto, hooked on drugs, in the bankruptcy court, abandoned by his spouse, unskilled and unemployed. He is in the intensive care ward or overwhelmed with a chronic case of depression. He is a defenceless refugee.

So what does God do about the situation? He raises the poor from the dust. He exalts the needy from the dunghill. He makes them sit side by side with the princes of his own people.

Has not God chosen the poor of the earth to be rich in faith? (James 2:5). Does not the Messianic King have pity on the poor? (Psa. 72:12-14). Doesn't he reach into broken homes and shattered lives to restore them to health, dignity and abundance of provision? Even in their weakness, doesn't he lift their spirits by assuring them of their abundant inheritance as the sons and daughters of God?

Where are you today in the rise and fall of human fortunes? Are you among the self-made proud ones who are sure to be brought low, as was splendid King Nebuchadnezzar? Are you among the humbled who sit in physical and spiritual poverty and want? Are you among those who have been lifted by his grace to enjoy the fulness of the riches that are in Jesus Christ? Wherever you are, turn as servants of the Lord and praise him. Praise him for his greatness as displayed in his power and his humility. Praise him for his help to the needy. Give him the glory due to his name.

A unique image climaxes this hymn of praise to the Lord. It pictures God's blessing on a simple domestic scene:

> He makes the barren woman
> dwell in her home
> as a mother of sons rejoicing.
> Hallelu Yah!
>
> (verse 9).

Remember the story of Hannah, the mother of Samuel? She came into the temple praying and weeping because she had no children. Eli the priest concluded that she was drunk, defiling the temple by her presence. But when he understood the true cause of her disturbed appearance, he sent her home with a message of hope. Shortly afterwards, she conceived and gave birth to a son whom she named Samuel, which means 'asked of the Lord' (1 Sam. 1:20).

Hannah's heart was so filled with joy that she composed a poetic prayer of praise to the Lord for helping her when she was in such a humbled state. She said:

> He raises up the poor from the dust;
> He lifts the needy from the ash heap
> To make them sit with princes
> And inherit a seat of honour
>
> (1 Sam. 2:8).

Do these words sound familiar? They should. They reappear almost identically in Psalm 113. Because of the consistency of God's help for the humbled over the ages, the theme proved to be worthy of celebration in the regular worship services of God's people. So the words of Hannah were incorporated into this psalm.

Over and over again the Lord has shown his sensitivity to the heart-hurts of his people. Sarah, the wife of Abraham, was barren, and God gave her Isaac (Gen. 11:30). Rebekah, the wife of Isaac, was barren, and God gave her twins (Gen. 25:21). Rachel, the wife of Jacob, was barren, and God gave her Joseph and Benjamin (Gen. 29:31). Manoah's wife was barren, and God gave her Samson (Judg. 13:2). Elizabeth, the wife of Zechariah, was barren, and God gave her John the Baptist (Luke 1:7).

In this history of deliverance from barrenness, the Lord shows how redemption works for God's people. This history teaches us not only about how he answers prayers over certain disappointing circumstances in our lives. More significantly, it teaches a lesson about how God works to fulfil his promises. Just as the promised seed leading to Christ the Redeemer could not be produced by human effort, so no one becomes a part of God's kingdom through the natural efforts he makes himself. Neither Sarah nor Rebekah nor Rachel nor Elizabeth could bring forth children by natural processes. God had to intervene on their behalf. Just as the line that led to Christ was preserved over and over again by divine intervention, so God directly intervenes in the lives of lost sinners to bring them into his kingdom.

As Paul explains it, Abraham had not one but two sons. What is more, he had two kinds of sons. One son was produced through man's natural powers when Abraham resorted to his concubine Hagar. But the other son was born by the supernatural intervention of God after Sarah was past the age when it was possible for her to conceive. The first child, the product of natural human effort, was born a slave. But the child that came as a gift produced and given by God was born free (cf. Gal. 4:21-23).

Paul makes a point from this crucial principle that has repeated itself over and over again in redemptive history. All those who have been born into God's kingdom are like Isaac, children produced by God's supernatural intervention as a fulfilment of his promise (Gal. 4:28). Every son and daughter of God has been born supernaturally by the work of God's Spirit in their hearts. Like that long line of barren women that could not conceive, the human heart is incapable of experiencing life with God apart from his re-creative grace.

If you have been born into God's kingdom by the Spirit of God, say 'Hallelu Yah' along with the psalmist. You have experienced the greatness of God when you could do nothing to save yourself.

The male counterpart to the barren woman is described in the vivid words of the prophet Isaiah:

> Let not the eunuch say,
> 'Behold, I am a dry tree.'
>
> For thus says the LORD:
>
> 'To the eunuchs who keep my Sabbaths,
> who choose the things that please me
> and hold fast my covenant—
> I will give in my house and within my walls
> a monument and a name
> better than sons and daughters;
> I will give them an everlasting name
> that shall not be cut off'
>
> (Isa. 56:3-5).

Jesus Christ had no offspring. He had no sons or daughters to carry on his name. He experienced not only the absence of any offspring; he also was deserted by every one of his twelve disciples. He had poured his life into these twelve men. They were more than children to him. Yet when the testing-time of his crucifixion came, they all abandoned him. He was left utterly barren.

On the night of his desertion and betrayal, Scripture says that he celebrated the Old Testament Passover Feast with his twelve disciples. According to Jewish tradition, the celebration of the Passover meal included the reading of Psalms 113 through 118. On the very night that he agonized alone in the garden of Gethsemane, he chanted with his disciples the concluding words of Psalm 113:

> God makes the barren rejoice as a mother of sons.
> Hallelujah!

As he was going to the barrenness of the cross, these words of hope were ringing in his ears. God would make the barren rejoice over his sons. Perhaps he also remembered the prophetic words of Isaiah about God's suffering servant:

> Yet it was the will of the LORD to crush him;
> he has put him to grief;
> when his soul makes an offering for sin,
> *he shall see his offspring*;
> he shall prolong his days;
> the will of the Lord shall prosper in his hand
> (Isa. 53:10).

Jesus Christ has seen the fulfilment of God's promises to him. He has seen of the travail of his soul, and he has been satisfied. His sons and daughters now include a great multitude from every kindred, nation, tribe and people that no man can number.

Conclusion

With Jesus Christ you can live in hope. You can say, 'Hallelujah! Praise the Lord!', even in the most barren times of your life. For our great God helps the humbled. He never leaves his people in a state of barrenness.

The new covenant equivalent of the Passover meal is the Lord's Supper. Whenever you gather about the Lord's Table, remember the message of Psalm 113 as Jesus did. God will not leave his people in their lowly condition. He will lift them up. They will be seated with the princes of his people. With that confidence, you can add your own wholehearted 'Hallelujah!' to the celebration of this song of the centuries.

Psalm 118
A Eucharistic Psalm

1st Reader: 1Give thanks to the LORD of the Covenant,
for he is good;
his covenant love endures forever.

1st Congr.: 2Let Israel say,
2nd Congr.: 'His covenant love endures forever!'
1st Congr.: 3Let the house of Aaron say,
2nd Congr.: 'His covenant love endures forever!'
1st Congr.: 4Let those who fear the Covenant LORD say,
2nd Congr.: 'His covenant love endures forever!'

2nd Reader: 5In my distress I called out to the Covenant
LORD.
The LORD of the Covenant answered me
and gave me great liberty.

6The Covenant LORD is for me;
I will not fear.
What can man do to me?

7The Covenant LORD is for me
among those who help me;
so I shall look in triumph
on those who hate me.

1st Congr.: 8 It is better to take refuge in the LORD of the Covenant

2nd Congr.: than to trust in man.

1st Congr.: 9 It is better to take refuge in the LORD of the Covenant

2nd Congr.: than to trust in nobles.

2nd Reader: 10 All nations surrounded me;
in the name of the Covenant LORD I cut them off.
11 They surrounded me, swarmed about me;
in the name of the Covenant LORD I cut them off.
12 They swarmed about me like bees;
they were extinguished
as quickly as thorns that blaze up.
In the name of the Covenant LORD I cut them off.
13 You pushed me violently that I might fall,
but the Covenant LORD helped me.

14 'My strength and my song is the Covenant LORD,
and he has become my salvation.'

1st Reader: 15 Voices singing and shouting, 'Victory!'
come from the tents of the righteous:

1st Congr.: 'The right hand of the Covenant LORD

2nd Congr.: does valiantly!

1st Congr.: 16 The right hand of the Covenant LORD

2nd Congr.: is exalted!

1st Congr.: The right hand of the Covenant Lord
2nd Congr.: does valiantly!'

2nd Reader: 17 I shall not die, but live
and declare the works of the Covenant Lord.

18 The Lord of the Covenant has disciplined me severely,
but he has not given me over to death.

19 Open for me the gates of righteousness;
I shall enter through them.
I shall give thanks to the Covenant Lord.

Chorus: 20 Here is the gate of the Covenant Lord!
Righteous people can enter through it.

2nd Reader: 21 I shall give thanks to you,
because you have answered me
and have become my salvation.

1st Reader: 22 The stone which the builders rejected
has become the chief cornerstone.

1st Congr.: 23 Only the Lord of the Covenant could have done this thing;
2nd Congr.: it is wondrous in our eyes.
1st Congr.: 24 Only the Lord of the Covenant could have made this day;
2nd Congr.: we will rejoice and be glad in it.

1st Congr.:	25 O Covenant LORD, work salvation!
2nd Congr.:	O Covenant LORD, let us triumph!

1st Reader: 26 Blessed is he who comes
in the name of the Covenant LORD.

Chorus: We have blessed all of you
from the house of the Covenant LORD.

All: 27 The Covenant LORD alone is God,
and he has shone on us.

2nd Reader: Bind the festal sacrifice with cords
to the horns of the altar.

28 You are my God,
and I give you thanks;
You are my God,
I will extol you.

All: 29 Give thanks to the LORD of the Covenant,
for he is good;
his covenant love endures forever.

A Eucharistic Psalm—
Messiah's Deliverance from Death

Introduction

Since the days before Jesus Christ, this psalm has been used by the Jewish nation in conjunction with its celebration of the Passover. Every year for well over two thousand years Psalm 118 has been included with the group of psalms known as the 'Hallel of Egypt' (Psa. 113–118). It is fitting, therefore, that this psalm be remembered by Christians as they celebrate the Lord's Supper, which by Christ's appointment took the place of the Jewish Passover meal.

This psalm was crafted for congregational celebration. It has a number of refrains in which the same phrase is repeated several times, with varying responses interspersed. At several points a single speaker steps forward to rehearse the Lord's faithfulness to him at a time when he was in great distress. He speaks as the king of Israel, assaulted by his enemies. In prospect, he is the Messiah, the anointed servant of the Lord, who faces death. But he also experiences a wondrous deliverance at the hand of the Lord.

This facing of death followed by divine deliverance fits exactly the pattern experienced by Jesus Christ in connection with his institution of the Lord's Supper. He took remnants of the bread and wine from the Passover and instituted a new meal in which he identified his own body and blood with the elements of the Passover. Psalm 118 may be viewed as 'a Eucharistic psalm,' since it gives thanks for the Lord's deliverance of the King Messiah from death.

Let us now hear and respond to this ancient summons of God's word, which has meant so much to the people of God throughout all the ages: 'Give thanks to the LORD, for he is good; his covenant love endures forever.'

The covenant love of God

According to the psalmist, the goodness of God is seen particularly in his 'covenant love' (*chesed*). But what is 'covenant' love, and how does it differ from other loves?

Covenant love is not spasmodic or temporary. It does not come and go with the circumstances. God's love in the covenant means that he commits himself to love men while they still are his enemies. In the covenant he swears that he will love them, whatever it may cost him personally to achieve their salvation. This love of the covenant endures forever.

The King of Israel, the anointed Saviour of God's people, offers a threefold testimony of his experience of the covenant love of the Lord. By this testimony, he encourages the people of God through all the ages to register their own 'Amen' to this constant love of the Lord.

First the king declares that the Lord delivered him from the fear of those who hated him.

1. The Covenant Lord protects his own when they are the objects of men's hatred (verses 5-9)

> In my distress I called out to the Covenant LORD.
> The LORD of the Covenant answered me
> and gave me great liberty.
>
> The Covenant LORD is for me;
> I will not fear.
> What can man do to me?
> The Covenant LORD is for me
> among those who help me;
> so I shall look in triumph
> on those who hate me
>
> (verses 5-7).

When others hate you, you cannot help but experience a sense of confinement and restriction. You don't feel at liberty to speak, because you know your words will be twisted. Anything you do will be subject to misinterpretation.

Jesus lived constantly with that kind of pressure. From the day of his first sermon at Nazareth, the religious leaders of the day were listening to his every word, seeing if they could catch him in some erroneous or false statement.

But God gave him great liberty. He provided him with the sense of inner freedom necessary to speak in accordance with the truth. As a result he could say that he would not fear. For what could man do to him? Having received confirmation from the Lord, he spoke fearlessly in the face of all men, assured of the ultimate overthrow of his enemies.

Experience proves the truth of this perspective for every Christian. 'The Covenant Lord answered me … The Covenant Lord is for me … The Covenant Lord is for me,' says the psalmist. He recognizes that the Lord himself is behind each and every person, circumstance and event that provides relief from trouble.

So the congregation can express its own confirming testimony to these words of their king:

> It is better to take refuge in the Covenant Lord
> than to trust in man.
> It is better to take refuge in the Covenant Lord
> than to trust in nobles
>
> (verses 8, 9).

Consider God and man in terms of the deliverance they can provide from powers beyond your control. Man can hardly predict, much less determine the weather for tomorrow. Man cannot make himself grow one inch taller or shorter. Man can attempt to persuade or convince, but he cannot actually change the attitudes of another person's heart.

But God can do all these things. He sends the rain on one city and withholds it from another. He shortens the life of one man and lengthens the life of another. He causes the earth to rotate on its axis and stops it when he pleases. He changes the heart of a heathen king so that it is favourable towards his people.

So why trust men rather than God? When troubles threaten, man may or may not be able to provide a limited amount of help.

But God lives without the limits of men. When men hate you and oppose you, look to the Lord for your defence. Has not experience taught you over and over again that he can intervene where man is absolutely helpless?

2. The Covenant Lord delivers his people gloriously even when they are threatened by many nations (verses 10-16)

Sometimes the people of God face opposition not merely from individuals. A larger coalition may set itself against the Lord and his anointed. Israel had this experience when they were oppressed by the Egyptians during their sojourn. Infants were slaughtered, adults were enslaved. During the period of the judges, food was taken from God's people by the oppressing Midianites. Under David, neighbouring nations regularly formed coalitions for the purpose of destroying God's people. This opposition of the powers of nations climaxed in the joining together of the Romans and the Jews to crucify Christ.

The distress of the Messianic King as he faced heavy opposition to himself may be understood in this context:

> All nations surrounded me;
> in the name of the Covenant LORD I cut them off.
> They surrounded me, swarmed about me;
> in the name of the Covenant LORD I cut them off.
> They swarmed about me like bees;
> they were extinguished
> as quickly as thorns that blaze up.
> In the name of the Covenant LORD I cut them off.
> You pushed me violently that I might fall,
> but the Covenant LORD helped me.
> 'My strength and my song is the LORD of the Covenant,
> and he has become my salvation'
>
> (verses 10-14).

Four times it is stated that this suffering saint of the Lord is 'surrounded,' swarmed as though by menacing bees. He is not imagining things. Powerful nations and individuals threaten his life on every side.

But what happens? They fade away as quickly as they came. Like a brush fire that blazes hot for an instant and then as quickly dies away into its own ashes, so his oppressors threaten with their fierce wrath and then are brought to nothing overnight.

But the collapse of a determined enemy isn't something that 'just happens.' It is the Lord who intervenes to overwhelm those who threaten the safety of his own people. Nabal rises to rage against his wife Abigail for helping David, and crumples to the ground with a massive coronary. The handwriting on the wall indicates that Belshazzar's days are numbered, and Nebuchadnezzar eats grass like a cow. Haman hangs on the gallows he prepared for Mordecai, and Herod is struck dead because he gave glory to himself rather than to God. God's hand is in it all.

The most dramatic deliverance came for God's people of old at the Red Sea. While the Israelites passed through the waterbed dry-shod, Pharaoh' s host was swallowed up in the rushing, returning tides. On the other side of that deliverance, Moses and the people of God sang a song:

> The Covenant Lord is my strength and my song,
> and he has become my salvation
>
> (Exod. 15:2).

These identical words recur in this psalm (verse 14). This is the common experience of God's people through the ages, although it never becomes commonplace.

At the resurrection of Jesus Christ from the dead this pattern of deliverance for God's people reaches its climax. Even by his death he won a great victory, since by death he atoned for the sins of his people. But the climax comes at the resurrection, when he emerges victoriously on the other side. Death has forever lost its sting and the grave its victory.

Luke 9:31 says that at the time of Christ's transfiguration he spoke with Moses and Elijah about the 'exodus' he would accomplish at Jerusalem. Christ's reference is not simply to the fact of his dying. The term points beyond the dying to the rising. His coming out on the other side of death was just as much a part of his 'exodus' as was the emerging of Israel on the distant banks of the Red Sea. Their exodus would not have been complete without a safe landing on the other side.

It must never be forgotten that Christ's resurrection was not a lonely trek of a single individual, any more than Israel's exodus involved Moses alone. Jesus brought with him all those who would believe in him through all the ages.

So today by faith you can join in a salute to the power of 'the right hand of the Covenant LORD.'

> Voices singing and shouting 'Victory'
> come from the tents of the righteous:
>
> 'The right hand of the Covenant LORD
> does valiantly!
> The right hand of the Covenant LORD
> is exalted!
> The right hand of the Covenant LORD
> does valiantly!'
>
> (verses 15, 16).

Whenever the church remembers his death it should also rejoice in the victory of his resurrection. 'Eucharist' means 'the giving of thanks,' and because his death is joined inseparably to his resurrection, its memory always must be an occasion for thanksgiving.

This remembrance of the resurrection leads to the third testimony of the anointed King who speaks in this psalm.

3. The Covenant Lord establishes his chosen one as the cornerstone of his kingdom (verses 17-25)

Living in a sin-filled world involves always existing with the threat of death. But this anointed servant of the Lord has come to the verge of death's destruction and has been delivered. As a consequence, he intends to enter the temple of the Lord and offer an appropriate sacrifice:

I shall not die, but live
  and declare the works of the LORD of the Covenant.
The Covenant LORD has disciplined me severely,
  but he has not given me over to death.

Open for me the gates of righteousness;
  I shall enter through them.
  I shall give thanks to the Covenant LORD.

Here is the gate of the Covenant LORD!
  Righteous people can enter through it.

I shall give thanks to you,
  because you have answered me
  and have become my salvation

(verses 17-21).

These verses describe the king as a worshipper who brings a sacrifice to offer in the temple. The priests respond by showing him the way by which he can enter to offer his oblation. Rejected by men, he nonetheless will be accepted by God. As a matter of fact, God's intent is that he become the 'chief cornerstone' of his entire kingdom. All the weight of the kingdom's activities will rest on him. As the psalmist says:

The stone which the builders rejected
  has become the chief cornerstone

(verse 22).

Imagine a construction team in the process of erecting a massive stone structure. They look through the quarry for a large, solid boulder which can withstand the pressure of the entire building. It will be the chief cornerstone. Their eye falls on one particular stone that has already been rejected by the builders themselves. Because the builders had a wrong image of the shape of the final product, they could not recognize the potential for this stone to be the 'chief cornerstone.' But the foreman of the construction team recognizes it. This stone will be the one that bears the entire weight of the structure.

Jesus applies this verse directly to himself at the time of his most intense confrontation with the religious leaders of his day. As they are involved in plotting against his life, he indicates that this scripture points to him even as it exposes them. They are supposed to be the builders of God's kingdom on earth. Yet they have rejected him as the Messiah, the one who alone could serve as the 'chief cornerstone' for the entire structure. What is a kingdom without a king? And by God's own designation, he is the King of this kingdom.

God does this marvellous thing. He makes the wrath of men to praise him. He turns even the wicked plots of his enemies into a tool to advance his glory. For only by the crucifixion and resurrection of the Son of God could the Lord's plan for redemption be accomplished. As the psalmist says:

> Only the LORD of the Covenant could have done this thing;
> it is wondrous in our eyes.
> Only the LORD of the Covenant could have made this day;
> we will rejoice and be glad in it.
> O Covenant LORD, work salvation!
> O Covenant LORD, let us triumph!
>
> (verses 23-25).

Today is the day for thanksgiving, even as it was for Jesus Christ in the upper room with his disciples. As he celebrated the Last Supper with his disciples, he remembered these very words. For in the Jewish celebration of the Passover, Psalms 113-118 were recited as a regular part of the service. As the Gospels record, Jesus and his disciples 'sang a hymn' just before departing from the upper room (Matt. 26:30; Mark 14:26). Almost certainly the 'hymn' that they sang was Psalm 118.

Can you imagine Jesus leading his disciples in these climactic words?

> I shall not die, but live
> and declare the works of the Covenant LORD ...
> The stone which the builders rejected
> has become the chief corner stone.

> Only the Lord of the Covenant could have done this thing;
> it is wondrous in our eyes.

What must these words have meant to him? Even though he was facing the certainty of death, he could be confident that the last enemy could not keep its prey. Rejection by his enemies could not prevail against the purposes of the Almighty. He would not die but live, and proclaim the wondrous works of God.

Only the Lord could have done this kind of thing. Only he could make a day like this one. Triumphant victory has been won for his people, even as Satan and his hosts have done their worst.

Today we can say, 'Only the Lord of the Covenant could have made this day; we will rejoice and be glad in it.' As we eat the bread and drink the wine of the Last Supper, we are celebrating the victory of Christ over sin and death. God has done it, and we shall be glad.

Conclusion

As the King of Israel approached the temple to make his sacrifice, he was greeted by the priests who pronounced their blessings on him. But their blessing was not on him alone. All those who came with him and through him received the same benediction.

So the sacrifice of thanksgiving is offered. God receives the praise of his people for the salvation he has worked for them. All of us should enter into the same spirit of thanksgiving. The Lord's Supper is called the 'Eucharist' for a reason. For the term refers to the 'giving of thanks' associated with the victory accomplished by Christ's death and resurrection.

So let it be for us today. As the psalmist echoes his opening words by repeating them in his conclusion, so let us echo the thanksgiving that has come from the lips of his people from age to age as they have celebrated with the words of this psalm:

> Give thanks to the Lord of the Covenant,
> for he is good;
> his covenant love endures forever
>
> (verse 29).

Psalm 126

Rejoicing over Restoration

A song of ascents.

Reader: 1When the Covenant LORD returned the
captivity of Zion,

Congr.: we thought we must be dreaming.

Reader: 2Then

Congr.: our mouth was filled
with laughter,
our tongue
with singing.

Reader: Then
they said among the nations,

Chorus: 'The Covenant LORD has done great
things
for these people.'

Congr.: 3Indeed, the Covenant LORD has done great
things
for us.
How happy we are!

Reader: 4Turn, O Covenant LORD, our captivity

Congr.: as the torrents [rush into] the Negev.

Reader: 5They that sow
in tears

Congr.: shall reap
in joy.

Reader: 6The one who goes out weeping,
bearing seed for scattering,

Congr.: undoubtedly shall come back singing,
bearing his bundles of grain.

Rejoicing over Restoration—
Joy at Deliverance from Exile

Introduction

This psalm centres on the sheer joy that accompanies restoration after devastation. The psalmist jubilantly announces that God has turned back the captivity of his people. Then he prays that God will complete the restoration he has begun. Finally he declares his confidence that God will undoubtedly turn the troubles of his people to their great benefit.

A current heir of the reformation begun by John Hus in the fifteenth century quoted this psalm at a ministers' conference in England in the spring of 1990. He was describing the ecstasy that accompanied the collapse of Communism in Czechoslovakia. Previously Christians had lived under restrictive threats. Only one worship service a week was allowed by the government to some select groups. But after the tearing of the Iron Curtain, Christian pastors could preach openly in the streets. Teaching on Communism in the state schools was replaced with a course about God and Christianity. Long-repressed believers in Christ were ecstatic. As the pastor said, 'We thought we must be dreaming' (Psa. 126:1).

The psalm divides into three sections: a declaration that God has restored his people (verses 1-3); a prayer for God to complete the restoration of his people (verse 4); and an expression of confidence that God will restore his people (verses 5, 6).

1. God has restored his people (verses 1-3)

> When the Covenant LORD returned the captivity of Zion,
> we thought we must be dreaming
>
> (verse 1).

The Lord brings his people into captivity, and the Lord delivers them from captivity. Whenever the Lord leads his people through trial, he never intends to destroy them but only to refine their gold and consume their dross.

But what are this 'captivity' and this 'return' to which the psalmist refers?

In the first place, the reference is to the deportation of Israel to Babylon in 586 BC. The Lord raised up Nebuchadnezzar to chasten his people and he also raised up Darius to restore them. The King of Babylon commanded his army to destroy the temple in Jerusalem and the King of Persia issued the decree that it be rebuilt. But behind it all was the Lord who orders all things for the good of his people.

In the second place, this reference to a 'captivity' may be applied to any bondage that afflicts God's people in a fallen world. It could refer to enslavement to a form of work not suited to a person's gifts. It could refer to the self-imposed burdens that come from a spirit of covetousness, pride and jealousy. Or it could involve entrapment in a pointless life that results from an earlier dissipation of God-given resources.

Who is it that experiences this kind of captivity? It is 'Zion,' the city the Lord loves above all other places on earth (cf. Psa. 87:2). If the Lord lets Zion experience these distressing circumstances, then no one can expect to be exempt.

When the Lord restores his people from these various 'captivities,' everything is so good that it seems like a dream. Those who have been delivered cannot believe that reality could be so wonderful. No matter how great you might imagine your future to be, the reality may be greater. For he does 'far more than all that we ask or think' (Eph. 3:20). Because his ways are higher than heaven above earth, the realities of restoration appear as dreams when they actually occur.

Among the minor cast in Cecil B. DeMille's *The Ten Commandments* was an anxious man with a furrowed brow. God sent plague after plague on Egypt, always sparing his people. He finally delivered them from Pharaoh's domain. He opened the Red Sea so they could pass through dry-shod between walls of water. The glory-cloud guarded their rear, holding back Pharaoh's army. The only thing before them was an open road to safety on the other side of the sea. Yet despite all these wondrous provisions of God's goodness, the little man cried out in a seizure of anxiety, 'Hurry, hurry!' He could not believe that the grace of God would continue long enough for them to complete their passage through the opened sea.

It is quite appropriate to marvel at the wonders of God's grace. Things may be so great that you think you are dreaming. But don't let your wonder slip into unbelief and doubting. Be sure your wonder expresses itself in praise to your great Deliverer.

In the second verse the psalmist describes the reaction of God's people as well as the reaction of the surrounding nations to their restoration. Each of the two sections of the verse is introduced by an emphatic *'Then' (az)*.

The reaction of God's people

Then
our mouth was filled
with laughter,
our tongue
with singing

(verse 2).

Uncontrollable laughter and singing characterize the reaction of the people of God to their restoration. They simply cannot contain their joy.

The mouth 'filled' with laughter suggests an abandonment to the spirit of joyfulness that comes to a person only on rare occasions. Robert Penn Warren, in his prize-winning novel *All the King's Men*, talks about the kind of uninhibited laughter that may occur to a woman only once in her lifetime. But he knows nothing of the grace of Christ as it is manifested in the life of godly men and women who pray earnestly for the Lord's intervention in times of trouble. Every time they see his grace renewed, their mouths are filled with laughter and their tongues with singing. It almost makes a person want to undergo trouble so he can experience the joy of being delivered. But it would be simpler to remember the words of the waiting father to the elder brother in the parable of the prodigal son: 'Son, you are always with me, and all that is mine is yours' (Luke 15:31). You can have a feast whenever you wish.

The reaction of the surrounding nations

Then
  they said among the nations,
    'The Covenant LORD has done great things
      for these people'

(verse 2).

The second half of this verse describes the response of the nations to the restoration of God's people. This statement also begins with an emphatic 'then' (*az*).

The watching world can only stand amazed. People may be atheistic by profession. But when they see the things God does for his people, they have to admit that he works wondrously.

When God leads a heathen king to sponsor the rebuilding of the temple in Jerusalem, the world must acknowledge, 'The Covenant LORD has done great things for these people.'

The same principle holds true today. When God answers prayer and heals a cancer patient, when he makes the ideology of Lenin and Stalin fall to the ground in one great heap, the world is amazed.

In any case, all glory must go to God for the wonders he does. The LORD of the Covenant is the one who has done great things, not the people. Whatever experiences of salvation that are yours must be used to magnify the name of the Lord.

Indeed, the Covenant LORD has done great things
  for us.
How happy we are!

(verse 3).

Obviously God's people must add their 'Amen' to the wonder expressed by the heathen nations. It is undeniably true. God has done great things for us.

What a sin it is for God's people to go about moaning and groaning, failing to acknowledge the greatness of God's intervention on their behalf! God has redeemed them from sin and guilt. He continues to weaken the power of sin in their lives. He ultimately will free his people from all the evil in the world. Every day you may see God's blessings as divine acts of restoration done by the Lord for you.

'How happy we are!' should be the spontaneous exclamation of the believer at all times. Count your many blessings, and it will surprise you what the Lord has done. If deliverance from the Babylonian captivity provided a source of great joy for God's people in the past, how much more should deliverance from the destructive powers of death and hell today?

2. A prayer for God to complete the restoration of his people (verse 4)

Having rehearsed the blessing of restoration, the psalmist now offers a prayer that the Lord would complete this work he has begun.

> Turn, O Covenant LORD, our captivity
> as the torrents [rush into] the Negev
>
> (verse 4).

Not every Israelite in Babylon seized the opportunity to return to the land of promise. Only about 49,000 actually left the land of their captivity. Those who remained were reluctant to exchange their new-found prosperity for the dangers associated with a return to the land of Canaan. Those who made the trek did not find life easy. The returning exiles had many obstacles and adversaries to face. The psalmist therefore prays that the Lord will complete the work he has begun.

In everyday life, sin constantly robs men of the richness of life. Tempers flare and interrupt the harmony of personal relationships.

A sluggish approach to doing a job leaves it unsatisfying because it remains half done.

So the psalmist prays that God will send his abundant grace to rush into the desert of their lives as torrents of water sometimes rush into the Negev. He pleads that they may be restored by the grace of the Lord, just as refreshing waters make the desert flower.

The imagery of a torrent rushing down the wadi into the Negev corresponds to the refreshment God brings into the lives of his people. Travellers are warned never to bed down in a valley creasing the deserts of Judea, for overnight the undetected rainwater that has fallen in the mountains may sweep away all that is before it. In just such a way, the psalmist prays that the Lord will surprise his people by flooding their lives with his refreshing grace.

God's mercy is never finished. One blessing only primes circumstances for the sending of another. God causes torrents to rush into the desert constantly. Expect it. Pray for the transformation of those areas in your life that are experiencing the greatest barrenness. For there God makes the abundant wonders of his grace to work most impressively.

3. Confidence that the Lord will restore his people (verses 5, 6)

In the end the psalmist speaks of the Lord's chastening judgments under a more hope-filled figure. Instead of a 'captivity,' their scattering by the Lord is viewed as a 'sowing.'

> They that sow
>   in tears
> shall reap
>   in joy
>
> (verse 5).

This change of imagery communicates a message of hope. The experience described as a 'captivity' from one perspective can just as well be viewed as a 'sowing.' Even as God chastens his people, he prepares them for bearing abundant fruit.

Don't think of the season of your chastening as lost time. Even when he is correcting you, God simultaneously is situating you in a new place so you can bear more fruit for him. Like the corruption of a seed in the soil, your 'captivity' may involve a painful dying to yourself. But in the long run, it will bear much fruit. For 'Unless a grain of wheat falls into the earth and dies, it remains alone; but if it dies, it bears much fruit' (John 12:24). Don't despair. For they who sow in tears will reap in joy.

So the psalmist has used two different images for the expectation of renewal. Renewal from the hand of the Lord is like a stream that bursts into the desert, and like a sowing that leads to reaping.

Improve your times of affliction. A tear has the shape of a seed, and weeping can be a form of sowing. As trials incline you to repent and humble yourself before the Lord, yield to his good purposes.

> The one who goes out weeping,
> bearing seed for scattering,
> undoubtedly shall come back singing,
> bearing his bundles of grain
>
> (verse 6).

As you trudge forwards under the burden of your captivity, bear some seed for sowing. Picture David leaving Jerusalem, forced out of the royal city by a rebellious son. Shimei curses him as he goes, but David responds in meek submission to the Lord's chastenings. By his response to Absalom's rebellion and Shimei's cursing, David sows the seed of faith in the Lord that eventually bears fruit in his triumphant return. Israel sends for him, asking that he come back as king. He re-enters the city more gloriously than ever before.

In a similar way, as Jesus bore our chastening he went outside the gate under great affliction. But his words from the cross demonstrate his gracious spirit, which was his means of sowing seed. He asks the Father to forgive them. He cares for his mother. He saves the dying thief. So you can be sure he will return one day in triumphant glory.

This same pattern will prevail for the believer in every generation. 'Going he shall indeed go,' but 'returning he shall indeed return,' as this verse literally reads. The farmer may sow in tears and also reap in tears. But you may lift your spirit in its darkest hour with this thought: you will return with rejoicing, bearing your bundles of grain.

Conclusion

The labours done for Christ under the greatest tensions ultimately will produce the greatest joys. 'It is the repenting, reforming people that are, and shall be, the rejoicing people.'[1]

> So came Messiah, friend of men,
>   (A man of sorrows He),
> To fight with grief, and tears, and pain,
>   That we might conquerors be.
> Behold, He comes the second time
>   To wipe away our tears,
> And takes us up along with Him
>   For everlasting years.[2]

[1] Matthew Henry, *Commentary on the Whole Bible,* vol. III, p. 733.

[2] Barclay, as cited in Bonar, *Christ and His Church in the Book of Psalms,* 1861, p. 393.

Psalm 128
The Happy Hearth

A song of ascents.

Reader: 1How happy is everyone
who fears the LORD of the Covenant,
who walks in his ways!

1st Congr.: 2The fruit of your hard work
you shall enjoy;
2nd Congr.: blessings and prosperity
will be yours.

1st Congr.: 3Your wife shall be as a fruitful vine
encompassing your home;
2nd Congr.: your children as olive shoots
around your table.

Reader: 4Look at him!
See how the man is blessed
who fears the Covenant LORD!

5May the Covenant LORD bless you
out of Zion,
and may you witness
the good of Jerusalem
all the days of your life.

6 May you enjoy your children's children.

All: Peace be on Israel.

The Happy Hearth—
Blessings in Life's Basics

Introduction

Human beings tend to think of life in large, grandiose terms. In Napoleonic fashion people evaluate their lives in terms of worlds to conquer. In modern jargon, the common man looks for health and wealth, the blessing of prosperity.

But the great and the meaningful things of human life centre instead on the basic simplicities. If a man gets adequate return from his labour so that his needs for food and shelter are met, he is greatly blessed. If he has a good domestic situation with a loving wife and happy children, he should count himself extremely blessed. But these things mean nothing if they are not experienced in the context of the blessings of the Covenant. For all true blessing comes 'out of Zion' and from 'Jerusalem' (verse 5). The blessings that flow from the house of God in the end must be the focus of all human happiness. This joy over the fulness of life is multiplied almost beyond human comprehension when a person has the privilege of seeing God's blessing passed on to the coming generations. That is the message of Psalm 128.

Only five psalms begin with a pronouncement of blessing on God's people (Psa. 1; 32; 41; 119; 128). The blessing in Psalm 128 centres on the creation ordinances of work, marriage and worship. All other blessings in human life radiate from these centres: your work, your domestic situation and what you do with your Sundays. If you are not being blessed in these foundational areas of life, you will not enjoy any other blessing you receive.

The happiness of the man who fears the Lord

The first verse of this psalm provides a general statement of the happiness of the man who 'fears the Covenant Lord,' who 'walks in his ways.' These two descriptions are inseparable. If you fear the Lord, you will walk in his ways, and if you walk in his ways, you show that you fear him.

This happiness is not for only a few of those who fear the Lord. It is specifically stated that 'all' who fear the Lord will go through life with this happiness. This declaration does not present the 'happiness batting average' for the church. It describes the experience of each and every person, without exception, who walks in the fear of the Lord. All these blessings are for all of you who trust in Christ.

But what does it mean to fear the Lord? It means recognizing that he judges in righteousness and without partiality. It means not attempting to compromise his holiness and righteousness with his love.

Fearing God is not a superstitious dread that thinks of him as an arbitrary, irrational being whose actions have no rhyme or reason. Instead, the person who fears the Lord understands that he blesses those who trust him and live out their lives in accord with his standards for work, marriage and worship.

From a new covenant perspective, this same concept is expressed in terms of loving God and doing his will. The fear of the Lord and love for the Lord are one and the same thing. Both have their concrete manifestation in doing his will. As the apostle John says, 'And by this we know that we have come to know him, if we keep his commandments. Whoever says "I know him" but does not keep his commandments is a liar, and the truth is not in him, but whoever keeps his word, in him truly the love of God is perfected. By this we may be sure that we are in him: whoever says he abides in him ought to walk in the same way in which he walked' (1 John 2:3-6).

Do you fear the Lord? Are you committed to walk in his ways and not your own? If you want the blessings of happiness and prosperity, you must begin by fearing the Lord, loving him and walking in his ways.

Having declared the happiness of all who fear the Lord, the psalmist then describes this happiness in three areas of life: happiness in your work (verse 2); happiness in your home (verse 3); happiness in your worship (verses 4, 5).

1. Happiness in your work (verse 2)

> The fruit of your hard work
>   you shall enjoy;
> blessings and prosperity
>   will be yours
>
> (verse 2).

We have heard enough of the 'health and wealth' gospel! Some tele-evangelists offer the certainty of prosperity to anyone who will exercise faith and pledge a large portion of his or her pension to support their programme. 'Where's your faith?' they ask. If you will have enough faith to send them a large gift, then you have their assurance that God will prosper you. But as long as you hold back your contribution, God will hold back his blessing.

No wonder the onlooking world reacts negatively to Christianity. For many non-Christians, the only form of 'Christianity' they know is what they see on television. You can hardly blame them for having a bias against the gospel.

The same holds true for the promise of health held out by the healers. 'The only reason you are sick,' they say, 'is because you do not have enough faith.' 'It is God's will that every Christian should be healthy all the time,' they assert. 'Your only problem is a lack of faith.' How cruel! How self-blinded they are to the fact that every Christian who has ever lived on the face of the earth has died! Without exception, all men have been ill, have suffered pain and have died.

But now the question arises: how, then, is the promise of prosperity in Psalm 128 to be fulfilled? Does not God's word explicitly say you will enjoy the fruit of your hard work and that blessings and prosperity will be yours?

At the outset, remember that the prosperity promised by the Lord never corresponds to the desires and expectations promoted by the ungodly. The world's idea of 'prosperity' is one in which a person is so well off that he works only if he wants to. He invests a little money in the right stock, or he wins the lottery jackpot, or by some fluke he gets much more income than his labour deserves. Then he is happy. Who of the world would count himself 'happy' so long as he is in a situation in which his maintenance in life hinges on his own consistent hard work?

But the fanciful idol of the covetous heart is the furthermost thing from the Lord's promise of prosperity. You may not think it a happy situation to have to go out and work for your daily bread, but it is! You will be a happy man if you work with contentment, trusting that the Lord will supply enough bread for your table every day. Even if it is only bread with nothing else, you still will be a blessed and happy person if you are trusting him. If he gives you more, you can count yourself doubly blessed.

This promise of prosperity is explicitly denied to those among God's people who live in laziness or selfishness. He who does not work shall not eat (2 Thess. 3:10). In the days of Haggai the prophet, God's people worked hard but had nothing to show for it. Why? Because they spent all their energies on building their own houses, while the house of the Lord was a shambles (Hag. 1:9). The same thing can happen to you. Seek first the kingdom of God, and the Lord promises that you will have blessings of food, clothing and shelter. But if you do not seek first his kingdom and his righteousness, you may find yourself not even enjoying the basics of life.

This promise of blessing in the material realm receives its fulfilment on several levels.

Firstly, the Christian enjoys every achievement in his work, whether small or great, because he does it for the Lord and not to be seen of men. He relishes every accomplishment as a token of God's love and grace to him. He savours his successes in a way the world cannot understand, because he celebrates accomplishment in the presence of the Lord.

If you have seen a proper production of *Swan Lake*, you have witnessed the quintessence of human beauty as expressed in the arts. The grace of every movement, the splendour of Tchaikovsky's music is rapturous. After the performance, the prima ballerina takes her bow. She receives her bouquet. The applause rises to a crescendo. She bows again, and again, and again. But then it is all over. The hours, the months, the years of tedious drill and discipline have paid off. But then the cheering stops. What then? Does she plunge from the dizzy heights of human praise to the dark doldrums of depression? If she performs for the praise of men, she has received her reward. But then it is all over.

Only if you do your work out of the fear of the Lord, out of trust in him, will you experience true happiness. Only then will you enjoy the fruit of your labour over the long haul of life.

Secondly, the natural powers of the believer in Christ are enhanced by his faith in the Lord. He is free from a conscience that hounds him to distraction. He transacts his business with a basic integrity that keeps him out of many troubles. His motivation for work is not self-centred, but God-glorifying, and so he can pursue his goals with unbridled vigour.

Thirdly, it is a simple fact that the Lord promises to provide for your temporal needs in this life if you trust in him. To the extent that legitimate needs are not supplied, it must be assumed that the larger purposes of God are at work. The reason for the deprivation will be made plain one day. The widow of Zarephath must have struggled with doubts many times as her food supplies dwindled to the last measure of meal for herself and her son. But in a moment she was immortalized by the sudden appearance of God's prophet Elijah.

Fourthly, the believer in Christ can handle the disappointments and setbacks that are sure to come along life's way, because he rests by faith in the sovereign purposes of God. Joseph could endure the dungeons of Egypt because he knew that though men intended evil, God meant it for good. Paul and Silas could sing in prison at midnight because they knew men could do nothing to them but what the Lord intended as a means for the advancement of the gospel. They were bound, but the word of the Lord could not be bound.

Finally, you will enjoy for eternity the blessings of the Lord for the work you do during your time on earth. The current disappointments are not worthy to be compared with the glory to be revealed in us.

The promise of prosperity is fulfilled in many different ways. Do your work in the fear of the Lord, and you will not be disappointed.

2. Happiness in your home (verse 3)

Many devoted Christians have grown up in unhappy families. The Lord delights in 'snatching brands from the fire.' These people experienced the turmoil of seeing father and mother quarrelling, arguing and even coming to blows. The place called 'home' was to them anything but a sanctuary from the strife of life.

Increasing numbers of children bear the scars of family break-up. The pain of appearing as witness in a court of law, the agony of choosing to stay with one parent or another, the distress of leaving the family home and moving to a flat, of entering another school midway through the year with only one parent to provide support, the strain of lessened financial security—all these experiences go along with the break-up of the family.

The inspired psalmist paints an entirely different picture of the family blessed of the Lord. Husband, wife and children live in harmonious happiness. The idealized vine-covered cottage finds its realistic counterpart at the place where the Godfearing man resides. According to the psalmist:

> Your wife shall be as a fruitful vine
> encompassing your home;
> your children as olive shoots
> around your table
>
> (verse 3).

There it is—the picture of paradise, heaven come to earth! Isn't it fascinating? When our Lord Jesus Christ wished to paint a vivid picture of heaven, he did not project an image from heaven down to earth. Instead, he chose the commonplace, earthly image of the home and transposed it to heaven. 'In my Father's house are many rooms,' he said to his distressed disciples (John 14:2).

A word to the unmarried and childless

In his little book on the psalms, C. S. Lewis begins by indicating his intention to deal with the difficult elements of the Psalter first.[1] As any child with his wits about him knows, you clean the spinach and the onions off your plate first. Then you can suppress those bitter tastes with the scrumptious flavour of roast beef and mashed potatoes smothered in gravy!

So as you consider this picture of the blessings of the ideal home, think first for a moment of those who feel hurt when this picture of the perfect domestic situation is painted so vividly. Many people are in pain because more than anything else in this world they want a husband or a wife, children and a home of their own. But they have none. Does this mean that they do not fear the Lord, and so cannot expect the blessings promised in this psalm?

As the apostle Paul was in the habit of saying, 'God forbid!' He himself was a bachelor, as was C. S. Lewis for most of his life. The same was true of that great theologian John Murray until he reached the age of sixty-five and retired to his native Scotland with his new bride, where he subsequently became the father of two children.

In response to those people who find it painful to read this psalm, the first word is, 'Be patient!' Be patient in terms of what God may yet do for you in the domestic scene. If you are unmarried and wish you were married, be patient. If God wants you to have a loving spouse, he will provide the perfect one for you. If you are childless and wish you had children, be patient. God may want you to go the adoptive route and learn that in a very special way this child was formed by God just for you.

The second word to any who may be troubled by this psalm is, 'Be broadminded.' Recognize that as a single person you may be a

[1] *Reflections on the Psalms*, 1958, p. 19.

participant in many families. The homes of the church are yours. The children of the church are yours. The joys of the entire church family are yours.

Remember that in heaven there will be no marriage and no giving in marriage. The disappointments of this brief time on earth are not worthy to be compared with the glory that is to be revealed in you. After all, as a single person you may be closer to the final goal of perfect union with Christ than married people.

Remember also that you have a right to view your hurts in this area as a form of suffering for Christ. It is not just the pain of the martyr that represents trial for Christ. All the believer's hurts are sufferings for Christ. By being present in this world rather than being taken up to glory you are providing a witness for Christ. Simply living in mortal flesh inevitably involves pain. This pain you endure is for Christ's sake. So the question is, can you endure these hurts just a little longer for the sake of Christ? Will you bear patiently as a way of serving the one who endured so much pain for you?

Remember also that the married status has its pains as well. Some people who are too anxious to get married jump from the frying pan into the fire. Even in the most idyllic circumstances, marriage is not without its distinctive pains.

Again, remember that so long as the Lord determines that you are to be in a single or childless state, he makes this determination because he knows it is for your best. He will bless you in it. He will provide great happiness for you in your present situation. His grace will be sufficient for you.

The blessings of family life as seen in the psalm

Now look on the other side of things. Consider the blessings described positively in this psalm.

First, the blessing of a fruitful wife. Children are not the only 'fruit' the wife bears. A vine provides not only grapes. It also produces leaves, shade, beauty and soil conservation. The fruitful wife manifests many graces from Christ in her life. She offers wise counsel to her husband. His heart safely trusts in her. She provides companionship, social relationships and an unspeakable joy for all of life. The image of a vine about the sides of the house suggests an all-encompassing companionship that comes with the godly wife.

Secondly, the blessed man in this psalm has a 'house' for himself and his wife. A better translation is 'home' rather than 'house.' For the emphasis is not on the possession of an imposing place of residence, but on the blessings of God in the domestic scene, however modest it may be. For thousands of years, God's people lived in tents that meant constant movement from place to place. They lived in caves and dens of the earth. Yet even in those circumstances, the Lord blessed their homes.

Robert Burns, the Scottish bard, immortalized the humble abode of the godly Covenanters of his native land in 'The Cotter's Saturday Night':

> Then kneeling down to Heaven's Eternal King
> The saint, the father, and the husband prays;
> Hope 'springs exulting on triumphant wing,'
> That thus they all shall meet in future days;
> There, ever bask in uncreated rays,
> No more to sigh, or shed the bitter tear,
> Together hymning their Creator's praise,
> In such society, yet still more dear,
> While circling Time moves round in an eternal sphere.
>
> Compar'd with this, how poor Religion's pride,
> In all the pomp of method and of art;
> When men display to congregations wide
> Devotion's ev'ry grace, except the heart!
> The Power, incens'd, the pageant will desert,
> The pompous strain, the sacerdotal stole;
> But haply, in some cottage far apart,
> May hear, well pleas'd, the language of the soul.

How many Christian couples can look back to their early days of marriage and fondly remember the apartment above the garage! How is it possible to duplicate the special blessings of those simpler days of early marriage? A humble home blessed of the Lord is better than a mansion.

Thirdly, this blessed man enjoys children around his dinner table. He has something to feed them, and they provide promise for his future. To the godly, his children are like olive plants, not like brambles. Like potted shoots that promise to become trees rich with olives later in life, his children embody a promise of innumerable blessings for the future that will last until his old age. What a blessing it is to see children showing not only deserved respect but also loving interest towards their parents even in their latter years! God meant it that way, and both parents and children are blessed through this ordering of the Lord.

But the whole truth must be told. The same kinds of tensions associated with the blessings of work manifest themselves in this promise concerning children. Just as it is totally wrong to preach a 'health and wealth' gospel, so it would be a grave mistake to declare that every married person will be blessed with numbers of godly offspring gathered about his or her table.

Often it is the single person, or the married couple without children, who enjoys the blessings that flow from children more than the parents who have them at home. Personally, some of my fondest memories from youth go back to two older couples with no children of their own who essentially 'adopted' me as the child of their special interest. Although they have been in heaven with the Lord for years, I sometimes think I still am running on the prayers they offered for me while they were on earth.

It is not our place to dictate to the Lord the way he will manifest his grace in the world. He alone has the wisdom to coordinate all the factors by which he will bless a universe confused by the sin of men. But you can be sure that if you knew all that God knows about your deprivations, you would give thanks to the Lord for everything you have been denied as well as all you have been granted.

3. Happiness in worship (verses 4, 5)

The psalmist has spoken of the blessings of work. He has depicted the happiness of the home. Both of these blessings originated at the beginning of the world when God created man. Now the psalm climaxes with a description of the blessings of worship, which are associated also with creation by God's pronouncing of his benediction on the day of rest (Gen. 2:3). The psalmist says:

> Look at him!
> See how the man is blessed
> who fears the Covenant LORD!
>
> (verse 4).

Contemplate this marvellous thing! Think about it! It is absolutely remarkable! As wondrous as the stars of heaven may be, the wonder of the blessing of God on the man who fears him is even more fantastic. Everywhere he turns, this person is blessed of the Lord. How could it be that hardships and trials, as well as moments of prosperity, would end up blessing the person who fears the Lord? It is a mystery that inspires wonder.

And what is the explanation of it all? This man is blessed so richly because he 'fears the Covenant LORD.' He knows that God is a righteous Judge, and so he avoids sin at all costs. His fear is not directed towards God in the abstract, but towards the one true living God, the God and Father of our Lord Jesus Christ.

The psalmist offers a benedictory prayer to be pronounced over God's people in worship. As they assemble at the Lord's house, the Lord's blessing is declared over them. Because the 'you' of this benediction is singular, this blessing is directed towards each and every individual of the worshipping community. On you and you and you this benediction comes:

> May the Covenant LORD bless you
> out of Zion,
> And may you witness
> the good of Jerusalem
> all the days of your life.
> May you enjoy your children's children
>
> (verses 5, 6).

All blessings in life ultimately come from 'Zion' and 'Jerusalem,' names representing the place where God is worshipped by his people. As the church assembles for worship, God communicates his blessings on the whole of life.

Don't think you will be blessed in your labours by working seven days a week and making it to church only occasionally. Don't think better grades will bring good into your life if you have to study on Sundays to get them. Don't think that by taking your family out into the woods instead of taking them to church you will create the blessing of 'family togetherness.'

No! It is out of Zion and Jerusalem that the blessings pour forth on your work and your family. Only God can give these blessings, and you must seek his blessing in his house, among your brothers and sisters in Christ.

As you seek the Lord's blessing among his people, be sure you are not looking out only for your own prosperity. It is the 'good of Jerusalem' that you must desire. A repulsive selfcentredness seeks blessings for oneself without giving equal consideration for the whole of Christ's body. Come to church loving and caring for your neighbour just as you love and care for yourself.

All the days of your life you will be blessed if you seek first the kingdom of God and his righteousness. You will enjoy your children's children. And don't forget it: happiness is being a grand-parent! Nothing could be better in life than seeing God's blessing extending from you to your children's children.

Conclusion

The man who fears the Lord, who worships regularly in his house, will experience all these blessings from the Lord. He will eat the fruit of paradise, and will experience the Creator's blessing on his work, his home and his worship.

So, 'Peace be on Israel.' May the blessings of wholeness in life be yours. By faith in Jesus the Christ you are a part of the Israel of God. As a result, all you do will be blessed by him. Happiness, blessedness is forever yours.

Psalm 132
From Cross to Crown

A song of ascents.

1st Reader: 1Remember, O Covenant LORD,
David
and his afflictions.

1st Congr.: 2He swore to the LORD of the Covenant,
2nd Congr.: he vowed to the Mighty One of Jacob:

1st Reader: 3'I will not go
to the tent where I reside;
I will not stretch out
on the bed where I recline;
4I will not allow
my eyes to slumber
or my eyelids to sleep
5until I find
a place
for the LORD of the Covenant
tabernacles
for the Mighty One of Jacob.'

1st Congr.: 6Indeed, we heard of it
in Ephratah;
2nd Congr.: we discovered it
in the fields of Jaar.

1st Congr.:	7 We will go up to his tabernacles;
2nd Congr.:	we will bow down at his footstool.
1st Congr.:	8 Arise, O Covenant LORD, into your resting-place,
2nd Congr.:	you and the ark of your strength.
1st Congr.:	9 Your priests will be adorned in righteousness,
2nd Congr.:	and your devoted ones will shout for joy.

All:	10 Because of David your servant,
	   do not turn away the face of your
	      anointed one.

1st Reader:	11 The Covenant LORD swore the truth to David; He will never turn away from it:

2nd Reader:	‘From the fruit of your loins
	   I will establish heirs to your throne.
	12 If your sons will keep
	   my covenant,
	   and my testimony which I teach them,
	then their sons will sit on your throne for
	   ever.’

1st Reader:	13 For the Covenant LORD has chosen Zion; he has claimed it for his dwelling-place:

2nd Reader: 14This is my place of rest forever;
Here I will reside, for I have claimed it.
15Its provision
  I will greatly bless;
its poor
  I will satisfy with bread;
16its priests
  I will adorn with salvation;
its devoted ones
  will shout for joy continually.
17There I will make sprout
  a horn for David;
I have prepared
  a lamp for my anointed one.
18His enemies
  I will cover with shame,
but on him
  his crown will glisten.'

From Cross to Crown—
God Confirms the Covenant with David

Introduction

This psalm concentrates on the two elements that were at the heart of God's covenant with David: the building of a 'house' (temple) for the Lord, and the confirming of a 'house' (dynasty) for David. Looking across the generations, this psalm anticipates the coming of Jesus Christ as the climactic descendant of David by which this covenant reaches its final fulfilment. This psalm also points towards the establishment of the house from which the Lord himself would rule over the entire earth. From the heavenly Mount Zion he controls the destinies of the nations of the world.

Two separate speakers declare their solemn intentions in this psalm. First David speaks to confirm the oath he had made to the Lord. Then the Lord declares publicly his formal commitment to David and his descendants. Mutual vows bind David and the Lord to one another.

The cross entails intense suffering. The crown brings exalted glory. Passing from cross to crown is an experience that both David and his greater son, the Lord Jesus Christ, have in common. You who hear about this transition are called to follow the anointed Lord, your leader. Your experience of submitting to him will begin when you take up your cross daily and follow him. But in the end you too will receive the reward of an eternal crown.

1. Remember the commitment of the Lord's anointed leader (verses 1-5)

The psalmist begins with a prayer for the Lord to 'remember':

Remember, O Covenant LORD,
  David
and all his afflictions

(verse 1).

Remember David's trials on behalf of the Lord? His own brothers mocked him when he sought to preserve God's honour in the face of the mockery of the giant Goliath. He wandered from one place to another because he was the object of Saul's jealousy and hatred. He suffered silently while his servant Shimei mocked him by shouting curses and throwing dirt from the crest of the hill above.

Despite all these sufferings and many more, David would not be content when the Lord gave him rest from all his enemies. He could have exploited his kingship by seeking relaxing pleasures for himself. But when he began to experience some prosperity he stuck by his commitment to the Lord:

I will not go
  to the tent where I reside;
I will not stretch out
  on the bed where I recline;
I will not allow
  my eyes to sleep
  or my eyelids to slumber
    until I find
      a place
        for the LORD of the Covenant,
      tabernacles
        for the Mighty One of Jacob

(verse 3).

Most people are careful not to get carried away with their religion. But David put the worship of the Lord above everything else. He would not enjoy the comforts of home, he would not take a well-deserved rest at night, until he had done all he could to establish God as Lord of all the earth.

Obviously David speaks in figurative terms. He did enter his house. He did sleep in his bed. But he declares his priority in no uncertain terms. Above the daily necessities of human existence will be the glorifying of God. As Jesus said, 'My food is to do the will of him who sent me and to accomplish his work' (John 4:34). He missed eating without thinking about it because he was so intently involved in doing the work of the Lord.

A place for the Lord

In this psalm David swears that his priority is establishing a 'place' for the Lord. But what is the point? Does Almighty God need a 'place'? At the time of the dedication of the house of the Lord for which David had made such extensive preparations, Solomon prayed: 'Heaven and the highest heaven cannot contain you; how much less this house that I have built!' (1 Kings 8:27).

No, it was not for God's sake that a 'place' on earth had to be built. Instead it was for man's sake that a particular point had to be located where God could be worshipped on earth.

Cooks need a kitchen. Mechanics need a garage. Musicians need a studio. Computer operators need a workstation. And worshippers in this sinful world need a place where the holy God can be honoured as they gather together in his name. This need of a centre for the worship of the God of redemption was made apparent through the temporary forms associated with Old Testament worship. The Lord commanded Moses to build for him a house exactly as the pattern was delivered on Mount Sinai. Central to that worship was the offering of a sacrifice.

Today the true nature of the sacrifice has become apparent. It is the Lamb of God that takes away the sin of the world. He must be the centre of our worship. The 'place' on earth towards which God's people once directed their adoration has been replaced by the reality of the Lamb's rule from heaven, where he is seated at God's right hand in glory. That place must be the focus of man's worship and adoration. It is towards Christ in heaven, towards the Christ who has suffered and now is reigning that our worship now must be directed.

Determination

David, the anointed of the Lord, was determined. When he himself was denied the privilege of building a house for the Lord, he committed himself to getting everything ready for his son Solomon. One way or another, the Lord would be honoured by all he had.

In an even fuller sense, the Lord Jesus Christ showed his determination to establish a place that would become the focus of the Lord's worship. Jesus faced enemies that were even more determined than David's. Remember all his afflictions? From the outset of his ministry, enemies were plotting to destroy him. But he responded with a determination equal to theirs: 'Destroy this temple, and in three days I will raise it up' (John 2:19).

This determination of Christ's became evident in his death and resurrection. He gave up his body to be crucified. He suffered the greatest of agonies, that God might be glorified in him. Then he triumphed by his resurrection from the dead. To doubting Thomas he said, 'Put out your hand, and place it in my side. Do not disbelieve, but believe' (John 20:27). Thomas gave the only appropriate response: 'My Lord and my God!' (John 20:28). In the resurrected Christ Thomas recognized God himself residing among men.

David and Christ were determined. They moved from cross to crown for the sake of the glory of God. They had an unshakeable commitment.

Are you determined? Are you committed to suffer all personal inconvenience for the advancement of the glory of God in this world? Is the establishment of the glory of God your top priority, no matter what sacrifice it requires of you? Can you say with David, 'I take a solemn vow before God that each day I will not return home until I have established a little more of your glory in the world'? Can you say with Christ, 'My food is to do the will of him who sent me, and to finish his work'? I will miss meals, I will not sleep at the end of the day until I am sure that I have glorified and served him above myself.

The commitment of God's anointed leaders is clearly established. Next the psalmist calls for a similar commitment by the people.

2. Establish the same priorities for your life (verses 6-10)

David and the Lord shared a common experience of humiliation. David was born in the lowly little town of Bethlehem Ephratah, and the Lord's throne was left forgotten in Kiriath-Jearim, the 'woods of Jaar.' As the psalmist says:

> Indeed, we heard of it
> in Ephratah;
> we discovered it
> in the fields of Jaar
>
> (verse 6).

For years the ark of the covenant, representing the throne of God on earth, was housed and forgotten in the woods of Jaar, at the town of Kiriath-Jearim (1 Sam. 7:2). Even though Abinadab and his family prospered as a result of the ark of the Lord being with them, the rest of the people went about their business as though God did not exist.

How could it be? How could God's people forget the symbol of his lordship and leave it in obscurity? It seems almost unthinkable that the ark of God could remain forgotten for decades. Yet the same thing happens today. Professing Christians go out into the ways of the world and forget the sacrifice of Christ on their behalf. They ignore his lordship over their lives. Priorities are set according to personal convenience rather than according to a willingness to suffer for the Lord. But David made a commitment. He will bring the ark of God from the woods of Jaar to Mount Zion, the place where he himself has been enthroned. All his authority as king he gladly will bring under the greater authority of the Lord.

David's leadership inspires the Lord's people. They discover the ark, symbolizing the throne of God, buried in an obscure village. It is not that God has been absent from his throne of glory; it is that men have gone their own way, totally neglecting his sovereignty over their lives.

But now the people of the Lord make a commitment that corresponds to David's:

We will go up
　　to his tabernacles;
we will bow down
　　at his footstool.
Arise, O Covenant LORD,
　　into your resting-place,
you
　　and the ark of your strength
(verses 7, 8).

Did not our Lord Christ suffer enough humiliation while he was on earth? Was not it enough for him to humble himself, take on the form of a servant and endure the humiliation of a shameful crucifixion? Must we now add insult to injury by failing to bow before him even though he reigns in glory?

Let us make the right response to his exaltation to the right hand of God. Let us determine that we will bow down at his footstool. For sooner or later every knee must bow and every tongue confess that Jesus Christ is Lord, to the glory of God the Father. Just as the ark of the Lord was brought up from obscurity and neglect to the place of prominence prepared by David, so our Lord Christ was brought from the humiliations of the cross to the glories of the right hand of God. That is the place where he will rest and from which he will reign for eternity.

The consequences in the lives of God's people

The consequences of this movement from humiliation to glory are seen in the righteousness and joy that flow into the lives of God's people. The psalmist says:

Your priests
　　will be adorned in righteousness,
and your devoted ones
　　will shout for joy
(verse 9).

It was the humiliation of their God and king that inspired the people to change their perspective on life. The ark of God had waited patiently for many years, and now it must be brought up from obscurity to glory. For decades David suffered the threats of Saul as he fled for his life. But in the end both the king and the ark were brought to their proper glory by the plan and purpose of God. In time they moved from cross to crown.

This pattern of the past gives hope to God's people for the future. It inspires a prayer in their hearts:

> Because of David your servant,
> do not turn away the face of your anointed one.
> (verse 10).

David said he would not enter the comforts of his own home, he would not let himself sleep, until the Lord's house had been established in glory. The people joined him in this commitment of priorities by their prayer. Above everything else, they wanted the Lord and his anointed one to rise in glory. What about you? Have you entered into the commitment made by David? Do you have an overwhelming desire that God's house be built? Is it more important to you than eating or sleeping?

Jesus' disciples saw in Christ's commitment to establish God's house a fulfilment of the words of David: 'Zeal for your house will consume me' (John 2:17; cf. Psa. 69:9). Can you say the same of your own attitude towards building God's house? Let us leave the Lord in obscurity no longer. Let us stretch ourselves beyond the level of our own comforts for the sake of his glory.

3. Trust the Lord's sovereignty in designating your anointed leader (verses 11-18)

David took a solemn oath that settled his priorities. This oath receives proper recognition in the first portion of the psalm. But God also took an oath. He settled firmly on certain priorities. As a matter of fact, the Lord's oath has a far greater prominence than David's oath. The psalmist underscores the significance of the divine oath for the ongoing drama of redemption:

> The Covenant LORD swore the truth to David;
> He will never turn away from it:

'From the fruit of your loins
I will establish heirs to your throne.
If your sons will keep
my covenant,
and my testimony which I teach them,
then their sons will sit on your throne forever.'
For the Covenant LORD has chosen Zion;
he has claimed it for his dwellingplace:
'This is my place of rest forever;
Here I will reside, for I have claimed it'
(verses 11-14).

David's sons were not in themselves an impressive lot. But God promised to raise up heirs to David's throne from among them. For he chose David and his city to be his resting-place forever.

For four hundred years the line of David remained on the throne in Israel, a most remarkable dynastic record in the history of the world. Because of God's oath, not because of their fidelity to him, the Lord maintained the descendants of David on the throne for this length of time.

With a vacuum created by the termination of the Davidic dynasty, the stage was set for the coming of Jesus the Christ, son of David according to the flesh. In him the oath of God continues to be fulfilled. David's descendant continues as King and Head of the church. His grace sustains the people of his domain even today.

The concluding section of the psalm rehearses the blessings for God's people and the priority of God's Messiah.

The blessings for God's people

First, consider the blessings for God's people:

Its provision
I will greatly bless;
its poor
I will satisfy with bread;
its priests
I will adorn with salvation;

its devoted ones
  will shout for joy continually
(verses 15, 16).

Because of the oath God has taken, certain blessings are guaranteed for his people. The Lord will greatly bless their provision and will satisfy their poor with bread. As the psalmist says,

I have been young and now am old,
  yet I have not seen the righteous forsaken
  or his children begging for bread
(Psa. 37:25).

Salvation and shouts of joy will be the experience of all who are devoted to him. It is not that God's people will face no difficulties. If the world hated Christ it will hate his disciples as well. But God will be in it all, triumphing for his people and giving them joy in their salvation.

The priority of God's Messiah

All these blessings will come to God's people because of the Messiah and his work. The priority that belongs to the Messiah may be seen by the three symbols used to indicate that God's blessing flows through him.

There I will make sprout
  a horn for David;
I have prepared
  a lamp for my anointed one.
His enemies
  I will cover with shame,
But on him
  his crown will glisten
(verses 17, 18).

Consider first the symbol of *the sprouting horn.* An animal's horn represented to the ancients a concentration of power. All the force of the rhinoceros is located in the horn projecting from his snout. The 'sprouting' of a horn in the psalm changes the figure to the idea of a tender shoot that sprouts from the ground. This modification of imagery may be intended to suggest the gentleness with which Messiah would exercise his power. During his ministry on earth, Christ would not quench even the smoking flax of the misplaced piety of the Pharisees. Though he could have eliminated his enemies instantly, he bore gently with them throughout his ministry.

So today Christ continues to hold 'all authority' over the nations. This power he exercises with great patience and restraint. Yet the mighty fall and the lowly are lifted according to his purpose and plan in showing grace to a fallen world.

The second symbol of priority is a *lamp*, representing the perpetuity of Messiah's life as reigning monarch. At the Gettysburg battlefield in Pennsylvania and at the gravesite of John F. Kennedy an eternal flame burns, even though the persons symbolized by these flames live on earth no longer. But the perpetual flame appointed by God for the Messiah symbolizes his incorruptible life and his eternal reign. God prepared for him a resurrection body that can never die. Through him the promises given to David stretch across eternity. They anticipate a resurrection body for all the redeemed. An athletic woman contracted a disabling disease that severely limited her physical movements. Yet she remained joyful in the Lord. She expressed confidence that one day her body would be healed completely. She knows that Christ, the possessor of eternal life, will infuse new life into her body at the resurrection. Because of his possession of eternal life, he can impart that same life to others. The light of his lamp brings hope to the faltering.

Finally, the priority of the anointed Messiah is symbolized by *the glistening crown*. This regal symbol represents the honour that must be accorded to Christ. As Paul says, 'that in everything he might be preeminent' (Col. 1:18).

Join the myriads that have gone before you and cast your crowns, wreaths and honours at his feet. Whatever glory comes to you must be given over to him.

Conclusion

The message of this psalm begins with a cross and ends with a crown. It begins by referring to David and all his afflictions. It ends with a glistening crown placed on the head of great David's greater son.

You too will have your crosses. But at the end of the road is a crown—not one that you have earned, but one that Jesus Christ gives as a consequence of his sovereign grace. By that crown you will be enabled to give greater glory to him. In your small way you can 'crown him with many crowns.'

Psalm 146

Praise the Covenant Lord, Help of the Helpless

A song of ascents.

Reader:

1 Hallelu Yah!
Praise the Lord of the Covenant, O my soul!

Congr.:

2 I will praise the Covenant Lord
throughout my life;
I will sing to my God
as long as I live.

Reader:

3 Don't any of you put your trust
in men, however noble;
in a son of man
who cannot save.

Congr.:

4 His life-breath will expire;
he will return to the dust;
in that very day his plans perish.

Reader:

5 How blessed is the man
who has the God of Jacob
as his help;
his reliance
is on the Covenant Lord his God.

Congr.:	6 He made heaven and earth, the sea, and everything in them. He remains faithful forever; 7 he enacts justice for the oppressed; he gives bread to the hungry.
Reader:	8 The LORD of the Covenant looses
Congr.:	the prisoners;
Reader:	The LORD of the Covenant opens
Congr.:	the eyes of the blind;
Reader:	The LORD of the Covenant raises
Congr.:	the bowed down;
Reader:	The LORD of the Covenant loves
Congr.:	the righteous;
Reader:	9 The LORD of the Covenant sustains
Congr.:	the sojourners.
Reader:	The orphan and the widow he will uphold;
Congr.:	but the way of the wicked he will frustrate.
Reader:	10 The LORD of the Covenant shall reign forever;
Congr.:	your God, O Zion, from generation to generation.
All:	Hallelu Yah!

Praise the Covenant LORD, Help of the Helpless— *Praise God for His Mercy to the Needy*

Introduction

This psalm begins the final sub-collection of the Psalter. Psalms 146 to 150 are appropriately designated as 'Hallelujah' psalms. Concerning these last five psalms, C. H. Spurgeon says, 'We are among the Hallelujahs. The rest of our journey lies through the Delectable Mountains.'[1]

Each of these psalms begins and ends with the Hebrew phrase: 'Hallelu Yah,' which means literally, 'All of you, praise Yah,' using the poetic abbreviation for the name 'Yahveh.' But this similarity of beginning and ending by no means indicates that a dullness of repetition characterizes this collection. Each of these five psalms has its own distinctive reason for summoning God's people to praise their Covenant LORD.

Psalm 146 says, 'Praise the Covenant LORD, help of the helpless.' Man perishes, and so the help he might provide cannot be trusted. But God is the Creator of all things and continues forever. He always is ready to help those in need. Furthermore, as God of the covenant, he has bound himself by his word to preserve his people. That word can be trusted, for he will do as he has promised.

Several elements of the help provided by the Lord may be noted in this psalm: the alternative to help from the Lord (verses 3, 4); the kind of help that comes from the Lord (verses 6-9a); the way to get his help (verses 5, 9b); the proper response to his help (verses 1, 2, 10c).

[1] *The Treasury of David*, III, p. 400.

Sooner or later you will need help—and it may be sooner than later. You may be oppressed by work, by sickness, or by financial necessity. You may be forced to become a wanderer with no job and no home. Although you are an adult, you may sense that you have been orphaned by the death of your parents. You may find yourself in desperate need of companionship by the loss of your spouse. One way or another, you will find yourself in severe need.

Yet in all these circumstances you can say with all your heart, 'Hallelu Yah,' 'Praise the Lord!' As the apostle James says, 'Count it all joy when you meet trials of various kinds' (James 1:2), not because of the trials themselves, but because you know God will help you through them all. You can be joyful even when under the pressures of need and necessity because the LORD of the Covenant helps the helpless. Now enter into the spirit of this psalm so that you can praise the Lord because of his help to you. Consider first the alternative to help from the Lord, which is where most people look.

1. The alternative to help from the Lord (verses 3, 4)

The psalmist contrasts help from the Lord with the help that is available through men:

> Don't any of you put your trust
>   in men, however noble;
>   in a son of man
>   who cannot save.
> His life-breath will expire;
> he will return to the dust;
> in that very day his plans perish
>
> (verses 3, 4).

The psalmist sets men over against God as the principal alternative to God's help. Why? Because man is the highest of resources on earth that might meet your need. Men are the channels through which help from the rest of the world flows. To make his point as strongly as possible, the psalmist encourages you to imagine the best-case scenario. You know there are good men and there are bad men; there are influential men with great resources, and there are other men who have little 'pull' in the world. Picture in your mind the best man you can imagine. He is a truly 'noble' man, as the psalmist designates him. He is reliable in all he does and has plenty of influence with others.

Yet the message of the psalmist is the same: don't put your trust in him. There is no exception to this principle. Though you should be ever so careful in selecting the one you would trust, you will be disappointed. Man without God is a helpless creature, and has in himself no capacity to help others. His life breath expires and he returns to the dust.

Breathing seems to be such a small part of the activity of men. You are hardly conscious that you are breathing unless you do some strenuous exercise. Yet as soon as you stop breathing, your life is over.

Once your life is over, all your plans perish. A man may have large intentions to help the poor and needy of the earth. But the moment he dies, those plans are set aside. He may leave a will or trust fund that manifests the best of intentions. But he has no power to supervise its administration.

Do not put your confidence in men, however noble they may be. You might think they can save you, but they cannot. After World War I, Europe hailed Woodrow Wilson as the saviour of the world. He returned to America with a plan for perpetual peace. Back and forth across the country he went, expending his energy in superhuman ways. In the end, he apparently had a massive stroke, and was handicapped for the rest of his life. Historians think that his wife actually ran the White House until the end of his term as president. His plan for peace failed, and the world was again at war within twenty years.

> Put no confidence in princes,
> Nor for help on man depend;
> He shall die, to dust returning,
> And his purposes shall end.[2]

[2] *Trinity Hymnal*, 1990, No. 57.

Instead of looking to the help that men can give, look to the help that comes from the Lord.

2. The help that comes from the Lord (verses 7-9a)

Nine different needs are listed to illustrate the help the Lord gives. The overriding point is just the opposite of the old adage: 'The Lord helps those who help themselves.' Instead, the Lord helps those who cannot help themselves. For:

> The LORD of the Covenant looses
>   the prisoners;
> The LORD of the Covenant opens
>   the eyes of the blind;
> The LORD of the Covenant raises
>   the bowed down;
> The LORD of the Covenant loves
>   the righteous;
> The LORD of the Covenant sustains
>   the sojourners.
>
> The orphan and the widow
>   he will uphold;
> but the way of the wicked
>   he will frustrate
>
> (verses 8, 9).

Two aspects basic to the Lord explain the kind of help he gives. He gives help as your Creator and as your Redeemer.

The Lord gives help as Creator

As Creator, he made heaven and earth, the sea and everything in them (verse 6). So he is fully capable of giving bread to the hungry. Providing bread is a symbol of the Lord's supplying all the daily needs of his people. Hungry people may be quickly satisfied, but they are soon hungry again. The more you eat, the hungrier you get. Stuff yourself with a big meal, and you are ready to eat even more the next day.

Hunger constantly reminds you that you are a dependent creature. You cannot survive without the food given by the Lord. As Maker of heaven and earth, the sea and all that is in them, God provides food for the hungry.

When Jesus fed the five thousand, he was only dramatizing what goes on all the time. First he showed that man could not provide this most basic need for himself. 'You give them something to eat,' he said to his disciples (Mark 6:37). The disciples did not have enough money to buy food for the multitude, much less the ability to produce the food themselves. But Jesus multiplied five loaves and two fishes to feed five thousand.

No doubt it would be fascinating to witness a miracle like Jesus' feeding of the five thousand. But every day God opens his creative hand and provides food for the whole world. It is absolutely amazing! He opens his hand and gives food for every living thing. From the mites that feed on dust particles to the elephant that tramps through the jungle, he sees to it that they all have enough every day. Only man's greed, brutality and selfishness keep many people of the world from feeding in abundance.

But daily bread is only one of the commodities the Lord provides for his people. He gives air to breathe, clothes to wear, shelter from the heat and the cold. He gives you daily strength to get all necessary work done and to find enjoyment in doing it.

Don't be a practical atheist. Don't receive all these benefits from the hand of God every day without recognizing that he is the one who gives them. He made everything in the world, and he gives you all these benefits.

The Lord gives help as Redeemer

The Lord also gives help as your Redeemer. For:

> He remains faithful forever;
> He enacts justice for the oppressed
>
> (verses 6, 7).

All God has promised he will do. When Solomon dedicated the temple he had built in Jerusalem, he said, 'Blessed be the Lord, who ... has fulfilled what he promised with his mouth to David my father' (1 Kings 8:15). You can say the same today. God has a will; he is not just an 'it.' With his will he has made a commitment, and he is not like a man who is unable to hold to his commitments.

With great fervour Peter pledged his readiness to go with Jesus to prison and to death (Luke 22:33). But when Jesus asked the inner core of three to pray with him for one hour, Peter fell asleep. Paul experienced great disappointment in men. Writing to the Philippians from jail, he said, 'They all seek their own interests, not those of Jesus Christ' (Phil. 2:21). To Timothy he had to say, 'All deserted me.' He could cite only one exception: 'But the Lord stood by me' (2 Tim. 4:16, 17).

Has the Lord promised to give you enough strength for each day as long as you live? He will do it! Has he promised to give you the resources for your daily spiritual battles? He will do it. Has he promised not to hold a grudge against you for your sin? He will be true to his word. The curse of sin that weighs on you like a great burden he will lift.

The Lord helps those with special needs

More specifically, he helps people with many kinds of special needs. He helps prisoners by loosing their bonds. Those who have lost their basic human freedoms he sets free. Even if their suffering is caused by their own sin, he opens the doors of their prison and gives them liberty.

In the realm of the soul, imprisonment is an awful thing. Sin ensnares with promises of pleasure. The price it exacts from the soul is very high. For whoever commits sin becomes the slave to sin. Tell a lie, and you are bound to tell another. Steal something you covet, and possessing it will haunt you for the rest of your life.

But say, 'Hallelu Yah!' The Lord helps those who cannot help themselves. It is just those kinds of people he helps. He gives help to the needy, and to those who have no might he increases strength.

He also helps the blind by opening their eyes. When Jesus came on earth, it could be said, 'Never since the world began has it been heard that anyone opened the eyes of a man born blind'

(John 9:32). Neither Moses nor Joshua, Elijah nor Elisha opened blind eyes. These words were spoken by a man who had been born blind, but who had been made to see by Jesus. The man was utterly amazed at the religious leaders of his day! Could they not perceive who Jesus was, when he had done something no other human being ever had done since the foundation of the world? They were indeed the blindest of them all! Yet Jesus opened the spiritually blinded eyes of many of them, like their leader Nicodemus.

God also raises those who are bowed down. Are you weighed down with responsibilities? Do you feel totally worn out at the end of every day? Does the lessening of your strength by the process of ageing burden you?

The Lord raises up those that are bowed down. For:

> They who wait for the Lord
> shall renew their strength;
> they shall mount up with wings like eagles;
> they shall run and not be weary;
> they shall walk and not faint
>
> (Isa. 40:31).

You may sink under your load. But look to the Lord. He said, 'Come to me, all who labour and are heavy laden, and I will give you rest. Take my yoke upon you, and learn from me, for I am gentle and lowly in heart, and you will find rest for your souls' (Matt. 11:28, 29).

The psalmist also says that the Lord 'loves the righteous.' But how does this point fit into the list of people that the Lord helps? Before and after this phrase, the psalmist has been talking about poor and needy people who are desperate for the Lord's help. He speaks of the hungry, the oppressed, prisoners, the blind and the bowed down, orphans and widows. The 'righteous' do not seem to fit this list of needy people.

But they do. Because of the fallen condition of the world, the righteous are desperately needy. They are not loved by men. They need God's loving reassurance that they are doing right. Of all people, they are in need of the Lord's love. When no one else loves the righteous, the Lord loves them. The world loves its own; but the Lord loves the righteous.

See that dirty, worn, torn and faded rag doll? No one would select it as the object of his love and affection. But one person does. The child to whom the rag doll belongs loves that doll above all others. So the Lord loves the righteous. No one else may love them. But for that very reason, they receive the unique love of the Lord.

The Lord also sustains the sojourners. He recognizes that they have special needs. The traveller does not know what he will meet around the next bend. When on a journey you need special grace, and the Lord provides it. As a stranger you are subject to all sorts of rip-offs. But the Lord sends his guardian angels to protect you.

On one family trip, we arrived late in the night at a friend's house. The next morning we went out and there it was: a flat tyre. The Lord had preserved that tyre all through our travel time on dark and winding roads.

More recently, someone in the family left a wallet in a restaurant miles away from home. The loss was not discovered until the evening. But even before the search had begun, God appointed a person who lived just a few blocks away to bring it all the way home.

All of us as Christians spend our lives as strangers and pilgrims in this world. We don't belong. It is often obvious that we are misfits. But the Lord has promised to protect us. He will see that we are sustained in our spiritual pilgrimage throughout life.

The Lord also upholds the orphan and the widow. Almost all of us will feel abandoned one day. Your father and your mother will pass away, and you will be left without parents. You will lose your spouse, and become a widow or a widower. How will you stand it?

The Lord can meet that need. He promises to sustain you in all your losses. He will make gracious provisions for you.

So there we have a sample of the kind of help the Lord gives. Whenever his people have a need, whatever their need, he steps in to provide.

And who is this Lord? How do you get in contact with him? He is the Lord Jesus Christ. It is not God in the abstract who helps the needy. Jesus Christ, the Son of God, has come into the world for the particular purpose of seeking out the needy. In response to the doubts of John the Baptist Jesus said, 'Go and tell John what you hear and see: the blind receive their sight and the lame walk, lepers are cleansed and the deaf hear, and the dead are raised up, and the poor have good news preached to them' (Matt. 11:4, 5). He is the helper of the helpless. If you want help from the Lord, you must turn to him.

3. How to get the Lord's help (verse 5)

But how do you get the Lord's help? What must you do to know that he will be with you when you are in need?

You must do two things. You must know him as the God of Jacob, and you must rely on him. The psalmist says:

> How blessed is the man
> who has the God of Jacob
> as his help;
> his reliance
> is on the Covenant Lord his God
> (verse 5).

You must know the God of Jacob

Jacob was a sinner and a scoundrel. Yet the Lord helped him. Jacob coerced his brother to forfeit his birthright by playing on his weakness. Then he deceived his own father in an effort to get his blessing. As a consequence of his sin, he had to flee the country to escape the wrath of his brother.

Yet while on his sojourn, the Lord prospered him greatly. Jacob returned with a large family and great possessions. But he still was a sinner and a scoundrel. As he re-entered the land, he sent ahead the women and children with gifts to appease the wrath of his brother while he stayed behind in safety. But the Lord met him in the form of an angel. Jacob wrestled with this angel all night long, and the angel wrestled with Jacob. At break of day, the Lord blessed him. Though he was slow to change from his sinful ways, the Lord continued to work change within him.

Later in his life, Jacob lost his favourite son. Joseph was sold into slavery by his brothers because of their jealousy. But in the end, the Lord restored this son to Jacob, and the once bereaved patriarch had the privilege of placing his blessing on the heads of his grandchildren.

That is the God of Jacob. He is a God who has committed himself by the covenant to save sinners and scoundrels like Jacob. His commitment to this goal has lasted over the centuries, and will continue until the end of time.

If you are going to get the help you need for life, you must know the God of Jacob. You cannot limit yourself to calling on God only when you think you deserve his help. Instead, you must call on him as the God of Jacob, the one who helps sinners even when they create their own problems.

You must rely on the Lord

Secondly, to get the help of the Lord, you must rely on him. It is not enough simply to know the Lord, or even to call on him. You also must put your trust in him. It is only as you ask in faith that the Lord will supply your needs. The blessed man is the one who relies on the Lord in his time of need.

But how can you know he will answer you if you call on him? You have the universal promise of his word. Whoever comes to me I will never cast out,' says the Lord Jesus Christ (John 6:37). For:

> God never yet forsook in need
> The soul that trusted him indeed.

We tend to panic. The slightest trouble threatens, and we become desperate. But God's word tells us to keep on trusting, no matter how dangerous the situation may appear. That is how you get the Lord's help.

How far can you trust the Lord? The psalmist says you can trust him beginning now and continuing forever after:

> The LORD of the Covenant shall reign
> forever;

your God, O Zion,
    from generation to generation
                                        (verse 10).

So long as the Lord reigns, you can count on the help he gives. As one commentator says, 'The world has always been governed, is now governed, and shall to the end of time be governed by him who makes no mistakes, and has no vicegerents, and no successful rivals'[3]

From generation to generation you will see God's blessing on your family. On your children's children you will see the help of the Lord. What greater blessing can be imagined in life than a person seeing God's blessing on his children and his children's children! It is the promise of the Lord to you.

4. Response to his help (verses 1, 2)

Seeing what the Lord has done and continues to do, how should you respond? The psalmist makes his point very plainly:

Hallelu Yah!
[All of you, praise the Lord!]
Praise the Covenant LORD, O my soul!

I will praise the Covenant LORD
    throughout my life;
I will sing to my God
    as long as I live
                                        (verses 1, 2).

All of you, praise the Lord! When you realize all the help he gives, then join together constantly with his people to praise him. Don't wait for some massive miracle to move you to praise him. Every day he gives you food, friends and shelter. See his common-place providences as plenty of reasons to praise him.

Not only as a group, but each of you individually should praise him. The psalmist will not ask others to do what he is not doing

[3] W. S. Plumer, *Psalms*, 1867, p. 1196.

himself. So he urges himself on. He addresses his own soul and says, 'Praise the Lord, O my soul.'

You need to work at praising the Lord if you are going to give him the glory he deserves. Whoever you are, you will not offer the Lord the amount of praise he should receive without concentrating on it, committing yourself to it. Stir up all the powers you possess. Train your mind to meditate on all the ways he helps you. Prod your memory to bring up the earlier blessings he has brought into your life. Call on your affections to love him for all the things he continues to do for you.

As long as you live, say, 'Hallelu Yah!' Continually praise the God of the covenant for what he has done, is doing and will do for you. Praise the Lord, help of the helpless.

Appendix
On the Translation of the Divine Name

A special word of explanation must be offered regarding the rendering of the old covenant name for God, known among academicians as the 'Tetragrammaton.' As a sign of reverence, some Jews have substituted 'Lord' (*Adonai*) or 'The NAME' (*haShem*) wherever the Tetragrammaton appeared. Perhaps the strangest effort to deal with this word that would not be pronounced was the imposition of the vowels for *Adonai* onto the consonants of this special name for the deity. But the resulting hybrid 'Jehovah' certainly has no resemblance to the original word in Scripture. The King James Version of 1611 rendered this divine designation as 'LORD,' using all capital letters to distinguish it from the more common 'Lord.' But it is doubtful that very many English readers actually noted the difference between 'LORD' and 'Lord,' while even fewer people understood the reason for the distinction. More recently the effort has been made to acclimate the English-speaking world to the representation of the name as '*Yahweh*.' But most likely this vocalization never will seem natural to the English-speaking world.

The current translation has worked with the generally accepted understanding that this special name for God is related directly to his revelation to his people as their 'Covenant LORD.' In association with his oath-bound commitments, God has revealed himself as 'LORD of the Covenant.' So this translation has used the designation 'Covenant LORD' for the distinctive name of God. The use of all capital letters for LORD reflects the distinction made in earlier English translations, but the additional specification that this God is uniquely the 'Covenant' LORD brings out the personal relation of this God to his people. Where the flow of the language favours it, the designation has been represented as 'LORD of the Covenant'.

It may be felt that too much of the distinctive revelation of God to his people is lost by a failure to approximate the original vocalization of the divine name. But even the rather wooden *Yahweh* is only a 'scholar's guess' as to how the consonants of the Tetragrammaton originally were sounded.

One additional thought may be appended to this discussion, which relates to the legitimate question as to why such a critical thing as the vocalization of this distinctive name for God would have proven to be so difficult throughout the ages. It just may be that God intended it that way for a special purpose. The revelation that came in the person of God's Son burst onto the scene of human history with greatest brilliance because of the 400 years of divine silence that preceded it. In a similar way, the obvious blank at the place where God's name might have been heard made the way clear for the name *Jesus* to receive the full honour it deserved. Without a rival even from Scripture itself, it is clearly and exclusively 'at the name of *Jesus*' that 'every knee should bow and every tongue confess that *Jesus* Christ is LORD' (Phil. 2:10, 11). In the present age, what better way could be found for preparing the way for the exaltation of Jesus' name than by translating the name of the God of the fathers as 'Covenant LORD'? For it is none other than *Jesus* who was, is and forever will be the 'LORD of the Covenant.'

OTHER BOOKS BY O. PALMER ROBERTSON PUBLISHED BY THE TRUST

Jonah—A Study in Compassion

72pp. paperback, ISBN: 978-1-80040-421-2

The Old Testament story catches the imagination and tells of a prophet who disobeys God and of a great fish which can swallow a man; it describes a city-wide revolt in a pagan country and a wonderfully-sighted prophet sulking in the sunshine. What does it mean?

In *Jonah–A Study in Compassion,* Dr O. Palmer Robertson's masterly knowledge of the Hebrew language, his vivid sense of the grace of God and the twisted state of man's heart, his ability to retell historical events and see their significance, all combine to explain what the message of the book of Jonah really is, and—since there is a sting in the tail—what it means for us today.

The Final Word

A Biblical Response to the Case for Tongues and Prophecy Today

172pp. paperback, ISBN: 978-1-80040-452-6

A call for freshness, spontaneity and life in worship has been resounding through the churches of the English-speaking world, together with a desire to hear God speaking here and now to his people. Many have called for a return to the pattern of worship found in 1 Corinthians 14, merging the biblical emphasis of the Reformation with the vitality of the modern Pentecostal and Charismatic movements.

Dr O. Palmer Robertson, pastor and Seminary teacher, currently Director of African Bible College, Uganda, argues from Scripture that preoccupation with tongues and prophecy shows a failure to grasp the fullness of New Testament privileges. The Christ of the Scriptures is the Final Word. All the church will ever need is to be found in him.

A Way to Pray

A Biblical Method for Enriching Your Prayer Life and Language by Shaping Your Words with Scripture

440pp. cloth, ISBN: 978-1-84871-860-9

Most evangelical Christians know of Matthew Henry's Commentary on the Bible, but few are as familiar with his *A Method for Prayer, with Scripture Expressions Proper To Be Used Under Each Head*. This work consists almost entirely of Scripture, arranged under various headings, to help Christians to pray in harmony with the truth of God, revealed in his word. First published three hundred years ago, it has been revised and updated by O. Palmer Robertson to allow the language of prayer to be expressed in today's idiom. It is sent out in the confidence that God will continue to honour his own word, as it is redirected back to him in the form of heartfelt prayer.

BANNER
of TRUTH

The Banner of Truth Trust originated in 1957 in London. The founders believed that much of the best literature of historic Christianity had been allowed to fall into oblivion and that, under God, its recovery could well lead not only to a strengthening of the church, but to true revival.

Interdenominational in vision, this publishing work is now international, and our lists include a number of contemporary authors, together with classics from the past. The translation of these books into many languages is encouraged.

A monthly magazine, *The Banner of Truth*, is also published, and further information about this, and all our other publications, may be found on our website, banneroftruth.org, or by contacting the offices below:

Head Office:
3 Murrayfield Road
Edinburgh
EH12 6EL
United Kingdom

Email: info@banneroftruth.co.uk

North America Office:
610 Alexander Spring Road
Carlisle, PA 17015
United States of America

Email: info@banneroftruth.org